Motor V
Workshop Organization
and Administration

BY
BERNARD CHANDLER
Chesterfield College of Technology

FOURTH EDITION

OXFORD UNIVERSITY PRESS
1983

Oxford University Press, Walton Street, Oxford OX2 6DP

Oxford London Glasgow
New York Toronto Melbourne Auckland
Kuala Lumpur Singapore Hong Kong Tokyo
Delhi Bombay Calcutta Madras Karachi
Nairobi Dar es Salaam Cape Town

and associated companies in
Beirut Berlin Ibadan Mexico City Nicosia

Oxford is a trade mark of Oxford University Press

© Oxford University Press 1972, 1975, 1977, 1983

ISBN 0 19 832720 X

Reprinted 1979 (with corrections), 1981, and 1983

Fourth Edition

All rights reserved. No part of this publication may be reproduced, stored in a retrieval system, or transmitted, in any form or by any means, electronic, mechanical, photocopying, recording or otherwise, without the prior permission of Oxford University Press

This book is sold subject to the condition that it shall not, by way of trade or otherwise, be lent, re-sold, hired out, or otherwise circulated without the publisher's prior consent in any form of binding condition including this condition being imposed on the subsequent purchaser.

Printed in Hong Kong

PREFACE

Modern garage operation requires considerable knowledge and skill. The days when a garage could be managed with little or no management knowledge are over.

To be an efficient manager of any motor vehicle workshop or service station, a man must have a good practical motor vehicle servicing background, an adequate knowledge of management practice, and a working knowledge of the law affecting the motor vehicle retail and repair trade. A manager's practical experience will come through his training as a motor vehicle mechanic or technician. His training for management must come through the careful study of techniques suited to his needs.

This book has been prepared to meet the requirements of existing managers wishing to extend their knowledge, prospective managers and trainees, as well as mechanics, receptionists, and others interested in the general operational requirements of service stations and workshops. To students taking the Full Technological Certificate of the City and Guilds of London Institute, the Institute of Motor Industry intermediate supervisory studies and final examinations, this book will prove to be a very useful aid as it follows closely the syllabuses covering all matters for the examinations of these bodies.

I am very grateful to all members of the trade, trade organizations, manufacturers, training schools, and all others who have supplied the information so necessary for a book of this kind.

Metric sizes converted to English in the text are not necessarily precise conversion.

C.G L.I course numbers are those currently allocated by the Institute in 1983. However, older courses covering similar topics but with different numbers are listed in Appendix III for reference purposes.

CONTENTS

ACKNOWLEDGEMENTS

The author would like to thank the organizations listed below for permission to publish the illustrations mentioned.

C. H. Allen Ltd.	Fig. 4.1
British Leyland Motor Corporation	Figs 2.1, 2.2, 2.13
Chrysler Motor Corporation	Figs 2.6, 2.7, 2.12
Garage Equipment Association	Fig. 1.3
Jessups Ltd.	Fig. 2.5
Kalamazoo Ltd.	Figs 2.3, 6.1
R.T.I.T.B.	Figs 5.3, 5.6
University Motors Ltd.	Fig. 2.8
Vauxhall Motor Co.	Figs 1.10, 2.4, 2.12, 2.14, 5.5

CHAPTER 1

LAYOUT

Selection and planning of a service station site

Main dealerships now change hands at prices in excess of £1 000 000! A new service station incorporating all the usual major facilities—for repairs (including bodywork repairs), for servicing commercial vehicles, for car and truck sales, for vehicle body building, for the sale of parts, for the petrol forecourt, for car hire and so on—can well cost £1 000 000 or more, taking into account the cost of land and building materials. The amount of capital available must therefore play a major part in site selection; and the type of land tenure—whether freehold or leasehold etc.—must be considered too. Planning permission from the local authority was also to be obtained; this involves complying with the various regulations governing building, petroleum, highways, etc.

Thus we can state that initial selection of a site depends upon (a) capital available, (b) land tenure, and (c) planning permission. A solicitor should be engaged for all legal work, and an architect for building work.

If all these requirements are met, then the layout of the site would have to be covered in detail and would be required for planning purposes. Actual layouts will be considered later.

Whilst capital, land tenure, and planning may be acceptable, the actual site might not be suitable. For instance, occasional trade may be severely limited by motorists' preference for alternative routes, provided by motorways or other main roads which bypass the site. Sites near blind corners and busy cross-roads are also unsuitable. Further consideration is given to site selection later in this chapter. In some cases, the need to arrange services such as electricity, gas, water, and so on can put prohibitive costs on an otherwise suitable site. It must be decided at an early stage what services will be offered. (As mentioned later, the M.A.A. have grades of membership according to work completed, etc.) Here are a few services which could be considered:

Services for motor vehicles

(1) Petrol and other fuels for private cars, motor cycles and scooters, commercial vehicles, motor coaches and, in some cases, motor boats, aircraft, and farm tractors.   1

(2)   Lubricating oils.
(3)   Water service for radiators and distilled water for batteries.
(4)   Radiator cleansing service; anti-freeze.
(5)   Parking space for vehicles, private or commercial.
(6)   Open garaging facilities for temporary parking of vehicles.
(7)   Lock-up garages.
(8)   Lubrication.
(9)   Washing, cleaning, polishing, and vacuuming.
(10)   Attended or fully automatic car wash.
(11)   Battery maintenance.
(12)   Brake testing and adjustment.
(13)   D.Tp. Vehicle testing.
(14)   Complete car and commercial maintenance contract service.
(15)   Decarbonizing, valve grinding, and engine tuning service.
(16)   Cylinder reconditioning.
(17)   Tyre repairing and tyre vulcanizing.
(18)   Wheel alignment and balancing.
(19)   Headlamp adjustment.
(20)   Overhaul and repairs of complete electrical equipment.
(21)   Car radio installation and maintenance.
(22)   Running repairs and minor adjustments.
(23)   Heavy repairs and breakdown salvage.
(24)   Crash repair work.
(25)   Body renovation and refinishing.
(26)   New tyres and accessories for sale.
(27)   New cars for sale.
(28)   Facilities for used car purchase and sale.
(29)   Facilities for the sale and hire of motor caravans and camping equipment, motor boats, and boat engines.
(30)   Car hire service.
(31)   Van and lorry hire service.
(32)   Facilities for vehicle body building.
(33)   Motor cycle repairs.

Personal service for drivers

Provision of:
(1)   Waiting room.
(2)   Washroom and W.C.
(3)   Shower baths and dressing rooms.
(4)   Writing accommodation.
(5)   Telephone facilities.
(6)   A clock.
(7)   Light refreshments.

(8)   Complete catering.
(9)   Automatic or canteen services of cigarettes, matches, tobacco,
      chocolate, soft drinks, tea, coffee, handkerchiefs, analgesics, and
      contraceptives.
(10) Personal accessories such as gloves and driving coats.
(11) Hostel or cabin accommodation (bed cubicles and breakfast) for
      motorists or commercial vehicle drivers.
(12) Driving instruction.
(13) Local guide books and detailed information as to trains, hotels, thea-
      tres, amusements, sports, beauty spots, historical places, roads, routes,
      and so on.

   The existing local provision of services for vehicles and drivers will have a
great influence on the planning of a dealership.
   If the site is especially promising (e.g. there is expanding local industry, or
the population is increasing as a result of housing developments, and it is
also easily visible and on an unrestricted road with good access, and there is
room for expansion in the future) then any adjacent spare land should be
purchased.
   Many dealerships have regretted not having further space for expansion—
especially in the parts department. Students should assess their local conditions and draw up a list of proposed services to meet local needs.
   When all basic services have been agreed then the actual physical layout
of the site can be considered. Some gross errors in the design of buildings
have occurred in the past. Vehicle inspection pits have been placed too close
to boundary walls of workshops, with the result that, whilst vehicles may
drive over the pit, it is impossible to withdraw half shafts or have enough
room to work on wheel hubs. Vehicle pits have been sunk in totally unsuitable ground, resulting in semi-permanent flooding. Entrance doors have
been made too narrow and too low. In one case the Department of Transport
(D.Tp.) refused a vehicle-testing station licence because the entrance door
was three inches short of the required height. Thus D.Tp. requirements should
be considered if vehicle testing is to form part of the dealership. The provision
of building heights adequate to the purposes of the buildings, suitable lighting, etc., which should be governed by the practical requirements of motor
vehicle work, is a major responsibility of the architect, who should always
bear it in mind.

Layout of a service station

The layout of a service station in its entirety is a crucial factor in its profitability. No matter how efficient management and staff may be, no one will
induce a customer to buy petrol from a service station which has difficult
access points. Narrow entrances and badly placed petrol pumps mean time

spent shunting a car in and out with the possibility of scratching it and, consequently, potential customers are lost. This however is only one aspect of service station layout. Reception area, accessories sales, workshop area, offices, toilets, and parts department all form part of the layout.

The site of the service station plays a very important part in its success. Very many factors have to be considered when an entirely new garage is being planned. Above everything is the obtaining of planning permission from the local council. Then there is traffic flow, existing competition, access points (that is whether entry is from one road or the service station is on a corner site, on cross roads with access from two roads), floating population either into or out of the area, and subsidies from oil and petrol companies for certain sites, to mention a few important aspects of site selection. Certain sites should be avoided; for example, sites where the population is dwindling, steep hills where it is dangerous and difficult to turn into a service station, one way street areas where access is obtainable from one side only, and similar situations are all poor and possibly disastrous choices. However, given a suitably accessible site with adequate car population the layout of the site must include the items listed.

Any progressive service station must consider new developments in garage repair and service work. The innovations of flow-line servicing and diagnostic centres as aids to speedy and efficient work now form part of many service stations. A standard service station layout using a triangular site is shown in Fig. 1.1 and a variation to include a flow-line installation in Fig. 1.2

1 Workshop with repair and service bays
2 Used car showroom
3 Petrol and oil sales island
4 Offices
5 Stores
6 New car showroom
7 Car wash
8 Accessory shop
9 Toilet for customers
10 Toilet for staff
11 Open space for car park

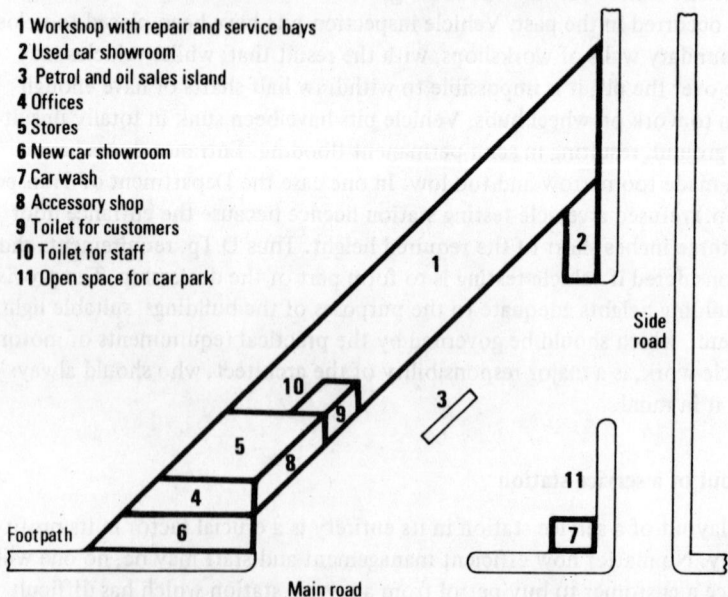

Fig. 1.1 Service Station Layout on a Triangular Site

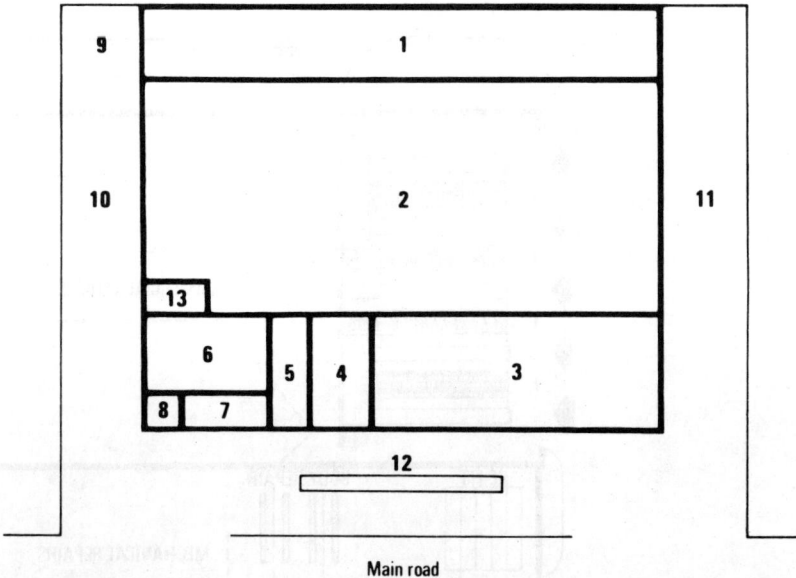

1 Flowline servicing area
2 Workshop area with repair bays
3 Car showroom
4 Stores
5 Accessory shop
6 Offices
7 Reception
8 Toilets for customers
9 Open car park for flowline
10 Open car park for cars awaiting repairs
11 Open car park for cars awaiting collection by customers
12 Petrol and oil sales island
13 Toilets and rest room for staff

Fig. 1.2 Service Station Layout with a Flow-Line

In both cases large parking areas are shown. From these areas cars are taken to the workshop area for major repair work or into the flow-line or fast service bay for servicing.

The reception area is clearly indicated by large clear signs, as are all areas including parking, toilets, and accessories, so that a customer can easily see where he wishes to go: this suggests efficiency. Customers like clear-cut signs without any confusion. Reception areas should be clean at all times and provide adequate seating where customers can wait, along with such amenities as tea-vending machines, magazines, and, very importantly, the accessories shop close by.

Offices should be sited as shown so that accounting, invoicing, and other work can be efficiently executed with minimum delay to the customer. A suggested site layout by the Garage and Equipment Association is shown in Fig. 1.3. This needs little explanation and is a layout suitable for most types of service station work. The Motor Agents Association have grades of service stations which determine the type of work a service station will do, and most

COMMERCIAL VEHICLES

RE-FIT   BODY REPAIR

MECHANICAL REPAIRS

SHOWROOM

STOVE   PAINT PREPARATION

SPRAYROOM

VOUCHER SERVICE

OFFICES   REST ROOM AND TOILETS   T.B.A.   WAITING M & F

TOILETS

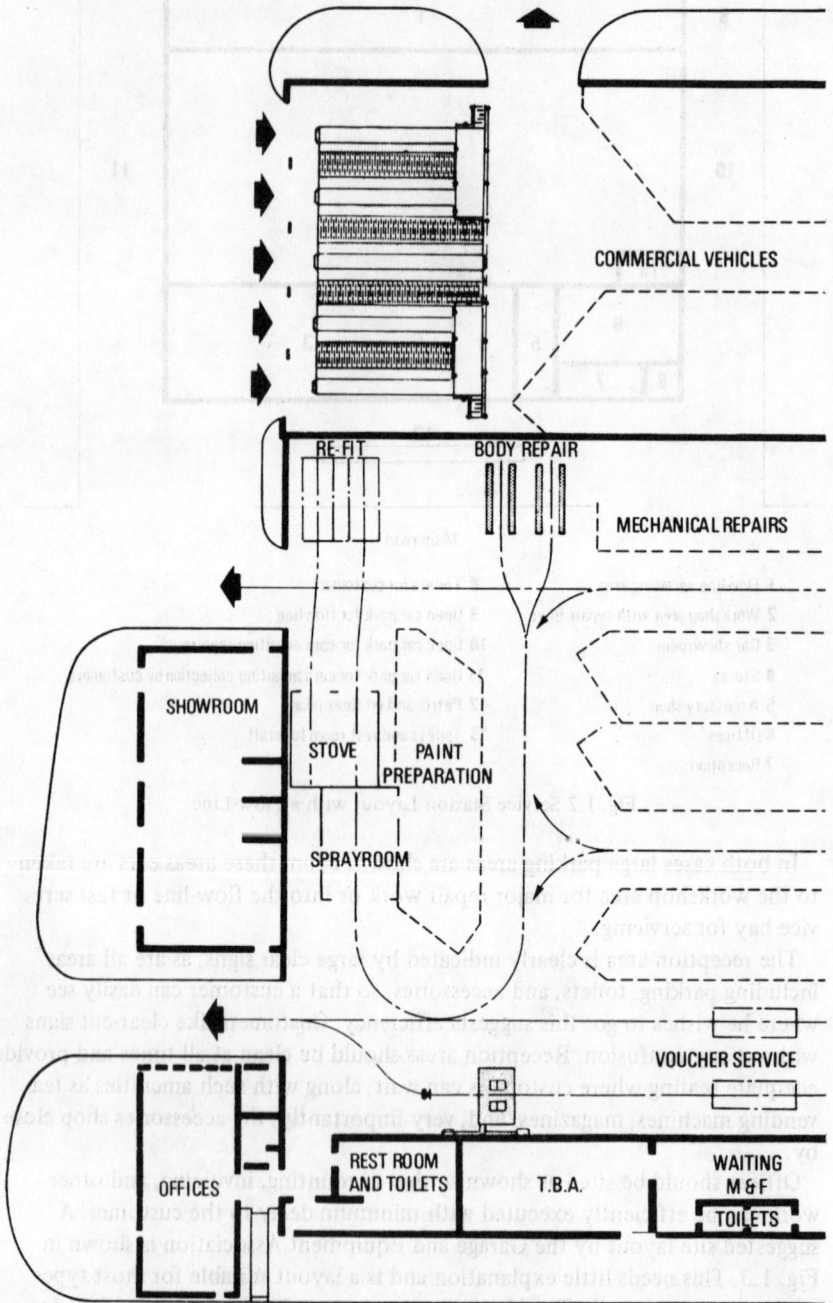

Fig. 1.3 G.E.A. Garage Layout

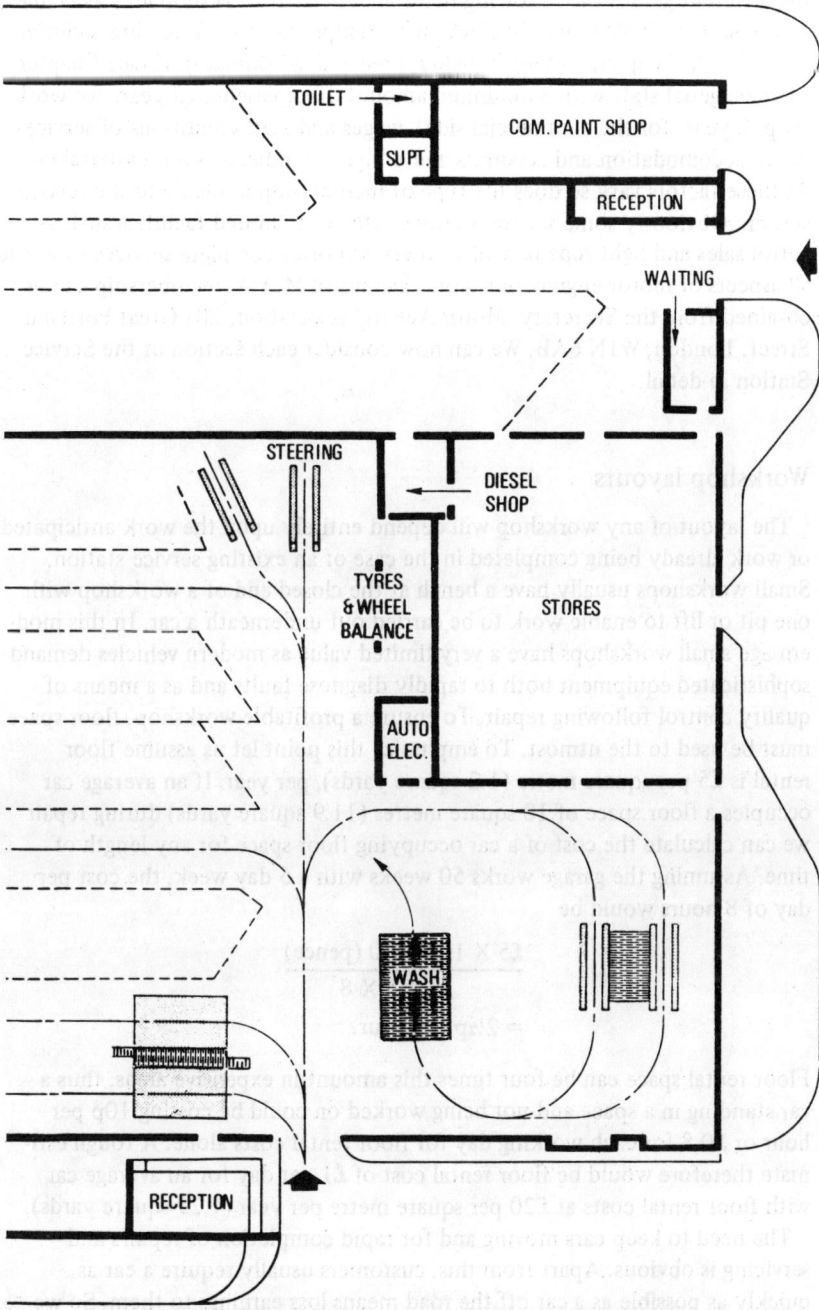

TOILET

SUPT.

COM. PAINT SHOP

RECEPTION

WAITING

STEERING

DIESEL SHOP

TYRES & WHEEL BALANCE

STORES

AUTO ELEC.

WASH

RECEPTION

service stations are registered with the M.A.A. under a particular heading. For the different grades the following items are covered: workshop area available, equipment available (which includes lifts, ramps, and tools), towing facilities, stores-stocks held, staff—which includes recognized skilled staff (see Chapter 5), managerial staff with a minimum amount of experience (5 years for workshop, 2 years for the commercial side), wages and staff conditions of service, office accomodation and accounts and a 'sign' to indicate work undertaken. As these factors vary so does the type of membership available to the service station. Obviously some service stations offer very limited facilities such as petrol sales and light repairs whilst others will offer complete services to include all aspects of motor engineering work. Details of M.A.A. membership can be obtained from the Secretary, Motor Agents Association, 201 Great Portland Street, London, W1N 6AB, We can now consider each section of the Service Station in detail.

Workshop layouts

The layout of any workshop will depend entirely upon the work anticipated or work already being completed in the case of an existing service station. Small workshops usually have a bench at the closed end of a workshop with one pit or lift to enable work to be carried out underneath a car. In this modern age small workshops have a very limited value as modern vehicles demand sophisticated equipment both to rapidly diagnose faults and as a means of quality control following repair. To ensure a profitable workshop, floor space must be used to the utmost. To emphasize this point let us assume floor rental is £5 per square metre (1.2 square yards), per year. If an average car occupies a floor space of 10 square metres (11.9 square yards) during repair we can calculate the cost of a car occupying floor space for any length of time. Assuming the garage works 50 weeks with a 5 day week, the cost per day of 8 hours would be

$$\frac{£5 \times 10 \times 100 \text{ (pence)}}{50 \times 5 \times 8}$$

$$= 2\tfrac{1}{2}\text{p per hour.}$$

Floor rental space can be four times this amount in expensive areas, thus a car standing in a space and not being worked on could be costing 10p per hour or £0.8 for each working day for floor rental costs alone. A rough estimate therefore would be floor rental cost of £1 per day for an average car with floor rental costs at £20 per square metre per year (1.25 square yards).

The need to keep cars moving and for rapid completion of repairs and servicing is obvious. Apart from this, customers usually require a car as quickly as possible as a car off the road means loss earnings to them. So we have seen some major changes in service work to meet these demands. Flow-line servicing and diagnostic centres are but two innovations which we shall discuss in detail later. In the meantime, they must form part of large workshop layouts.

With a large workshop we can consider an area of, say, 50 metres (160 feet) by 30 metres (100 feet), that is 1500 square metres (16 000 square feet). Utilization of an area of this size is shown in Fig. 1.4. Workshop areas with painted lines on a slope of 60° make it easy to run in and back out. Benches with steel tops and a 150 mm (6 in) jaw vice for every bay constitute basic equipment for repair work of a general nature. Jobs requiring use of a lift

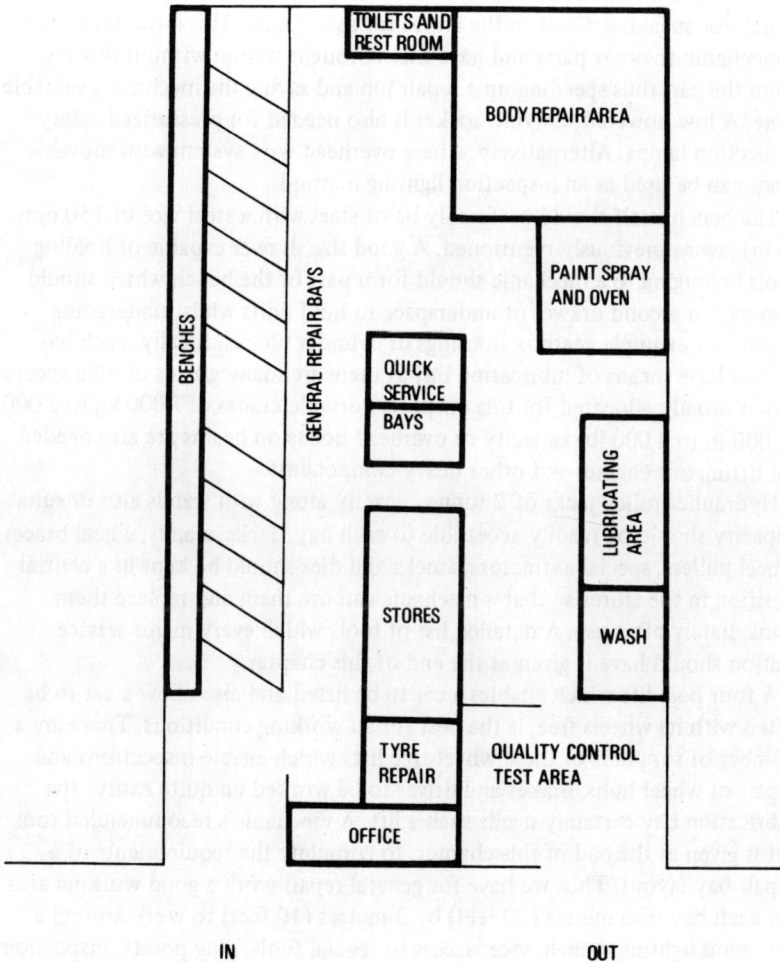

Fig. 1.4 Workshop Layout

will move into the work area where lifts are part of standard equipment in the repair bays. At this point it should be stressed that wheel-free lifts are to be preferred and pits are to be avoided. Many serious accidents have occurred with pits when fumes have accumulated and caused serious poisoning. Other accidents have occurred when petrol has spilled into pits and gone unnoticed until a naked flame eventually ignited the vapour with terrible results for mechanics working underneath vehicles. Where pits are used they should be as wide as possible and have very easy access and exit points at frequent intervals.

With each repair bay there must be certain services. A power plug with 13 amp fuse, an air line connection, an inter communications connection at the bench for speaking direct to the stores for spare parts. This latter item enables a mechanic to order parts and have them brought to him without moving from the car; thus speeding up a repair job and saving the mechanics valuable time. A low powered, 24 volt, socket is also needed for pressurized safety inspection lamps. Alternatively, a bare overhead wire system with movable leads can be used as an inspection lighting method.

The bench itself should preferably be of steel with a steel vice of 150 mm (6 in) jaw as previously mentioned. A good size drawer capable of holding tools belonging to a mechanic should form part of the bench which should also have a second drawer or underspace to hold units whilst undergoing repair, for example gearbox housings or cylinder blocks. Ideally, each bay should have means of lubrication but as there are many grades of oil a special bay is usually allocated for this purpose. Portable cranes of 1 000 kg to 2 000 kg (2 000 lb to 4 000 lb) capacity or overhead hoists on beams are also needed for lifting out engines and other heavy components.

Hydraulic trolley jacks of 2 tonne capacity along with stands also of suitable capacity should be readily accessible to each bay. Jacks, stands, wheel braces, wheel pullers, special extractors, stocks and dies should be kept in a central position in the stores so that a mechanic can use them and replace them immediately after use. A detailed list of tools which every major service station should have is given at the end of this chapter.

A four post lift which enables a car to be lifted and also allow a car to be lifted with its wheels free, is the best for all working conditions. There are a number of suppliers of these wheel-free lifts which enable inspections and repair of wheel hubs, brakes and drives to be worked on quite easily: the lubrication bay certainly needs such a lift. A mechanic's recommended tool list is given at the end of this chapter, to complete the requirements of a repair bay layout. Thus we have for general repair work a good working area for each bay of 6 metres (20 feet) by 3 metres (10 feet) to work around a car, good lighting, bench, vice, access to special tools, plug points, inspection lamp point, intercommunication system to stores, air line point and other special items which may be necessary for working on certain types of cars or commercial vehicles. B.S. AU 161: 1973 Vehicle lifts is a useful document.

The servicing area

Now we must consider the type of servicing we are going to do. Is it to be (a) a single-speed bay servicing or (b) flow-line servicing? Also to be considered (a) cars (b) commercial vehicles. Both cars, and, especially, commercial vehicles will be longer, heavier and possibly wider in the future and due allowance must be made for these factors when planning any service area either on a single-speed bay or on a flow-line principle. It would be useless, for example, to plan a bay to service commercial vehicles on the present restricted length and tonnage.

Before we proceed to describe a flow-line system of servicing in detail let us consider the merits of the single bay and the idea behind flow-line servicing.

Flow-line servicing. This may be defined as the application of time and motion study to the servicing of cars and commercial vehicles. It can be seen to be derived from manufacturing methods on production lines. Similar terms which apply to production lines can also be usefully employed in garage workshops. Such terms are:

Job production. The completion of one particular type of job only, that is a 'one off' job. This is done occasionally in motor repair shops but usually repeat jobs are the case.

Batch production. This is the repeating of a few types of jobs of a similar pattern or nature. In production work repeat of identical jobs of small numbers comes under the heading of batch production.

Flow-line production. This is the continuous repeating of the same job, on production lines of several hundreds or thousands of the same kind of job. Applied to repair shops flow-line servicing does result in a continuous repeat of certain types of servicing work.

We must consider whether it is worth setting up a flow-line or not. Some manufacturers maintain it is not a practicable proposition and recommend the use of a well laid out service bay as being just as good or even better. On the other hand very good use of flow-lines has already been made to both garage, customer and mechanic. For example, some service stations have operated excellent flow-lines since 1966 and these will be referred to again later. One line can service 40 cars per day with 8 personnel but before we say this is not very impressive, the service given at this particular station far exceeds normal servicing requirements for very little extra cost.

Before a flow-line is considered, the volume of cars or commercial vehicles must merit the use of space and capital investment involved with equipment needed on the line. How can this be assessed? An obvious place not to put a flow-line is in a rural or country area where traffic is light. On the other hand a heavily congested area, such as any major city or large town, provides a source of supply of cars or commercial vehicles to feed a flow-line. Feeding the lines has proved a problem on occasions but overall they have been very successful. Further consideration must be the type of vehicle to go on the line. It is highly desirable to keep to one type of vehicle thus obtaining a constant supply of similar vehicles for example Ford Cortina or Leyland Mini. A little research into any area will reveal the popular type of car in the district. How many cars are needed to keep a line fully operational? If we say 25 cars a day on average making 125 per week, then for a 50 week year this will mean 7 250 cars of the same type in a particular district.

This number of course is with one service per year. As leisure time increases at least 2 services per year will be required by each car, thus reducing the number of cars to 3 625. Furthermore, it is not unlikely that all cars will eventually require an inspection and test certificate *every 6 months* or 12 000 miles whichever comes first. Bearing it in mind that lifting tackle and similar equipment which can involve danger to life and limb have been inspected and reports filed every 6 months for many years, is it unreasonable for the fast modern car and heavy commercial vehicle to be inspected and a report filed? Whilst not at present a practical proposition because of lack of D.Tp. facilities, it could eventually become a feature of future motor transport. Flow-lines are already used very successfully for pre D.Tp. Testing of Commercial Vehicles. Inspection at D.Tp. Testing Stations is also completed on a flow-line system. Cars and commercial vehicles can use such lines for checking new vehicles for pre-delivery checks. Manufacturers do rely on dealers to complete pre-delivery inspections and flow-line systems are ideal for this purpose.

Where other garages already offer a flow-line service close by, a reorganization would have to be considered, if customers are to be retained. The innovation of such lines in a district heavily populated with cars is certain to draw customers and, as will be seen when we inspect an actual service sheet, it also leads to more work in the workshop by detecting worn or dangerous parts when servicing and inspection is taking place. This repair work inevitably goes to the workshop where the flow-line is operating. It is quite possible to offer a service for all makes of cars on a flow-line basis but this can lead to problems as a flow-line must be operated on a time and motion study basis. Changing an oil filter on one car can take 3 minutes and on another 10 minutes, even longer on commercial vehicles. Thus it would be possible to create a blockage on a flow-line but once again we shall refer to this possibility later.

Perhaps a problem associated with flow-lines is the manning of the various stages. Men can get bored on one type of job and can lose interest in the work involved. For example a man constantly employed on one job, say checking an adjusting tappets, tightening cylinder head bolts and similar associated jobs on one stage of a flow-line, is bound to become bored and this can result in careless work. Production lines in car factories can suffer in a similar way. The way to overcome this is to have men on each stage 2 weeks at a time. If 6 stages are involved then 12 weeks on the line will be required before a man reverts back to stage 1. Some flow-line operators allow men to go back into a workshop after 4 or 5 weeks on the line. All men in the workshop take a turn on the flow-line. It is true to say, however, that some mechanics once having worked on flow-line servicing prefer to stay on the line rather than go back into a workshop on general repair work. Now if we look at the single bay system of servicing and compare this with a flow-line we can assess its merits. We have already seen that single bay operation is bound to operate when car population density does not merit flow-line operation. In areas where car density is heavy a single bay will, when operated efficiently, produce very good results. Some garages employ two mechanics in the bay to speed up service. Whilst one mechanic works on one part of the car the other works on another part. Where possible more than 2 mechanics can be employed but a stage is reached when too many mechanics can get in one anothers way. However, the judicious use of mechanics ina single bay can reduce considerably service time schedules set up by manufacturers. However, full flow-line operation usually includes many more items than those included on normal service and a customer gets very good value for money. A single service bay cannot usually employ all the equipment necessary for some services and cars have got to be shunted from the single bay to another area for a brake test, chassis dynamometer test or other specialized part of a service check. Single bay servicing has been in use for many years, almost since the invention of the motor car and has been successful. It still is successful but the future of service work is bound either to make service bays fully comprehensive for all equip- ment or lead to the adoption of a flow-line system. A speed bay fully equipped means one bay occupied with one or two mechanics working on a car. On a flow-line the equipment is distributed along the line with mechanics at each stage: a continuous flow of cars move along the line and this system must result in greater productivity. Cars in a single bay have to be driven in and out. If the bay is against a wall the car has to be backed out following a service and shunted about with loss of time as the car is handled. Each car has to be handled this way. Some workshops now employ a drive-in—drive-out service bay saving time by having good access and exit points and approaching the idea of a flow-line.

So we have now assessed the objects and ideas of single bay and flow-line servicing. Only the garage owner can decide if a flow-line will pay. In a heavily populated area any service station owner would do well to dwell on what has been written. Furthermore since the end of the 1939—1945 war the car population has steadily increased, almost doubling every 10 years. In 1969 10 million cars were registered, in 1983 over 18 million vehicles are on the roads in Britain. The Electrical Development Association along with some motor manufacturers, estimate that 20% of all vehicles may eventually be electrically driven vehicles. Who can say in this fast changing but constantly expanding industry what we can expect by the year 1990 or 2000. Progressive

garage owners must be prepared to meet the present and future demands of
the car servicing industry and one of the ways to meet these demands is
either by installing a flow-line or by reorganizing existing premises and equipment to operate on a flow-line system. Many service stations have installed
equipment on a piecemeal basis over the years to meet immediate needs and
consequently have equipment located in various parts of a workshop which
really needs to be re-organized to obtain a much better return for the owner.

Let us assume then that a flow-line is to be considered. Here is the procedure
to be adopted.

Planning a flow-line

As motor manufacturers issue service requirements for all vehicles the implementation of the work on a flow-line basis should be considered as follows:
1) Decide and list the problems to be solved. Include the following items:
    a) All the jobs requiring attention, i.e. oil changes and/or checks, tappet
        adjustments, contact breaker point adjustment, etc.
    b) Location of each of these jobs on the flow-line.
    c) The time required to execute each job: where not given by the manu-
        facturer a stop-watch check should be made to obtain an average time.
    d) The staff required for each job so that a smooth flow can be obtained
        and bottle-necks avoided. For example, if 6 stages of 10 minutes are
        envisaged then work for 10 minutes in each stage must be carefully
        allocated. Car inspection and lubrication can cause congestion and
        duplication of this section is sometimes required, for example two
        lifts or pits. Such duplication allows a car on a minor service to bypass
        one on a larger service.
2) Assess the benefits to be gained for having a flow-line in your workshops
    i.e. skilled, semi-skilled and unskilled workers placed at correct places
    with minimum waste of time. Also, equipment placed in a logical order
    to obtain maximum use and profitability from it can be considered.
3) Calculate the *area* to be required for such a service, the *capital expenditure*
    needed for equipment or removal of existing equipment, *overheads* in-
    volved for rental, services etc., and the *total staff* required, so arriving at
    the cost.
4) The *revenue* which can be expected from the service should then be cal-
    culated. Operational expenses and depreciation of equipment should be
    deducted from the revenue, to calculte the total net *profit*.
5) When all calculations are complete and it is certain that a profit will be
    made and increased over previous servicing methods then installation of
    the line can proceed. Much useful advice and financial aid can be obtained
    from oil companies who have experience in this field. Personnel in charge
    of such work at the oil companies are usually referred to as 'Dealer Planning

Engineers'. These are the people to be contacted for all practical advice and any servicing or workshop manager would be wise to seek their advice.

Ideas for flow-line layouts

It is now necessary to see how a flow-line is arranged. We have considered the basic requirements and now the layouts themselves need some study. Ideally, a flow-line on a continuous straight line is best with sufficient width to enable a vehicle to be shunted off the line if necessary. Consider the service offered, layout and personnel required for a standard basic car of all makes bearing in mind some of the pitfalls involved where an identical make of car is not used on a flow-line. Here is a suggested service whihc has been used successfully.

Commercial vehicle standard service

1. Check rear axle and gear box, oil levels, top up as necessary. Visual inspection of suspension. Check wheel nuts.
2. Change engine oil and filters. Check fan belt and engine generally.
3. Jack up, check brakes and steering. Check lights and focus headlamps.
4. Check fifth wheel coupling and all fittings. Check tyres for pressure and for cracks, loose bolts etc.
5. Full lubrication of all grease and oil points. Check tyres for pressure and wear.
6. Smoke check.

Now these items need to be completed at six stages as indicated, each stage in this case taking about 30 minutes—a total of 3 hours. The line could be arranged as shown in Fig. 1.5 but such is not essential. In practice a line can operate by driving a vehicle from one bay area to another as shown in Fig. 1.6. Pits or lifts are required to carry out the service.

In Fig. 1.7 a further flow-line is shown to give an idea of variations that can be adopted.

At some service stations only one make of car is taken on the line. In addition to the usual service requirements many additions are made, making it very attractive to customers. This service is shown below and the work is executed in 6 stages as follows:

Stage 1. Remove wheels. Inspect tyres for wear and report. Balance wheels. Check tyre pressure. Check brake adjustments, mechanisms and linings. Inspect drums, discs and leaks from hub seals. Inspect dampers, road springs, Hydrolastic units, swivel pins. Replace wheels and check that they rotate freely. Check under bonnet. Adjust tappets and pull down cylinder head if required. Renew valve cover gasket. Clean or renew air cleaner element as required. Check fan belt condition and adjust.

Stage 2. Test braking efficiency (including hand-brake). Check and top up dampers. Tighten carburettor and manifold flanges. Clean or renew distribu-

FLOWLINE FOR COMMERCIAL VEHICLES

LINE	STAGES	EQUIPMENT	STAFF
	STAGE 1	(a) LIFT OR PIT (b) TOOLS FOR JOBS	1 SEMI-SKILLED MECHANIC
	STAGE 2	TOOLS FOR JOB	1 SKILLED MECHANIC
	STAGE 3	(a) TROLLEY JACK OR WHEEL FREE LIFT (b) STEERING ALIGNMENT EQUIPMENT (c) HEADLAMP ALIGNMENT EQUIPMENT (d) TOOLS FOR JOB	1 SKILLED MECHANIC 1 UNSKILLED WORKER
	STAGE 4	(a) LIFT OR PIT (b) TOOLS FOR JOB	1 SKILLED MECHANIC
	STAGE 5	(a) LUBRICATION EQUIPMENT (b) LIFT OR PIT (c) AIRLINE FOR TYRES (d) TOOLS FOR JOB	1 SEMI-SKILLED MECHANIC
	STAGE 6	SMOKE METER	1 SEMI-SKILLED MECHANIC

50 metres (165 feet)

7 metres (23 feet)

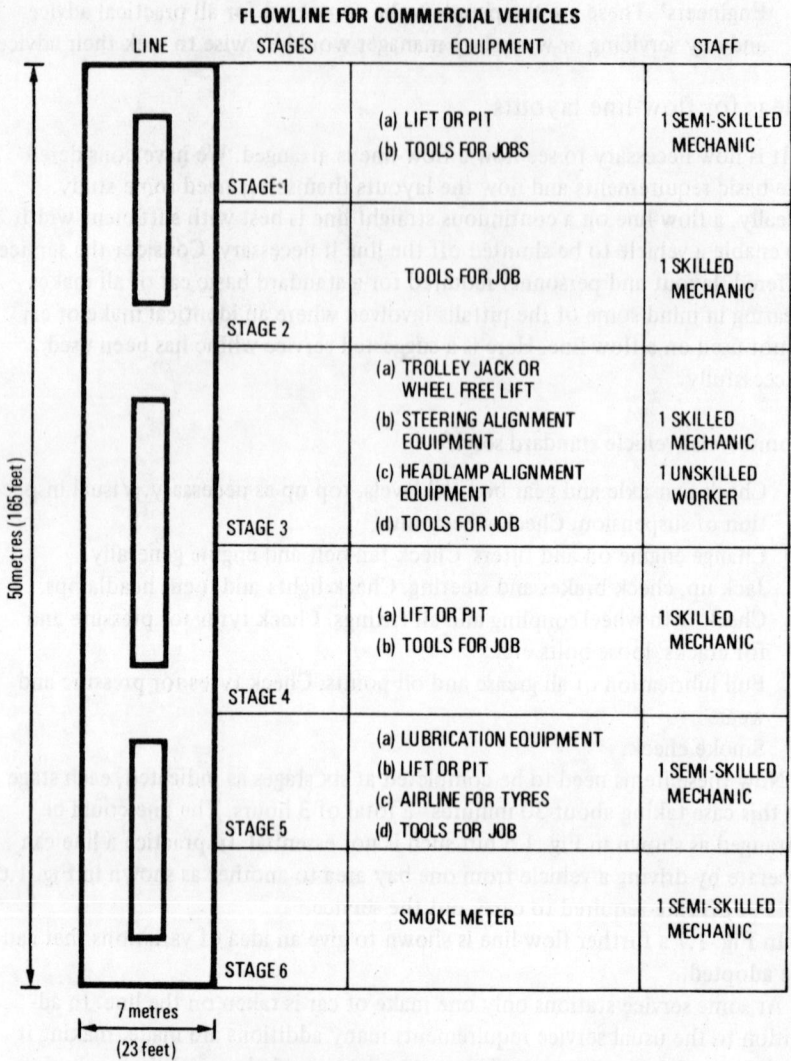

Fig. 1.5 Flow-line Layout (1)

tor points. Check and clean distributor caps and rotor arm, centrifugal spring tension, oil centre spindle. Check and tighten battery connections. Top up battery. Test horn, heater and windscreen wipers. Check seat and window mechanisms, wiper blades and windscreen washers. Check and adjust headlamp alignment and brilliance. Test all lamps, including indicators, interior lights and panel warning lamps. Lubricate door locks and hinges.

Stage 3. Clean or change plugs. Check compressions on engine and test cylinder head gasket for leaks. Test pressure system in radiator, all connections and

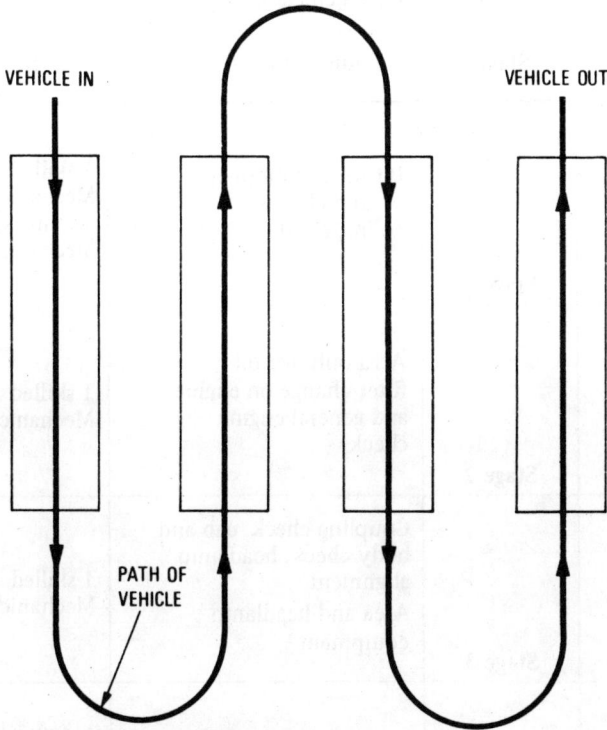

Fig. 1.6 Flow-line Layout (2)

hoses and top up if required. Top up windscreen-washer bottle. Check brake
and clutch master cylinders and slave cylinder. Check and adjust clutch pedal.
Check safety belt anchorages. Test for oil, petrol and water leaks throughout
vehicle. Test exhaust system and tighten brackets. Check pipes, cables, pro-
peller shaft couplings and bell ends. Check and top up oil and fluid levels in
engine, gearbox, rear axle, brake master cylinder, clutch master cylinder,
idler box, steering box, rack and pinion and automatic. Lubricate grease
points, dynamo, bearing and water pump. Change oils if instructed.
Stage 4. Adjust throttle and choke controls. Test battery voltage, cranking
    voltage, starter system, charging voltage and voltage regulator. Check coil
    voltage, voltage drop, points, primary windings in coil. Test distributor,
    condenser, coil polarity and secondary windings. Check h.t. leads, plugs.
    Adjust ignition timing. Check automatic advance, vacuum advance,
    centrifugal-advance, and air/fuel ratios at idle, intermediate and high speeds.
    Check power in each cylinder.
Stage 5. Test road performance. Acceleration test. Overrun test 100 kilometres
    per hour to 65 kilometres per hour (60 miles per hour to 40 miles per hour
    approximately). Record maximum power reading and speed in top gear.

Commercial Vehicle Flow-Line

Line	Stages	Equipment and Service	Staff
	Stage 1	Pit for full lubrication and chassis inspection	1 skilled Mechanic 1 semi-skilled Mechanic
	Stage 2	Area only for oil filter change on engine and general engine check	1 skilled Mechanic
	Stage 3	Coupling check, cab and body check, headlamp alignment Area and headlamp equipment	1 skilled Mechanic
	Stage 4	Steering and brake check Area and equipment	1 skilled Mechanic 1 unskilled Mechanic
	Stage 5	Quality control check for power output on dynamometer. Smoke meter check	1 skilled Mechanic
	Stage 6	Wash with vehicle washer polish	1 unskilled worker

Note. **Stage 6** can be suitably placed at **Stage 1**. D.Tp. work demands top and under cleaning. Thus, washing underneath before inspections is really essential.

Fig. 1.7 Flow-line Layout (3)

Test fuel consumption at 70 kilometres per hour (45 miles per hour). Check accuracy of speedometer at varying speeds. Test clutch operation, differential operation and engine rev/min.

Stage 6. Full wash.

In all these flow-lines, equipment to operate the service is placed at suitable points along the line to enable the work at the various stages to be completed. Equipment for one Service of Leyland cars is arranged as shown in Fig. 1.8 but not in the straight line shown because of space difficulties.

A final example is shown in Fig. 1.9

A standard service for any make of car is shown now. Care should be taken in planning the line to avoid bottlenecks as previously explained.

Standard service for cars and light vans

1. Check steering and wheel alignments.
2. Check brakes and adjust as necessary.
3. Check engine for loose, worn components, fan belt. Adjust as necessary.
4. Check plugs and points. Clean and reset. Electronic engine analyser check.
5. Full lubrication service.
6. Check chassis and body generally for deterioration.
7. Check suspension.

Diagnostic centres

Diagnostic Centres have been in operation in the U.S.A. a decade and have become popular in this country where they have been well promoted. Such centres not only diagnose faults as a normal rule, they are also used to check work done on a car as a means of quality control in the workshop. Diagnosis is made by performing inspections to discover what parts of a car or commercial vehicle require adjustment or repair. It is a useful aid to generate more business in the workshop. When diagnostic equipment is used as a means of quality control, any repairs executed are tested to ensure the finished job is satisfactory and operation is within certain limits. For example, if new contact breaker points have been fitted and the dwell angle is $57^{\circ}-63^{\circ}$ then the quality control check should reveal whether the mechanic has completed the work satisfactorily. Most jobs can be checked with correct type of equipment.

Note: 1) Difficult corners to negotiate—not recommended.

   2) Lifts placed in such a way cars cannot be shunted off the line if a serious defect is found.

   3) For preference a 6 metre width is desired so that cars on minor or major service can proceed to sections of a line or to enable one section to be omitted.

   4) A flow-line can be operated for part of a working day if considered suitable for prevailing custom and conditions.

Line	Stage	Equipment	Staff
Automatic Door Path of Car 50 metres	**Stage 1** All gaskets, parts etc. placed in a basket inside the car	Wheel free lift Wheel balancer Torque wrench and other suitable tools	One skilled Mechanic One semi-skilled Mechanic
	Stage 2	Brake tester Headlamp alignment equipment Tools as required	2 Mechanics
	Stage 3	One lift or pit Compression tester Radiator and cap tester Tools as required	1 Mechanic 1 unskilled worker
	Stage 4	Electronic engine analyser Tools as required	1 skilled Mechanic
	Stage 5	Dynamometer	1 skilled Mechanic
5 metres Wash-Finish	**Stage 6**	Car washing machine	1 unskilled operator

Fig. 1.8 Diagnostic Flow-line Service Layout

This line not only 'services' a car but many extra items are checked on the cars. 'Diagnosing' or 'fault finding' are part of the line. The customer can benefit by having defective parts replaced after service and not whilst out on the road! Because of diagnostic checks with servicework it would be true to say that this arrangement is *A Diagnostic Flow-Line Service Layout*. Staff are fully utilized for skill and time thus aiding efficiency and profitability.

WORKSHOP AREA

30 metres (100 feet)

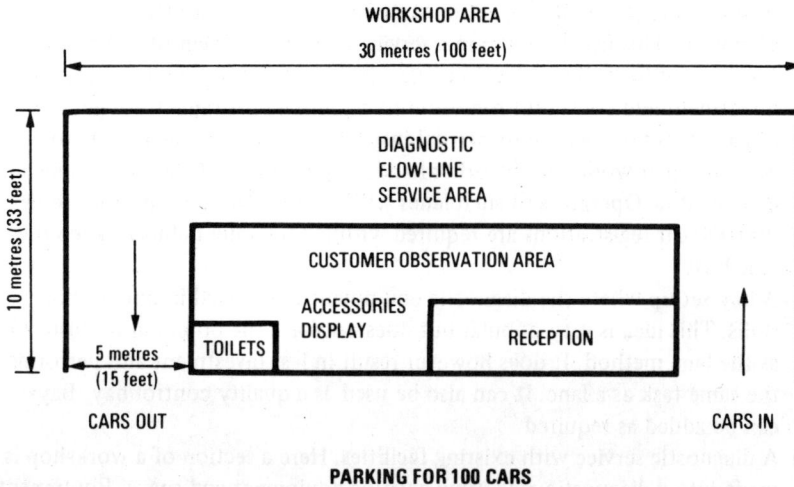

Fig. 1.9 Diagnostic Flow-line Service Layout

5) As with repair work, cars should be serviced away from commercial vehicles. Otherwise, car owning customers may expect damage to occur.

From the garage point of view advantages of diagnostic centres are as follows:
1) Equipment installed is useful for diagnostic and quality control.
2) Faults revealed are generally passed to the workshop thus increasing profit on labour and parts.
3) It is attractive to customers who appreciate checks for safety and efficiency.
4) Flexibility for partial inspections if of a bay type centre.
5) Use for checking second-hand vehicles prior to repair and selling.

The disadvantages from the garage owner's point of view could be summarized as follows:
1) Costly investment.
2) Mechanics have to be trained to use the equipment.
3) Space taken which otherwise could be used for repair bays.

However, all of these disadvantages can be nullified provided the centre is a well advertised in a reasonable area where car population is good, and gives an efficient service to attract customers back time and time again. Some service stations run diagnostic clubs offering two or three diagnostic checks per year for a fixed fee of £10 or so.

If it is decided to proceed with a diagnostic centre, the next decision is what type of layout should be considered. Space is the all-important factor but at least one of the layouts below will be suitable.

1) A diagnostic lane with inspection stations end to end for drive-through operation. This usually takes in a service as well as a diagnostic check but can be used for a diagnostic lane only. It does, however, require a sizeable investment and constant promotion to achieve a profitable throughput of of cars. It is not suitable for partial inspections and is not adaptable to general repair work. On the other hand, a large volume of work does mean large profits. Operators of such lanes without rivals have found that some 200 000 car registrations are required within a ten mile radius to keep the lane busy.

2) A bay set up where the diagnostic equipment is arranged in one or more stalls. This idea is very popular but does not have the potential of business as the lane method. It does however result in less investment and performs the same task as a lane. It can also be used as a quality control bay. Bays can be added as required.

3) A diagnostic service with existing facilities. Here a section of a workshop is made into a diagnostic area using existing equipment and space. Equipment can be supplemented as required. If this produces the custom a separate diagnostic bay can be installed at a later date.

Equipment for diagnostic centres

The equipment needed for any centre will depend upon the service offered. For a comprehensive diagnostic check the following equipment will be required.

Wheel-free lift/s, comprehensive electronic engine analysing equipment, headlamp alignment equipment, comprehensive wheel alignment equipment, wheel balancer, chassis dynamometer and brake tester, services to operate this equipment (air, electricity and water). This comprises all major equipment. In the future it is likely to be extended to include front wheel dynamic steering checks. This involves running the front wheels on rollers that can swivel and thus check the steering mechanisms. Likewise, mechanical tests on dampers (shock-absorbers) will be made. In the U.S.A. some tests of this nature are already completed along with such things as chemical analysis of automatic gearbox oils to determine whether the oil is contaminated and the type and amount of wear this could indicate.

In addition to the major items listed additional diagnostic service tools required are as follows: Brake drum micrometer, Calipers to measure brake lining thickness, cooling system and pressure cap tester also antifreeze tester, tyre tread depth gauge and tyre pressure gauge, height gauges for measuring torsion bar and spring heights, ball joint checking instrument, torque wrenches for various parts, air cleaner tester and hand tools as required.

Recently developed equipment which will probably find its way into diagnostic centres and now used in repair shops is the sonic leak tester. This quickly tests and traces leaks in brakes lines; slow punctures and body leaks can also be very quickly detected. Thus, a quick check of braking systems for slight leaks is possible and another addition to any diagnostic centre.

Washing and car valeting

Very recently car washers have become very popular in the retail motor trade. Washers of course are not new but certain events have taken place which must now make good car washers a part of any good service station layout.

Let us examine the reasons for investing in such equipment. First, the general public are beginning to shrink from the time-consuming messy job of washing the car as a Sunday ritual. Many people are more interested in leisure than in washing cars. Representatives, executives and many more people cannot spare the car for one to three hours and are anxious to have a clean car in 3 minutes or 10 minutes depending on the type of wash being made. Before the car wash is installed, a service manager will have a good idea of its possible use by assessing car population, existing customers, competition already in the area and so on. Use of the car wash could form part of the end of a flow-line or it could be used before any car is serviced, thus helping to keep the workshop clean and customers satisfied. With relatively low cost washing, custom must grow. A car wash then can be useful as a profitable side-line and as an aid to efficient workshop practice. Like all equipment, however, it must pay its way and budgeted for accordingly.

There are a number of washers available and selection must meet the needs of the service station where it is to be installed. Let us examine typical installations.

Coin operated car wash

With one attendant this wash proceeds as follows:
1) Coins or tokens are inserted in the meter which is positioned so that the driver need not get out of his car.
2) Red light changes to green indicating driver to proceed to a marked spot.
3) Conveyor chain is switched on by the vehicle by a contact switch and vehicle is pushed forward.
4) Shampoo spray arch loosens road film and dirt.
5) Brushing stage where 7 brushes move over the car, 2 on the wheels, 4 on the sides and 1 on the roof. Brushes are self-cleaning thus avoiding streaks on the paintwork.
6) As the car moves along parts of it are washed several times by different jets placed in different positions.
7) Rinsing arch—vehicle rinsed with water.
8) Wax spraying arch—vehicle paintwork fully sprayed with wax emulsion.
9) Vehicle rolls into drying zone which is completely separated by a special anti-splash door and which does not open until touched by the front of

the vehicle. High air pressure and air speed quickly dry the car avoiding streaks on the paint work. The horizontal air jets are suspended telescopically and glide close to the vehicle contours guided by photo-cell scanning. Other air jets are placed in suitable vertical positions.

10) A second green light comes on indicating the car can leave the wash— finished!

It takes two weeks to install this wash. The wash itself takes 3 minutes and 60 cars per hour can use the wash. The inside of the car is not cleaned but some service stations now have valeting for the inside as well; we shall discuss this later.

Fixed-car moving-gantry car wash

With this type of wash, the car remains stationery whilst a gantry on rails moves over the car, cleaning the car in a similar way to the wash described above. Certain items operate differently and the process could consist of clean water wash, detergent wash, rinse and dry without waxing.

Wall-mounted container wash

Simple car washers are still available which consists of a wall mounted container which has an electrically driven pump. The pump operates at pressures up to $3.12N/mm^2$ ($450lbf/in^2$). An operating lever with 'Off', 'Detergent' and 'Water Rinse' positions is used by the operator. By directing the jet on to various parts of the car cleaning is completed. The jet is sometimes replaced by a brush and mains water pressure only used. The high pressure referred to is especially useful for cleaning the underneath of cars. Warm or hot water gives better results with this type of wash which takes between 5 and 10 minutes. Care should be taken to avoid forcing water into door locks where subsequently it could freeze in cold weather.

Valeting

The washed car can now receive internal valeting (if required) as part of the service. American car valeting has operated like this for many years. To do this a good vacuum cleaner is essential. Special car vacuum cleaners are available and these have special nozzles to enable every part of the car to be cleaned thoroughly. Stiff brushes form part of the vacuum nozzles with some makes so that brushing cloth upholstery results in improved cleaning and appearance. An operator is necessary for this job and in some American valeting stations one operator vacuums the car, empties ash-trays front and rear whilst another operator applies a quick silicone polish to any metal parts as well as using a duster to wipe over the instrument panel. Difficult stains on upholstery are not removed in the wash area. The car is shunted off for this work if required and one of the many patented cleaners for leather or P.V.C. used. Upholstery

cleaners of this nature have improved greatly in recent years and various
cleaners are now available for all types of materials. The American car valeting
includes wash, wax, dry, polish, internal vacuum and polish. Taking about 15
minutes and costing up to 2 dollars it is a very popular service in America.

The layout and selection of the car-wash and valeting equipment will depend
on seven factors, namely (1) will customers use the wash and car valeting
equipment—a survey will indicate this, (2) is the car population sufficient to
merit installation, (3) could 'contract' work be obtained from local fleet
owners, (4) would the service station 'workshop' and 'car sales' benefit—
especially if cars stand outside for sales purposes and a lot of cleaning is
involved, (5) what is the cost of running the equipment and is it a profitable
proposition, (6) is a good space available to install the wash so that customers
can easily see it and use it, (7) what competition exists or is likely to exist in
the future?

As with all items of equipment, a careful assessment to make up a profit
and loss account should be made prior to purchase. The account, in this case,
would include (1) cost of installation and consequent loss of interest on
capital invested, (2) cost of running the wash, i.e. electricity, water rate for
water used and disposal of effluent from the wash, promotion costs, cost of
detergents/waxes, hidden costs such as cleaning out of the water-traps each
week, and the need of protection against frost damage if located outside,
depreciation costs of equipment on a 5 or 10 year life depending upon the
manufacturer of equipment being used and charges for maintenance of equipment.

On the credit side is the customer who pays for individual washes and
contract work. Other credits are of course the value to the workshop and car
sales in 'time saved' which is always difficult to assess.

Before installing any such equipment a service manager should examine as
many car-washes and car valeting items as he can in order to select the equipment best suited to his needs. A student would benefit greatly by visiting
service stations which have such equipment and obtaining comprehensive
answers to the questions listed below.

Visit to a car valeting area of a service station

1. How in detail does the car-wash operate, i.e. water used, detergents, wash/
   wax times, types of brushes, etc.
2. What quality of finish is obtained when a car comes through the wash and
   is presented to the customer (water-streaks, brush marks, etc.)? Is it
   necessary to provide brushes and detergent mixture for parts of the car
   missed in the wash?
3. What are the costs of installation, cost of running and return on investment
   expected over one year? Make out a profit and loss account.

4. (a) How would you promote a car wash?
   (b) How does this particular workshop promote the wash?
5. Once the car has been washed the complete valeting includes internal cleaning. Detail the jobs to be done then (a) how you would have them completed? (b) how does this workshop complete the jobs?
6. Why was the car-wash located in this position and what are the advantages and disadvantages of a car-wash on a service station site.

Breakdown equipment

A vehicle which breaks down on the road has to be moved as quickly as possible so that obstruction of the road is reduced to a minimum. The cause of a breakdown could range from a failed capacitor in the ignition system to a collapsed set of gears in a gear-box. Consequently, the mechanics going out on a recovery vehicle must be fully experienced, be able to diagnose faults quickly, be able to use all the recovery equipment (e.g. winch, crane, slings, shackles, tow bar, towing ambulance—a tow bar with wheels and cradle, the broken down vehicle is lifted onto the ambulance at one end and towed using the front or rear wheels of the vehicle as required—, fire extinguisher, first aid and all other appliances on the breakdown vehicle. Recovery crews should also be familiar with the restrictive speeds when towing which vary according to type of recovery vehicle, that is whether solid or pneumatic tyres which have 13 kilometres per hour or 26 kilometres per hour (8 or 16 miles per hour) limits). Breakdown vehicles, fully equipped, are now supplied by manufacturers specializing in this type of vehicle. However, the important thing is to ensure that recovery vehicle mechanics can use the slings and lifting gear safely and are fully aware that a safe working load marked on a lifting item means that this load cannot be exceeded. Thus a crane marked S.W.L. 1 000 kg (2 200 lb) means that nothing can be lifted that will exceed this amount. This also applied to the slings, shackles, hooks and all lifting devices which have a *safe working load* stamped on them or identified by tags attached to them.

When called out, a breakdown crew have to be prepared to pull vehicles out of ditches, tow wrecked vehicles and complete a host of repairs to get a vehicle back into a workshop. The breakdown vehicle should be equipped as stated previously and in addition should have the following: sledge-hammer, crow-bars, a length of rope 30 mm ($1\frac{3}{16}$ in) diameter and 40 metres long (130 feet), two or three wooden planks 80 mm (3 in) thick with widths of 10 cm (4 in), 20 cm (8 in) and 30 cm (12 in), at least 2 metres (6 feet) long, a trolley jack of good capacity, large steel levers, portable electric lamps, locking clamps for a steering wheel when a car has to be towed backwards, flashing beacon to indicate a breakdown, waterproof clothing for the breakdown mechanics, a suitable 'on tow' notice board for attaching to the vehicle, lengths of twin electric cable and spare lamp holders for attaching to the broken down vehicle for rear illumination if required and a normal mechanics' tool-kit. Many garages mark breakdown equipment kept on the vehicle with a special bright paint so that the equipment is kept on the vehicle and does not find its way into the workshop. Periodically, the breakdown vehicle's lifting equipment has to be inspected under the Factories Act, and at the same time it is useful to check that all breakdown equipment is correct by checking the inventory on the vehicle. The inspection of lifting equipment, incidently, is carried out by an independent inspecting engineer usually belonging to an insurance company. A report is then issued and has to be filed by the garage owner for inspection by the Factory Inspector as required. The condition of the equipment is recorded and these reports and any action required should receive immediate attention.

Finally, the size of the breakdown vehicle will depend upon its use. A car recovery vehicle will have a capacity up to 3 000 kg (6 600 lb) and a commercial recovery vehicle at least twice this amount to meet the needs of modern heavy vehicles. Consequently, commercial recovery vehicles often have high capacity engines to give very high tractive effort at their road wheels. See Appendix II for details of AVRO.

Budgeting—evaluation and selection of workshop equipment

When considering the purchase of equipment the correct approach is *will it pay*? Not *what does it cost*?

When tools or equipment are being thought about as *labour saving* devices, the costing must be marked out on the following lines. Let us assume a power tool is available to replace a hand tool.

Example
a) Cost of hand tool = £6 Power Tool = £60.
b) Cost of operator = £0.5 per hour.
c) Power tool halves job time.
d) Operating time 1 000 hours per year on hand tool.
e) Power consumption 0.5 h.p. per hour.
f) Power cost 1p per h.p. per hour
g) For the hand tool allow *20% of cost* for depreciation, maintenance and other cost. i.e. 20% of £6 = £1.20. Annual labour cost = 1 000 × £0.50 =
£500
Running costs of hand tool = £1.20 + £500 =
£501.20
For the power tool allow 10% for maintenance, 10% for depreciation, 3% per annum capital charge (which is the interest which could be obtained by putting the cost of the machine into a safe investment).
a) *Capital charge* interest (3% on £60) = £1.80
b) *Depreciation* (10% of £60)   = £6.00
c) *Maintenance* (10% of £60)   = £6.00

d) *Power costs* $\left(\dfrac{1\,000\ \text{hours}}{2} \times \dfrac{1\text{p}}{2}\right)$ = £2.50

   (half h.p. and half operating time)

e) *Labour* (500 hours × £0.50)   = £250

   £266.30
   _____

Use of hand tool costs   £501.20

Use of power tool costs   £266.30

£234.90 = *saving in costs per annum.*

Difference means

1) Reduction in price of job possible and a better chance in competition.
2) Increase in general turnover leading indirectly to greater profit.

This calculation assumes that other work would be found for the mechanic during the time saved otherwise labour costs would be the same and extra cost of power would be all loss.

Depreciation of equipment

All equipment wears out and due allowance must be made for this. The same applies to buildings, vehicles and so on. In connection with depreciation the following formulae can be used as a means of calculating annual depreciation.

Let P = original cost of machine, equipment, building etc.

N = number of years of estimated useful life of unit.

R = scrap or second hand value at the end of N years.

D = annual sum to be charged as depreciation.

Thus $D = \dfrac{P - R}{N}$.

Example– An electronic engine analyser when purchased cost £1 000 and its useful life is estimated at 5 years. The scrap value of the equipment is expected to be £30. What is the annual depreciation?

$$D = \frac{P - R}{N}$$

$$\therefore D = \frac{1\,000 - 30}{5} = \frac{970}{5} = £194$$

Annual Depreciation = £194.

Depreciation of all garage equipment and assets has to be considered in order to obtain correct profit and loss accounts. Depreciation of different items varies considerably. Here are some approximate rates of depreciation per annum.

Asset	Annual Rate of Depreciation (%)
Buildings	2.5
Boilers	5.0
Electrical cables	3.0
Electrical motors	8.0
Electrical transformers	8.0
Electrical dynamos	8.0
Diesel engines	10.0
Lorries	22.5
Coaches	15.0
Vans	20.0

From experience, depreciation values will vary from these given. For example, a temporary concrete building could depreciate to scrap value between 10 and 20 years. Suppliers will always be pleased to give this information. Similarly, *use* of a machine such as a pillar drill will affect depreciation as well as natural ageing of wiring and insulation. Machines such as drills, lathes, grinders etc. are usually depreciated at a rate of 7.5 to 10.00% per annum, whilst tools are depreciated at a rate of 5.0 per annum. Taking the latter as an example, it means tools should last 20 years before becoming scrap. Mechanics will know that some tools will last longer and some much shorter than this because usage, quality of material as well as natural ageing affect depreciation. Consequently, whilst the formulae and figures given are useful aids to calculating depreciation, the facts regarding the number of years of useful life should be carefully considered in all calculations.

Selection of equipment for a workshop

It will be obvious that the size of the workshop and the amount of work expected will have a strong bearing on the equipment to be purchased. No workshop can be efficient without suitable tools and equipment. The service station owner, service manager or other responsible person will decide which equipment is necessary as an aid to efficiency and profitability in a workshop. An entirely new layout gives a great opportunity for careful selection and placing of equipment to obtain maximum productivity from the repair shop. As stated previously the different types of garages perform servicing and repair operations according to size, and equipment must be of a certain standard if M.A.A. membership is being sought. An independent operator, however, will choose for himself from the tools and equipment listed below what exactly suits his needs.

A list of equipment and tool *suppliers* can always be obtained by looking at trade journals. Two journals which specialize in equipment and tools as well as small technical articles are: *The Service Station* and *Garage and Transport Equipment.*

Motor vehicle workshop equipment

Wheel Free and other types of *Lifts.*
Comprehensive wheel alignment equipment.
Air compressor.
Combined dynamometer and brake tester (or individual units if more suitable).
Lubrication equipment.
Brake servicing equipment.
Wheel balancer.
Lifting jacks.
Paraffin wash tanks and degreasing plant.
Hydraulic press.
Battery charging unit including hydrometer, 0–20 V voltmeter and High Rate Discharge Tester.
Steam cleaner or high pressure water cleaner.
Electrical testing equipment for starters, dynamo, ignition circuits and timing.
Electronic engine analyser equipment (comprehensive).
Power hacksaw.
Comprehensive engine overhaul equipment comprising engine stands, cylinder boring, grinding and re-sleeving plant, valve and valve seat grinding and re-seating equipment, connecting rod alignment jig, piston and piston ring service tools valve spring compressors, various cylinder gauges, micrometers and verniers.
Main bearing and big-end bearing boring equipment.
Tyre repair plant for tubes, valve vulcanizers, also includes tyre removing jig, tyre levers and vulcanizing unit for permanent repairs to tubeless tyres and inner tubes.
Oxyacetylene and metallic arc welding equipment (could include spot welding machine and/or continuous wire feed CO_2 welding equipment).
Headlamp alignment equipment.
Gas soldering ovens and irons with assorted bits.
Lathe, 15 cm to 24 cm (6 in to 9 in) centres with various tools and attachments, e.g. milling head.
Power drills–Bench pillar type with capacity up to 30 mm ($1\frac{1}{4}$ in) diameter drill. Portable drills, capacity up to 15 mm ($\frac{5}{8}$ in) diameter drill.
Power shaping machine (small).
Breakdown and salvage plant usually a vehicle completely equipped with a crane, winch and other tackle.
Shop benching with tool racks and steel tool cupboards and steel vices 7.5 cm and 15 cm jaws (3 in and 6 in).
Creepers for under car work.
Diesel pump and injector testing equipment, also includes reconditioning equipment for injectors and pumps. Smoke tester.
Body Repair Equipment, this can be very extensive, but should include *body*

jigs for checking car dimensions, hydraulic push and pull rams with assorted connections and heads, a comprehensive range of dollies and spoons, planishing hammers, sanders (air or electric) buffers and polishers, paint spraying equipment with suitable booths and paint baking ovens. Welding equipment to include oxyacetylene CO_2 Metallic Inert Gas, (MIG) metallic arc and portable spot welding equipment with variety of heads and cranked arms. Sheet metal cutting, folding and rolling equipment. Straight and curved tinsnip.

Forge or hearth can still be useful, but virtually obsolete. However, still essential for much workshop practice is a *gas brazing blowpipe* 2 cm (0.75 in) to use with a *small forge* and *swage block*.

Anvil with tongs (flat and round).

Marking out equipment comprising surface plate, scribing block, steel squares, surface gauges, scribing blocks, dividers, scribers, engineers' blue, sine bar, protractors.

Axle stands for cars and commercial vehicles.

Portable crane or hoists for lifting vehicles or units such as engines.

Fire fighting and first aid equipment.

Bench grinding-machine with coarse and fine stones 20 cm (8 in) diameter.

Shot-blasting cabinet for cleaning parts which have cavities in difficult positions.

Turntables for garages with restricted space.

Sparking plug cleaning and testing machine.

Motor vehicle workshop tools, these are tools normally held in stores or on steel racks for use by mechanics. A comprehensive tool kit for mechanics suggested by the R.T.I.T.B. is given on pages 29 to 31.

Lathe tools, right and left hand assorted cutters, boring tools, screw cutting, knurling and chaser tools.

Drills, assorted from 1 mm to 25 mm ($\frac{1}{32}$ in to 1 in) also drills to suit special thread diameters.

Reamers, taper and parallel, also expanding reamers essential for repair work. Reamer sizes most used range from 10 mm to 30 mm ($\frac{3}{8}$ in to $1\frac{3}{16}$ in).

Sets of screw-cutting dies and taps. Threads to be cut will depend upon choice of dies and taps. Most common for motor vehicle work are metric, U.N.C., U.N.F., B.S.F., B.A. with Whitworth and B.S.P. found occasionally.

Screw thread gauges are kept with these tools also thread restorers.

Hammers various shapes and weights. Steel, leather, copper and rubber faced. Sledge hammers of 4 kilogramme (7 lb) weight is a popular size.

Scrapers of various shapes and sizes for bearing and decarbonizing.

Bolt cutters up to 20 mm ($\frac{3}{4}$ in) capacity.

Torque wrenches with capacity up to 30 NM (120 lbf ft)

Oil cans large and small.

Tyre pressure gauges.

Sets of ring spanners, short and long reach, also open-ended spanners.

Socket spanners. Assorted sockets to suit bolt and nut sizes normally used.

Sets of feeler guages metric and english sizes as required with taper blades.

Portable electric pressurized safety *inspection lamps* with low voltage supply.
Hacksaws with 20 cm to 30 cm (9 in to 12 in) frames.
Extractors for bearings and bolts.
Cold chisels, 5 mm to 30 mm ($\frac{3}{16}$ in to $1\frac{3}{16}$ in) width.
Multi-wheel braces for assorted wheel nuts.

Recommended apprentice tool kit. (R.T.I.T.B.)

(Note: R.T.I.T.B. give English sizes for tools only except for open-end, sockets and ring spanners listed).

Box,
Tool kit, steel with lock.
Bar,
40 cm Pry (16 in).
Brushes,
Steel wire 2 row,
engine cleaning,
file cleaning.
Chisels,
cold flat,
    crosscut,
      diamond point.
Caliper,
firm joint inside,
        outside.
Drifts,
brass.
Dividers,
16 cm (6 in) Quick release.
Files,

flat safe	bastard 2nd Cut
edge	25 cm (10 in) 20 cm (8 in)
flat edge	15 cm (6 in)
round	20 cm (8 in)
half round	20 cm (8 in)
square	15 cm (6 in)
warding	10 cm (4 in)

Gauges,
engineers' feeler, imperial and metric.
Hammers,
ball pein engineers' 0.75 kg ($1\frac{1}{2}$ lb)
                0.25 kg ($\frac{1}{2}$ lb)
combination hide and copper 1.5 kg (3 lb).

Keys,
hexagonal (Allen type) imperial and metric.
Punches (Engineers')
centre
parallel (Set of 5) 1 mm to 8 mm ($\frac{1}{16}$in to $\frac{5}{16}$in).
Pliers,
Engineers' side cutting,
round or snipe nose,
diagonal nip.
Rules,
stainless steel 16 cm (6 in) and 24 cm (12 in) with in and mm graduations.
Saws (Engineers'),
hacksaw adjustable frame to take 10 in and 12 in blades,
   Junior,
pad handle.
Screwdrivers,
engineers' heavy,
   light
    chubby,
electricians' large,
    small,
cross head nos. 1, 2, 3 blade
and chubby.
Scriber,
Engineers' double point,
one straight and one right,
angled point.
Square,
engineers 16 cm (6 in).
Scraper,
engineers', hand flat.
Snips,
tinmans.
Spanners,
open jawed BSF−BSW $\frac{1}{8}$ in to $\frac{3}{4}$ in
    AF $\frac{3}{8}$ in to $1\frac{1}{16}$ in
    BA 0 to 10
    metric 8 to 22mm
  socket BSF−BSW $\frac{3}{16}$ in to $\frac{3}{4}$ in
    AF$\frac{7}{16}$ in to $1\frac{1}{16}$ in
  Ring,
  doubled end BSF−BSW $\frac{3}{8}$ in to $\frac{3}{4}$ in
    AF $\frac{3}{8}$ in to $1\frac{1}{16}$ in
 Metric 10 to 22 mm,

SAFETY PRACTICES CHECK FORM

Date . . . .

Item	Available Yes or No	Operation O.K.	Action Taken	Responsibility
Fire Extinguishers				
Water Buckets				
Sand Buckets				
Fireproof Paint Store				
Fireproof Oil Store				
Flash Proof Bulbs				
Steel Dust Bins (Oily Rags Etc.)				
Oxy-Acetylene Gauges				
Oxy-Acetylene Hoses				
Welding Goggles				
Oily Floors				
Jack Stands				
Garage Jacks				
Chain Hoists				
Emery Wheel Guards				
Emery Wheel Goggles				
Belt Guards				
Lift Opening Gates				
Earther Lead Lamps				
Earthed Electrical Tools				
Loose Pit Boards				
Complete First Aid Kit				

Reproduced by kind permission of Vauxhall Motors Co.

Fig. 1.10 Safety Practices Check Form

See Appendix IV for recommended layout of safety forms.

open jawed adjustable, Length 8 in Jaw Opening 1 in.
Wrenches,
Pipe 8 in for $\frac{3}{4}$ in pipe,
Mole Grips.

Inspection and control of tools and equipment

All tools and equipment should be recorded in an inventory. The inventory should detail the date of purchase, supplier and cost. Spaces should be provided to initial inspection date checks. Inspection is to ensure all equipment is correct and in good working order as well as recording any maintenance carried out. Depending on the size of the station 6 monthly or annual checks should be made. See Fig. 1.10 for a 'safety practices check form' which is recommended to service managers by Vauxhall Motors Training School.

Design of Stationery

Throughout the text, forms, invoices, cards and similar recording data are mentioned and illustrated. Sometimes it may be necessary to design a particular card or form to a special application. The procedure to follow could be: 1) Decide which items need to be recorded. 2) Collect all essential data which must go on the document. 3) Analyse the data, place in logical sequence and decide where and how it will be set out. 4) When a provisional document has been made obtain constructive criticism from qualified staff. 5) With all amendments considered and implemented as required, the document can be printed.

'Afterthoughts' can be very expensive and attention to detail in the first instance is essential. Existing forms, cards and so on from manufacturers of stationery can be perused before designing any document for use in a dealership.

Questions

1. As a Service Manager you are given the task of converting part of your Service Department into a flow line system. Describe how you would lay out this new service and how you would redeploy the staff to operate the service. (I.M.I.)
2. The time spent by skilled mechanics at the Parts Counter still appears to be too high in some repair shops. Describe any system that you know which will eliminate this waste of highly-skilled men's time, or at least reduce it to a minimum. (I.M.I.)
3. In recent years Fleet Owners have become more 'service' minded. How would you organize the regular maintenance of a fleet comprising ten cars and forty medium weight commercial vehicles? (I.M.I.)

4. From time to time it is necessary to take a look at the Repair Workshop to ensure that all available space is being profitably used. How would you layout a Workshop measuring 80 feet by 150 feet with entrance and exit both at one end, so that no floor space was wasted? (I.M.I.)

5. Much valuable workshop space is often taken up by vehicles waiting for spare parts. In many cases this should not have been necessary. How would you organize your parts stock and your Reception/Workshop/Parts Department relations in order to cut this waste to the absolute minimum? (I.M.I.)

6. With operating costs continually rising, discuss whether servicing costs could be reduced without reducing the standard of workmanship and without reducing wages. (I.M.I.)

7. Much emphasis has recently been placed on the importance of quick service to customers. Some garages have met this problem by setting up a flow line installation. Describe this method of operation and also an alternative method of obtaining the same results. (I.M.I.)

8. Describe a suitable system of inspection and control for all shop tools and equipment used in a garage. (I.M.I.)

9. As a service manager you are about to take over a newly built Repair Shop. It has an area of 8 000 square feet and lies behind a showroom and petrol station on a main road. Entry is from the main road and there is an *exit only* to a side road. Draw a sketch showing how you would lay out the shop for general servicing for customers and company vehicles. (I.M.I.)

CHAPTER 2

ORGANIZATION OF DEPARTMENTS

Invoicing

The need for speedy invoicing lies in the fact that many customers pay cash for repairs when the car is released from the workshop. Customers with accounts will also wish to have their bills delivered on time. The service station itself relies on prompt payment in order to meet its own bills for wages, materials, overheads and so on. The quicker an invoice is made out and the sooner payment is received cannot be anything but beneficial to the organization. In any case, when bills are delayed unduly, any dispute about items listed can become obscure, especially if more than one repair has been completed in a short space of time. It is grossly inefficient to present any bills in excess of 28 days from the date of service or repair; in effect this is loaning money free of interest.

To achieve rapid invoicing many innovations have been made. Kalamazoo Ltd., have produced three and five card job sets. Manufacturers' Service Schools such as those of Vauxhall Motors, Leyland and Ford, have produced their individual interpretations of the easy to complete job sets.

One of these 3 part job sets is shown in Fig. 2.1. The three copies are used together. Usually, the reception engineer will make out the work required on the top copy which is recorded on the second and third copies. The customer signs the form approving the work to be done and this is the customer's invoice. Accounts/Cost Office receive the second copy and the third copy goes to the workshop. The last copy is used by the workshop to make out a job card, record parts used and is filed at reception for use as a service follow-up. On the back of this hard copy shown in Fig. 2.2 is printed the job card for use by the foreman and mechanic. Also detailed is a very useful chart for quality control inspection. The body work section can be completed before work commences and can prevent argument about scratches on bodywork whilst the car was in for repair! New car quality control, that for pre-delivery inspection, will require all parts to be examined as listed. Any faults found being corrected before the customer receives the new car. Many dealers give this quality control check as part of a service, thus helping to promote the garage with customers who appreciate such checks. Any repairs required can be noted and the customer advised. Following repair and certain services, the 'road test

CUSTOMER'S INVOICE SALE

V.A.T. Reg No.

NAME
ADDRESS

BUSINESS:
'PHONE PRIVATE:
MAKE/MODEL   COLOUR
REG· No.   REG-DATE
CHASSIS No.
ENGINE No.
COMM. No.
SUPPLIED BY

RECEIVED   REQUIRED
DATE TIME DATE TIME

MILEAGE   ORDER No.

OPERATIONS ✓
1   LUB.
2   SERVICE
3   ENGINE WASH
4   CAR WASH
5   ROAD TEST & REPORT
6

ITEM	PART No.	QTY	U/P	DESCRIPTION	£

INVOICE No.

TAX POINT
CASH
ACCOUNT
CLAIM
INTERNAL

FOR OFFICE USE

ACCESSORIES

PETROL, OILS & ZERO RATED

MOT TEST

PETROL, OILS AND ZERO RATED

TOTAL MATERIALS
SUB-CONTRACTED WORK
LABOUR CHARGES (B/F wd)   £
SUB TOTAL   £
V.A.T. RATE   %
PETROL, OILS AND ZERO RATED
INVOICE TOTAL   £

Thank You!
We Appreciate Your Custom.

LABOUR CHARGES   (C/FWD) £

SUB-CONTRACTED WORK

REC. BY: COSTED BY:

OWNER'S SIGNATURE
(OR HIS AUTHORISED AGENT)

* I HAVE READ AND ACCEPT YOUR TERMS AND CONDITIONS FOR THE REPAIR
OF VEHICLES AND THE SUPPLY OF PARTS, AND AUTHORISE THE ABOVE
REPAIRS TO BE CARRIED OUT ALONG WITH THE MATERIALS REQUIRED. E. & O.E.

7

BRITISH LEYLAND

Fig. 2.1 Front of Leyland 3 Part Job Set

BODYWORK REPORT

FAULT SYMBOLS (PANEL & PAINT)
D DENT   C CHIPS   R RUST
S SCRATCHES

QUALITY CONTROL INSPECTION

UNDER-BONNET
ENGINE OIL LEVEL/LEAKS — COOLANT/HOSES LEVEL/LEAKS — HYDRAULIC/HOSES LEVEL/LEAKS — BATTERY LEVEL/CORROSION
FAN BELT — FULL THROTTLE CARB DASHPOTS — CHOKE CLOSING — SCREEN WASHER LEVEL

INTERIOR
DOOR HINGES OILED/FREE — COURTESY LIGHT — WARNING LIGHTS INSTRUMENTS HEATER — CHOKE OPERATION SLOW RUNNING
HEADLIGHTS FLASH/DIP — STOP/FLASHER SIDE/REVERSE — SCREEN WASHER WIPER ACTION — FOOT/HANDBRAKE EXCESS TRAVEL

ACCESSORIES
MIRRORS — RADIO — CIGAR LIGHTER

EXTERIOR
DOORS — BONNET — BOOT — WHEEL NUTS
SPOT/FOG LIGHTS
TYRES (INCLUDING SPARE) PRESSURE — CONDITION (TYRES)

OPERATORS SIGN   FOREMAN

ROAD TEST SUMMARY   REF. NO:
ENGINE
TRANSMISSION/CLUTCH
FINAL DRIVE
STEERING/SUSPENSION
BRAKES/WHEELS
BODY/CHASSIS
ELECTRICAL

CLEANLINESS   DOOR HANDLES — STEERING WHEEL — SEATS/CARPETS — ASHTRAYS — WINGS — SCREEN
FUEL READING
TESTERS SIGN.

	NO	OFF			**LABOUR**	
			MANS No.	ITEM No.	ELAPSED TIME	TIME	TIME CLOCK RECORD
	NO					OFF	
		OFF				ON	
	NO					OFF	
		OFF				ON	
	NO					OFF	
		OFF				ON	
	NO					OFF	
		OFF				ON	
	NO					OFF	
		OFF				ON	
	NO					OFF	
		OFF				ON	

TIME CLOCK RECORD — TIME — ITEM ELAPSED TIME — MANS No. — ON No. — REQ. No. — **TOTAL**

MATERIALS   LABOUR

Fig. 2.2 Back of Leyland 3 Part Job Set

summary' will be made and finally, the very important, cleanliness check on door handles, steering wheel, carpets, seats, ashtrays, wings, bonnet and screen. Forming as it does, part of the three part job set, invoicing is rapid and it cuts out other paper work. The only extra work is the requisition note from the foreman to the stores and from the stores to the account/costing section where the final bill is prepared.

The five part job set has copies as follows:
1. customer's invoice,
2. job card,
3. stores authority,
4. accounts/costing,
5. spare copy for retention at reception.

This type of invoicing means that one set of writing only is needed initially and this saves considerable time and expense. As stated previously, Kalamazoo Ltd., Northfield, Birmingham, B31 2RW, produce the five card job set which has different colours for each sheet so that identification is easy, e.g. blue for top copy for customer's invoice, yellow for job card and so on, depending on the system adopted. The Kalamazoo five part job set is reproduced in Fig. 2.3.

To use this set the procedure is as follows:
1. Reception engineer details work required on top copy and states if 'credit account' or not by deleting appropriate wording. This copy is retained at reception (No. 1).
2. The second and fourth copies which are the job card and stores authority are handed to the workshop foreman for attention as required.
3. Copy No. 3 is passed to Accounts/Costing to await final parts used. This is obtained from the stores from No. 4 copy when the job is complete. Every part used is charged to the customer.
4. The fifth and final copy is retained by the service manager for future reference.

To summarize the five part job set:

No. 1 copy is retained at reception and finally filed if required.

No. 2 copy—goes to the workshop foreman and then to the service manager for labour sales analysis and then filed.

No. 3 copy goes to Accounts/Costing with No. 5, is duly completed as an invoice when all details from No. 2 and No. 4 copies are to hand. Details of the bill are entered in appropriate accounts ledgers prior to dispatch.

No. 4 copy goes to the workshop foreman, then to the stores where all parts are listed and is then forwarded to Accounts/Costing.

No. 5 is sent to Accounts/Costing and is retained as a copy of the invoice to the customer along with No. 4 copy.

So finally—one copy is retained at reception (if required)
two copies are retained at Accounts/Costing
one copy is retained by the service manager
one copy is the invoice for the customer.

┌ ┐

Progressive
Garages
Limited

tel 246 - 732 5000
nat giro 623 1234
VAT no. 010 2159 04

└ ┘

Kalamazoo
BUSINESS SYSTEMS B-19D-635726-98

100 High Street Anytown Anyshire AN2 1ST

DATE	WANTED FOR	MAKE & MODEL			REG. NO.		MILEAGE	FUEL E ½ F	INTERNAL	CASH
									WARRANTY	CREDIT

Item	INSTRUCTIONS	✓	AMOUNT	Item	INSTRUCTIONS	✓	AMOUNT
					BROUGHT FORWARD		
1	Carry out miles Service						
2	Oil & Grease. Change/Oil/Filter			26	D.O.E. Test		
3	Adjust & Bleed/Brakes/Clutch			27	Fit accessories		
4	Remove & overhaul Clutch						
5	Overhaul Brakes, Reline/Fit Service Shoes			28	Repair Body Damage to		
6	Decarbonise engine, Grind in Valves						
7	Full engine tune/Plug/Points/Timing						
8	Adjust Valves/Tappets				ADDITIONAL OPERATIONS		
9	Carb/Fuel Pump. O'haul fit new/exchange						
10	Check/repair/Lights/Wipers/Bulbs Replace						
11	Fan Belt/Adjust/Replace						
12	Generator/Starter O'haul/Fit new or exchange						
13	Front end alignment Steering/Adjust/O'haul						
14	Balance Rd. wheels/Change around						
15	Repair/Replace Exhaust system						
16	Check/Repair/Overhaul Gear Linkages						
17	Remove/Overhaul Gearbox						
18	Reverse flush radiator/Check leaks/repair						
19	Fit new Top and Bottom Hoses					VAT Rate	VAT	VALUE
20	Water Pump O'haul/Fit new or exchange			Labour			
21	Repair/Replace Horn/Trafficators			Parts/Accessories			
22	Shock Absorbers O'haul/Fit new or exchange						
23	Battery Test/Charge/Fit new or exchange Check and adjust charging rate			Oil/Lubricants			
24	Wash/Polish/Wax				TOTAL		
25	Drain & refill including Anti-Freeze						
	CARRIED FORWARD				TOTAL DUE (Tax inclusive) ➡		

IT IS RECOMMENDED THAT THE FOLLOWING ITEMS BE GIVEN ATTENTION

WHILST TAKING ALL REASONABLE PRECAUTIONS AGAINST FIRE, THEFT, LOSS OR DAMAGE THE COMPANY ACCEPT NO RESPONSIBILITY FOR CARS OR OTHER PROPERTY BELONGING TO CUSTOMERS AND VEHICLES ARE DRIVEN AND TESTED AT OWNERS RISK.

AUTHORISED BY

19 N

INVOICE

Fig. 2.3 Kalamazoo 3 Part Job Set

Obviously, this procedure can be varied to suit the needs of each particular station. No. 1 copy is only needed at reception as long as the job is in hand and upon dispatch of the job it could be filed in Accounts/Costing with No. 4 and No. 5. These copies are needed where monthly accounts are kept so that customers can be reminded if payment is not forthcoming within 7–14 days of dispatch of the invoice to the customer.

Costing

Sales are vital to profit and so are expenses; they are necessary in order to do business. Expenses, however, have to be controlled and, as will be seen elsewhere in the chapter, they have to be recorded daily, totalled weekly and monthly. Costing, accounting, book-keeping are complicated subjects and this section of the book can only outline the principles involved. Each manager of each department will be responsible for its profitability and recording of sales and expenses will indicate a profit or loss. The modern practice is to allocate a proportionate amount of overheads and other costs to each department according to floor space occupied. Before labour costs can be charged to a customer the actual labour charge is calculated from the amount of overheads and other costs involved so that a profit is made on the sale of labour. The objects of a costing system is to provide accurate information for estimates and repairs, to compare the costs to prices in detail and to show the true earning capacity of each department. With such accurate data we can ensure each job can be made to pay without overcharging. Likewise, unprofitable jobs involving loss or waste are clearly indicated and can be avoided in future work. When departmental expenses are fairly distributed, flat rate prices can be established for many jobs and similar jobs will have similar prices thus avoiding suspicion from customers. Such are the objects and advantages of a costing system.

To assess the profitability of a department costs and expenses must first be placed under two separarate headings i.e. (1) *Direct costs* which include mechanics' wages, materials used for repair work such as parts, cleaning materials and so on: these can be accurately charged to each department according to amount being used. (2) *Indirect costs* which are referred to as 'overheads': these include rental costs, payment of rates, non-productive but essential labour costs such as office staff, advertising etc.

Before we itemize all the costs involved let us consider how each department will have such costs distributed to them.

Each department of a service station will occupy a certain ground area, for example, workshop 800 square metres, (950 square yards), stores 100 square metres, (120 square yards), car showroom 160 square metres (200 square yards), and so on. The total area of all departments may be 1 600 square metres (1 900 square yards). In this case the workshop would pay $\frac{800}{1600}$ of overheads that is 50%. In proportion to area each department can then be similarly assessed. However, some open parking areas will not have to pay the same rates as buildings and must be reduced accordingly, say to half or one third of their share of the indirect costs and all their direct costs, thus obtaining total costs involved.

If we take the workshop quoted as having to pay half the total indirect costs, then if the rates for the buildings were £60 then the workshop must pay £30, the stores $(100 \times £60)/1\ 600 = £3.75$. How much use is made of office staff and buildings will again be proportioned to the workshop, stores, car sales etc. unless each of these is self contained. In this case they will have their own direct and indirect costs. Overheads can also be apportioned according to capital investment of buildings and equipment and/or number of employees in each department but the area method is most popular with service stations.

Having seen how overheads are allocated, the actual overheads for a garage could include the following: rates, rent, electricity—power and lighting, government taxes, heating, water, advertising, insurance, licences, R.T.I.T.B. levy, depreciation of buildings and equipment, office wages and paper costs, national health insurance contributions, telephone bills and maintenance of buildings will also have to be included. All these items would give a total 'overheads' cost. All known facts must be considered to give a fair distribution of these costs to each department. For example, cost of lighting at night to advertise a showroom and use of toilets by customers. The first will generally be allocated to the showroom overheads and as toilets are usually in the forecourt area, then the forecourt overheads must meet this cost.

Now the usual way to recover these overheads is to apply the formula:

$$\frac{\text{total establishment expenses} \times 100}{\text{total chargeable wages}}$$

The establishment expenses include rent, rates, advertising etc. To check overhead charges, which are passed on to the customer, this formula would be used. For example, if total expenses per annum were £20 000 and total wages £10 000, then overhead charges would be calculated thus:

$$\frac{£20\,000 \times 100}{10\,000} = 200\%.$$

A workshop will recover overheads by applying the formula:

$$\frac{\text{workshop share of overheads} \times 100}{\text{labour costs.}}$$

If the workshop overheads were £100 per month and labour costs were £100 per month, then the percentage on the customers bill to cover the overheads would be $(100 \times 100)/100 = 100\%$. Thus if a man is paid £1 per hour and completes 4 hours work on a customer's car, the total cost to the customer would be $4 \times £1 + 100\%$ labour cost to meet overheads = £8. This would cover the employment of the man plus all other costs. To make a profit on labour, then a further percentage is added e.g. 100%. In this case the customer would pay £4 for mechanics wages, £4 for overheads, £4 for profit—a total labour charge of £12, i.e. £3 per hour. The profit addition on labour and materials usually averages at 25% so that a competitive labour charge is established. Having achieved the all round rate then a fixed charge for labour is established. Thus, paying a mechanic £1 per hour plus 100% overheads = £2 per hour, plus 25% profit, total labour charge per hour = £2.50. The number of hours on a job is recorded on the job card and on a Pay Claim Slip Form as shown in Fig. 2.4 to enable the wages of a mechanic to be calculated.

Referring to distribution of overheads again, for example to the car sales, they must ensure that sales will cover their share of the overheads as well as a suitable profit margin. About 20% profit on car sales is expected which results in a good net profit on turnover along with a suitable return on capital invested.

A typical Service Department Balance Sheet is shown in Fig. 2.5 which gives

PAY CLAIM SLIP
TO COST OFFICE DAILY

EMPLOYEE'S NAME						NO	DATE
N.R. Hours	Std. & T.T. Hours	Item Comp	Item No.	Job No.	Clock No.		Date
					OFF		
Auth. by					ON		
					Time Taken		
N.R. Hours	Std. & T.T. Hours	Item Comp	Item No.	Job No.	Clock No.		Date
					OFF		
Auth. by					ON		
					Time Taken		
N.R. Hours	Std. & T.T. Hours	Item Comp	Item No.	Job No.	Clock No.		Date
					OFF		
Auth. by					ON		
					TimeTaken		
N.R. Hours	Std. & T.T. Hours	Item Comp	Item No.	Job No.	Clock No.		Date
					OFF		
Auth. by					ON		
					Time Taken		
N.R. Hours	Std. & T.T. Hours	Item Comp	Item No.	Job No.	Clock No.		Date
					OFF		
Auth. by					ON		
					Time Taken		
N.R. Hours	Std. & T.T. Hours	Item Comp	Item No.	Job No.	Clock No.		Date
					OFF		
Auth. by					ON		
					Time Taken		

TOTAL	TOTAL	Adj.Hrs. Plus or Minus		TOTAL ATTENDANCE HOURS			
Col.1	Col.2	Col.3	Col.4	PAY	O/TIME	AUTHORISED	

Fig. 2.4 Mechanics' Pay Slip Form

SERVICE DEPARTMENT
PROFIT AND LOSS ACCOUNT

	Current Month	Cumu-lative	LAST YEAR Month	Cumu-lative
	£	£	£	£
RECEIPTS				
Repair Charges —Customer				
—Departmental				
—Warranty Claims				
Engine Department Sales				
Sub Contract Recharged				
Profit on Petrol Sales				
Discount on Parts Sold				
EXPENSES				
Productive Wages				
Deduct: Non productive labour				
Managers and Foremans Salary				
Reception and Tester				
Apprentices				
Tool Stores and Cleaner				
Government Taxes (if any)				
N.H.I. & G.P. (Employers Contribution)				
Engine Department Materials				
Sub Contract Charges				
General Time and Works Expenses				
Breakdown and Managers Car Expenses				
Minimum Warranty				
Service Office Salaries				
Total Direct Expenses				
Electricity Gas and Fuel				
General Overhead Apportionment				
TOTAL EXPENSES				
NET PROFIT/(LOSS)				

Fig. 2.5 Service Department Balance Sheet

a final net profit or loss at the foot of the page. All the expenses listed are self
explanatory but one or two items need more details. For instance, 'non-
productive time' means time paid to mechanics for 'idle time' when no jobs
are available or for correcting faulty work. Other non-productive labour charges
are involved when apprentices attend technical college, staff are on courses,
holidays with pay and sickness pay, maintenance of break-down vehicle etc.
all mean that 100% labour is virtually impossible. If 75% total labour time is
acheived this is considered satisfactory, although 100% should always be the
aim. Where a time-saved bonus scheme is in operation a minimum labour
efficiency is 120%. This must always be carefully watched by the service
manager as undue non-productive time is going to affect the profitability of

DAILY SALES RECORD
MONTH_____

DAILY SALES OBJECTIVE	
CUSTOMER LABOR	PARTS
$	$

DATE	NO. CUSTOMER REPAIR ORDERS	CUSTOMER LABOR ACCUMULATIVE		PARTS SALES ON R.O. ACCUMULATIVE	
		OBJECTIVE	ACTUAL	OBJECTIVE	ACTUAL
1					
2					
3					
4					
5					
6					
7					
8					
9					
10					
11					
12					
13					
14					
15					
16					
17					
18					
19					
20					
21					
22					
23					
24					
25					
26					
27					
28					
29					
30					
31					

Fig. 2.6 A Daily Labour Sales Record (Chrysler)

the workshop. Due allowance is sometimes made for unavoidable slack periods in the costing charge for labour by including 25% of the mechanics' wages in the overheads. A daily sales record can be kept by the service manager similar to that used by the Chrysler Co. (U.S.A.) in Fig. 2.6. The Chrysler Co. recommend a 'Monthly Service Department Expense Control Sheet' as shown in Fig. 2.7. The daily chart is completed from the Job Cards and the monthly chart is a total of the daily charts. As monthly charts are maintained a year by year check can be made each and every month to see how the garage is progressing and action can be taken as required.

MONTHLY SERVICE DEPARTMENT EXPENSE CONTROL

EXPENSE ITEM		JAN	FEB	MAR	APR	MAY	JUN	JUL	AUG	SEP	OCT	NOV	DEC
SALARIES AND WAGES—SERVICE DEPARTMENT	FORECAST												
	ACTUAL												
SUPPLIES AND SMALL TOOLS	FORECAST												
	ACTUAL												
POLICY ADJUSTMENT— SERVICE AND PARTS	FORECAST												
	ACTUAL												
ADVERTISING— SERVICE AND PARTS	FORECAST												
	ACTUAL												
LAUNDRY SERVICE	FORECAST												
	ACTUAL												
MAINTENANCE MACHINERY AND EQUIPMENT	FORECAST												
	ACTUAL												
VACATIONS AND TIME- OFF PAY	FORECAST												
	ACTUAL												
COMPANY CAR EXPENSE	FORECAST												
	ACTUAL												

Fig. 2.7. Chrysler Service Dept. Monthly Expense Control Sheet (This sheet is also known as a Budget Control Sheet).

To return to the costing of a job bearing in mind the points raised, the actual costing is completed by a cost clerk. As stated previously, certain repeat jobs will have standard prices and a typical standard price list offered by one large service station in 1969 is shown in Fig. 2.8. Needless-to-say, this will require modifying as labour charges, taxes, and other prices increase and need to be passed onto the customer. It is, however, much easier to modify such lists and certainly it avoids haphazard costing which can result in different prices for the same job! Manufacturers' Service and Repair Schedules also form a valuable aid to pricing a job. So many hours are allowed by manufacturers for certain services and repair jobs. These have been very carefully

1100 AND 1300 BLMC CARS FIXED PRICE REPLACEMENT SCHEME

Brake System			General/Other		
1 Reline front brakes	5	35	30 Adjust throttle linkage	1	10
2 Reline rear brakes	6	30	31 Throttle cable	1	55
3 Reline all brakes	11	60	32 Tighten all engine nuts and bolts	1	40
4 Clean & abrade front brakes	1	30	33 Tighten all gearbox nuts & bolts	0	85
5 Clean & abrade rear brakes	3	20	34 One drive shaft coupling rubber	4	25
6 Clean & abrade all brakes	4	50	35 Remote control adaptor	2	75
7 Free handbrake mechanism	2	50	**Cooling System**		
8 One brake drum	3	80	36 Fan belt	1	10
9 One brake disc	4	20	37 Top radiator hose	1	20
10 One front wheel cylinder			38 Bottom radiator hose	1	65
11 One rear wheel cylinder	4	15	39 Water pump by-pass hose	4	55
12 Overhaul one brake calliper	3	20	40 Treat with bluecol	1	10
13 Brake master cylinder	4	45	41 Flush out bluecol	0	55
Electrical System			**Suspension: Steering**		
14 Fit one bulb & check wiring	0	30	42 Steering column bushes	2	10
15 Indicator switch	4	50	43 Check and adjust hydrolastic pressures	1	80
16 Adjust indicator switch	0	55	44 Electronic steering check	1	65
17 Decorrode battery	1	65	45 One new tyre—standard	6	70
18 Battery earth lead	0	65	46 Front wheel bearings—one side	4	50
19 Battery negative lead	1	75	47 Rear wheel bearings—one side	4	30
20 Battery jumper lead			48 One front hub oil seal	2	05
21 Battery clamps	0	55	49 One rear hub oil seal	1	25
22 Charge battery	0	85	50 One half shaft gasket		
23 H T distributor leads	1	85	**General**		
24 Distributor rotor arm	0	35	51 One wiper blade	0	70
25 Distributor cap	2	60	52 Adjust w/washer jets	0	30
Engine			53 W/washer control pump	1	95
26 Distributor contact points	1	10	54 Clean out w/washer lines	0	85
27 Engine sparking plugs(set)	1	20	55 Exhaust bracket	1	15
28 Strip clean adjust one carb	1	10	56 Complete exhaust system	6	70
29 Overhaul one carburettor	4	20	57 Reposition exhaust system	0	85

Fig. 2.8 Standard Price List for Replacement of Units in 1970. With constant up-dating the prices in 1983 and onwards will obviously be very different!

analysed by work study methods and give a very fair number of labour hours for a particular job. They are not always available for each job however and, in this case, the job has to be carefully costed to ensure a profit. With such cases the procedure would be as follows:

1. Customer signs for work to be done. This is very important as (a) it is proof the owner authorized work to be done (b) it authorizes a road test if necessary (c) in the event of death or injury it may be necessary evidence for insurance or workmen's compensation.
2. An estimate of time can either be taken from a similar job completed previously by reference to old job cards or by consultation with the shop foreman. Retail cost of parts are added to the estimates. This will be completed by the reception engineer. The estimate should always be above that amount expected but not excessively high.
3. When the job card is completed and total hours and parts used are listed by the mechanic, the card is passed to the cost clerk.
4. The cost clerk then totals all labour costs, part costs and, as previously explained, obtains the final charge for detailing on the customers invoice.
5. The invoice or bill is a statement of work done and should clearly state the actual work done. The invoice layout is shown in this chapter. Where a 'one off' job is completed the invoice should include in the description of the work done a concise account of the operations completed along with the cost of each operation. For example:

Description of work

Job No.	Labour	Price
28	Removing and dismantling steering box, clean and examine parts	£1.75
	Replace cam and peg mechanism, thrust races, re-assemble and adjust	£0.75
	Refit steering box to car, refill with oil, test	£1.13
	Parts and materials	
	1 cam and peg assembly	£2.75
	2 thrust races	£0.75
	1 gasket	£0.07
	1 pint S.A.E. 80 oil	£0.20
	Total =	£7.40

V.A.T. at the current rate would of course be added (10% in 1974).

In the event of a dispute with a customer, the invoice is an essential part of a service station's evidence.

Thus, a job is costed through a garage and a typical repair order flow is shown in Fig. 2.9.

REPAIR ORDER WRITTEN ON 3 PART JOB SET

COPIES 1&2   HARD COPY NO.3

PARTS DEPARTMENT
Enters and prices all parts
as they are issued

FOREMAN AND THEN TO MECHANIC
who completes the job enters his time
and notes repairs made and parts used

COST OFFICE/ACCOUNTS
who cost the job and make out the invoice

ALL COPIES TO SERVICE MANAGER
for approval of invoice

RECEPTION ENGINEER
invoice to await collection
by the customer

COPY 1.
OFFICE
filed numerically
in job no. order

COPY 2
CUSTOMER
his receipted bill

COPY 3
SERVICE DEPARTMENT
placed in owner's file

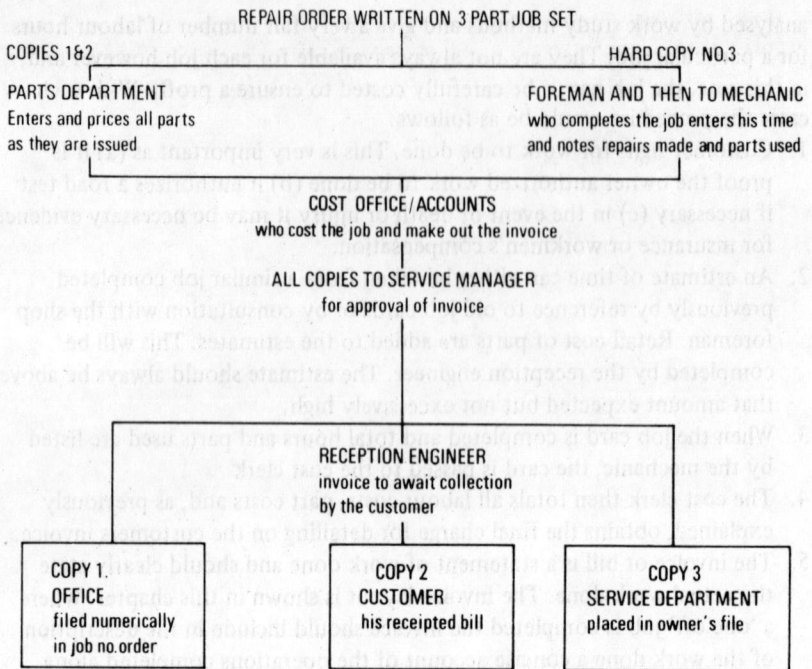

Variations to the above procedure can be made as required but this
is a typical method of handling repair in a dealership

Fig. 2.9 Repair Order Flow Layout

All consumable items are costed as shown. Control of these items is made
by having a signed requisition to the storeman and he in turn makes out the
parts issued on the appropriate form—which is passed to the costing section.
The storeman is responsible for recording receipt of such items and the issue
of parts and this is dealt with in a separate part of this chapter. All parts are
received by the garage at a trade price and sold at a profit at a retail price to
the customer. Part sales are credited to the Parts Department for their Profit
and Loss Account.

Accounts department

The keeping of good and accurate accounts is essential to enable any business to function efficiently. In a large dealership the complete presentation of
accounts to auditors and for other purposes, is usually under the control of a
qualified accountant. The accountant will have the responsibility of making
out the Profit and Loss accounts for each department of the concern, collecting all such information together and finally presenting a Profit and Loss
account for the entire firm. These accounts will normally be made up each
month with an annual account to cover the years' trading. To obtain this all

expenses and receipts are listed. As stated previously, the use of monthly trading accounts from each department enables a quick check to be made on profitability of a particular section. Thus, a full years trading account could indicate a loss even though say, two departments were successful and one unsuccessful. The remedy is obvious and action must be taken to correct the cause of failure in the department concerned.

Organization and administration of the parts department

The size of a dealership will determine whether the parts department has a separate manager or not. In most cases the parts department is an entirely separate unit, but in small concerns the overall administration of the parts department could be part of the duties of a service manager. With the tremendous increase of vehicle population in recent years, the sale of parts has become a specialized and major part of service station business. All parts personnel need to be trained in Parts Merchandising and should take the C.G.L.I. course No. 384 (or 376) which covers this subject. Managers of such departments need to have the Advanced PARDIC certificate. The PARDIC certificate is issued by the Society of Motor Manufacturers and Traders upon satisfactory completion of a course of study and success in examinations dealing with parts merchandising. PARDIC is an acronym built up as follows: PARts/ Distribution Certificated training. (Now replaced. See Appendix III.)

As with all other departments, the parts department must be well organized and efficient. The layout of a stores should be considered on—(a) its merchandising possibilities (b) the economic holding of stock (c) adequate area for stock and (d) future expansion, this latter item being very important bearing in mind that vehicle population is almost doubling every ten years.

A good and poor layout of a stores is shown in Figs 2.10 and 2.11. Access to all sections should be easy and time should not be wasted by having to wander round to poorly placed racks and bins. Bins should be arranged in symmetrical blocks and gangways. Lighting should be above storage racks and in the centre of gangways. Access to related departments such as the workshop and showrooms should be easy. Selling areas should be convenient for customers and be attractive to the public to induce them to come in and buy. Window space should not be blocked by racks and bins, thus obtaining good use of natural light.

The merchandising possibilities can be assessed by local vehicle population and volume of work normally taken into the workshop. Economic holding of stock is very important as all parts held in the stores means money standing idle. Parts department managers must obtain a turnover of all stock at least three times a year. Thus if a total of £210 000 turnover in stock is achieved each year, the actual holding of stock should be £210 000/3 = £70 000. Each item in the stores will obviously sell at different rates, e.g. sparking plugs and replacement engines. However, by trying to have a 4 month stock or annual

STORES-GOOD LAYOUT

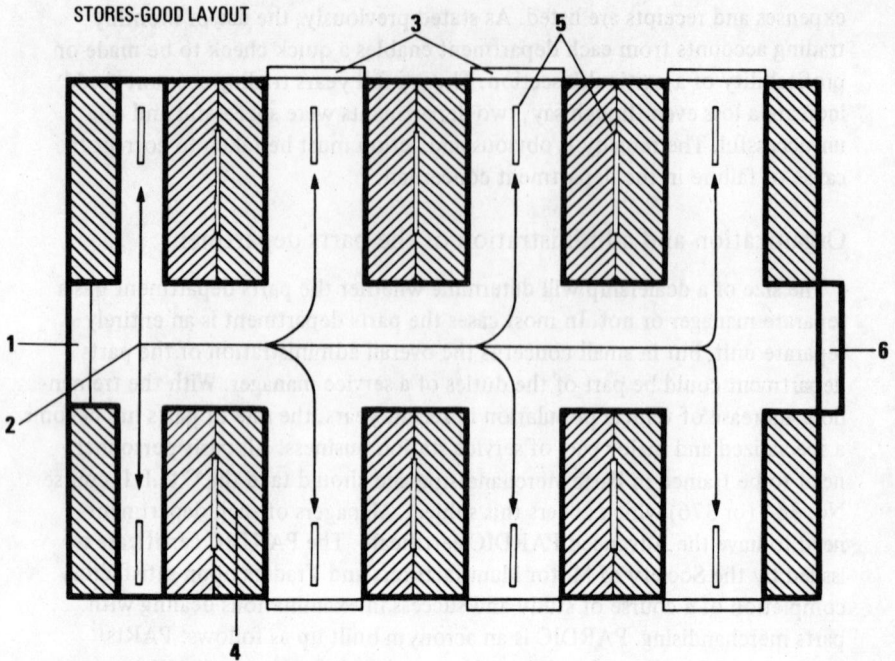

1. Adequate serving counter
2. Clear gangway giving access to racks and bins
3. Unobscured windows making maximum use of natural light
4. Well-placed bins and racks in symmetrical order
5. Fluorescent strip lighting above racks and in the centre of gangways
6. Well-placed "goods inward" area with rack to hold parts awaiting storage in bins

Access to showroom, service and other departments should be good. Any office
within a stores should give a clear view of most areas for the purpose of supervision

Fig. 2.10 Good Stores Layout

turnover of 3 times of all parts, we can assess how much stock to hold as
follows:

1. Check last 3 months sales—say 80.
2. Deduct parts in stock—say 25,
$$80 - 25 = 55.$$
3. Deduct parts on order—say 10,
$$55 - 10 = 45.$$
4. Add customers pending orders—say 15,
multiply this by 2 = 30.
5. Add this figure to 45 to obtain the total order required to be sent to the
manufacturer,
i.e. $30 + 45 = 75.$

STORES-POOR LAYOUT

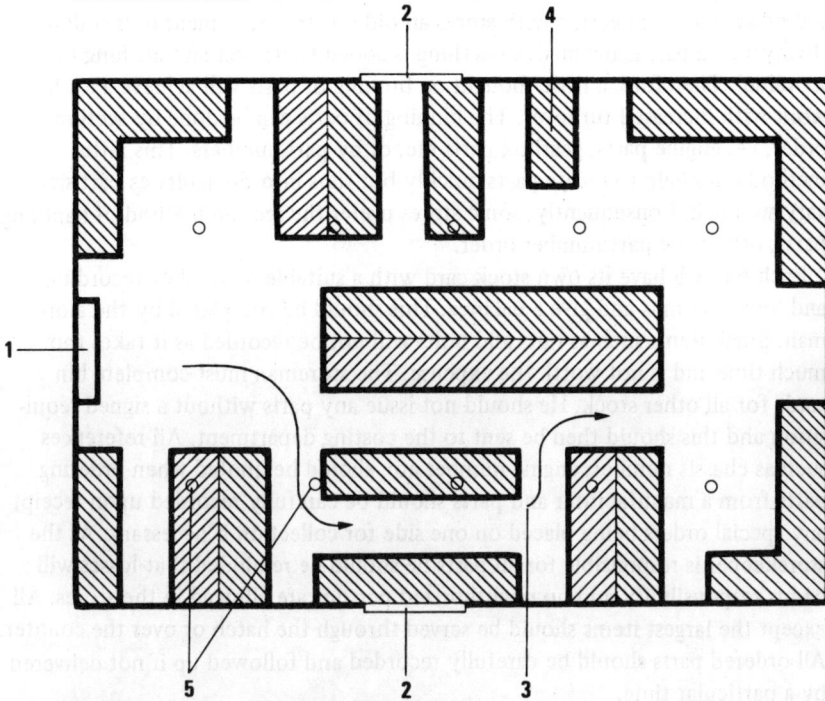

1. Serving counter and "goods inward" area causing confusion
2. Window space obscured-poor use of natural light
3. Devious, time consuming, path for assistants
4. Poorly-placed shelves at irregular intervals
5. Lighting placed in bad position

Fig. 2.11 Poor Stores Layout

No parts department can be expected to hold every part from the many thousands of parts that go to make up a modern motor vehicle. The department should, however, be capable of assessing the need for quickly-moving items and retain sufficient in stock by using a system similar to that indicated above. This system needs to be modified for seasonal changes, for example, anti-freeze solutions have a heavy demand in autumn but a light one in other periods. All departments should co-operate with the stores, for example car sales departments can mention accessories available in the stores to their customers and so on. Any window displays should *attract* attention by having a good central focal point which should *interest* a potential customer so that he has a *desire* to buy and will be able to take *action* by walking into the stores and purchasing the advertized item or items. Thus the principle of selling using the A.I.D.A. formula is followed. It is recommended that this principle should be used in all advertising including any circulars sent out by the garage.

Now all parts which are sold each and every day should be close to the selling area. In connection with stores an old but true statement is as follows: 'Everytime a part is handled, something is added to its cost and nothing to its value'. Therefore, a little thought on binning of parts will achieve a lot less work with increased turnover. The binning of parts can be done by section order, i.e. engine parts, gearbox parts etc. or by part numbers. This latter method does help to locate parts quickly but runs into difficulty as part sizes vary so much. Consequently, some stores prefer the section method of handling parts, others use part number order.

Each bin will have its own stock card with a suitable method of recording 'in' and 'out' columns and give a balance. This should be completed by the storeman. Small items such as nuts and bolts will not be recorded as it takes too much time and is not worth the expense. The storeman must complete bin cards for all other stock. He should not issue any parts without a signed requisition and this should then be sent to the costing department. All references such as chassis number, engine number etc. should be quoted when ordering parts from a manufacturer and parts should be carefully recorded upon receipt any special orders being placed on one side for collection if necessary. As the storekeeper is responsible for all parts he should be reminded that losses will be his responsibility and no unauthorized persons are allowed in the stores. All except the largest items should be served through the hatch or over the counter. All ordered parts should be carefully recorded and followed up if not delivered by a particular time.

Keeping a check on stock is vital so that (a) obsolete stock is not held taking up vital space, (b) parts are being ordered as required to meet a turnover of 3 times a year, and (c) to ensure that pilfering is not taking place. Stock checks can be completed twice a year noting parts ordered, sold and in stock. A few bins can be checked each day making a perpetual stock check and thus not requiring an annual stock check. A bin card contains headings of Part No., Description of Part, Location of Part. Columns underneath this comprise Date, Receipt or Issue, In, Out, Balance. This type of card and a 'Stock Consumption Record Sheet' showing monthly sales of all parts, can be obtained from various suppliers of essential stores paper work.

Where a small stores is operated under the guidance of a service manager, stock control can be operated by having a Purchase Book and Issue Book to record receipts and issues. The Purchase Book will contain columns indicating date, description of part, quantity ordered, supplier, advice note number, trade cost, retail price, bin number. An issue book will contain columns to indicate date, description of part, quantity issued, retail price, bin number, job number and signature of person issuing the parts. Providing all parts ordered and issued are recorded this can be an effective method of stock control.

There are many necessary forms, books, ledgers, and so on which must be used in all major parts department operations. Typical forms are Goods Received Notes which deal with inspection of goods coming into the department. These cover the specification, quantity, and condition of the goods. Damage and Shortage Reports deal with the reporting to the supplier of shortages, damage, and surpluses of goods received. The Parts Manager will despatch such reports promptly. A visit to a large parts department can be most useful for noting current methods of operation; and a prepared questionnaire may be answered in the form of a report. Typical questions might be:

1. What is the current 'stock-turnover' rate? What 'impulse' items are there at the point of sale?
2. Where are 'slow moving' and 'fast moving' items located?
3. State the names of all forms used in this department and the function of each one. Specially note the use of forms such as return-to-stores notes, copy orders, visible and non-visible card systems, and bound books.
4. What items make up the Profit and Loss Account of the department?
5. State the main changes that have occurred in the past ten years of parts merchandising at these premises.
6. How are parts received, checked, moved to bins, and collected by partsmen?
7. Make a scale drawing of the stores operation. Include in the sketch
    (a) width of pathways;
    (b) distance between shelves;
    (c) location of incoming stores, workshop sales, trade sales and retail sales, offices, exit doors.
    Obtain the height of shelving and number of shelves.
8. State how stock checks are completed.
9. If a bonus scheme is in operation, how does this work?
10. If sales promotions are used, which of these has proved to be most successful? How is the computer used to forecast sales?
11. Explain how the computer is used to obtain current stock holdings; state the time it takes to do this.
12. What advantages and disadvantages accrue when a parts manager controls forecourt operations?

Computers in dealerships

It is not the intention of this book to detail the operation and programming of computers. How computers can be used every modern manager must know. The time computers can save is now legend. Very few main dealers have any area which cannot benefit from computer control. Of course, like every machine, a computer is only as good as the person operating it. We can state that a computer is an electronic device which can add, subtract, multiply, divide, and make 'yes' and 'no' decisions according to the information it processes. For every department it has certain advantages such as that:

(1)   information is accurately recorded and stored;
       (N.B. The information given to it must of course be correct.)
(2)   the current financial position can be determined in hours instead of
       days;
(3)   the costs of individual departments, such as maintenance, can be ascer-
       tained in detail;
(4)   forecasts of vehicle, service, and parts sales can be made, thus assisting
       budgetary control;
(5)   by assessing all costs of operations, non-profitable operations can be
       eliminated and good operations can be extended;
(6)   staff can be utilized in a more efficient manner;
(7)   management reports and statistics are provided without additional
       effort, on a consistent basis and with cash-values shown.
(8)   Clerical errors are reduced because of extreme accuracy in the com-
       puter's processing and extensive checking of input data.

All departments can collect relevant data to feed into the computer.
Punched cards and paper tapes are fed into the machine and master files are
amended to include the new data. Manufacturers of vehicles and parts almost
unanimously recommend computer methods of control. Further details
about the implementation and operation of computers can be obtained from
the National Computing Centre, Quay House, Quay Street, Manchester 3.

Work study

Throughout this book emphasis has been placed upon efficiency in all aspects
of garage work. The use of work study methods is now applied in all industries
and has been used in many garages for a long time. Work study methods are
often applied without recognition as such. Take the apprentice mechanic who
is trained to replace all tools clean and on the same position on the tool board.
Supposing he leaves the tool dirty and in some obscure place: the next time he
requires the tool, considerable time will be spent trying to find the tool. Thus,
tidyness in a workshop is a form of training in work-study methods. The section
of this book dealing with flow-lines is the application of time and motion study
to the servicing of vehicles. Likewise standard repair schedules and standard
times for services offered by manufacturers are all based on work study methods.
Good stores layouts with rapid turn-over items near to the serving hatch is yet
another example of studying work and reducing time and effort to a minimum.

Work study is a subject which has many ramifications. The Institute of Work
Study Practitioners has evolved many time saving methods by the scientific
approach to job analysis. Correct use of principles can be applied to all aspects
of work, and, if this results in a job being completed quicker with more bonus
for employer and employee then this must be encouraged. The British Standards
Institution detail important definitions in connection with this subject and the
student would be well advised to study the appropriate sections as required.

For example:

Method study. A study of the suitability of the tools or work aids and the manner in which they are employed.

Motion study. The study of the physical characteristics of the job requirements.

Motion economy. The analysis of motion study to minimize waste of human energy and to ensure a smooth and rythmic performance.

Time study. The measurement of the speed and effort required to produce a fair day's work.

Incentives. These are rewards designed to operate at a certain level of performance.

Work measurement. This is a modern derivation of Time Study.

Work study. Work study embraces Time Study and Motion Study and conditions which influence the job such as heat, fatigue, lighting etc.

By applying these it is possible to analyse a job in detail, and, where appropriate, to adjust the work routine so that the job is completed in less time or with less fatigue on the part of the operator. Manufacturers who issue standard service and repair job times carefully analyse all work required. For example if a replacement engine is required for a particular vehicle, the job itself will be timed by having a mechanic remove all necessary parts such as bonnet, radiator and hoses, carburettor and manifolds etc., and recording each operation on a Motion Analysis Sheet. The total time taken to complete the job is then obtained. A standard time achieved by having a number of operators complete the same job to obtain an average time. With due allowance being made for various conditions which can prevail the standard time becomes a time in which any skilled mechanic can easily complete the work set. In practice as referred to elsewhere dealing with bonus and incentive schemes, a skilled mechanic will save time and thus achieve his reward.

Work study can be applied to all jobs and if an assessment of time to be taken is required or if improvement of performance is desired, then the procedure to adopt would be as follows:
1. Select the work to be studied or analysed.
2. Record all the facts about the work being done and the method being employed. This means recording times taken, where tools are taken from and replaced, physical movement of the operator i.e. where he walks, lifts and so on.
3. Examine all the facts critically and put in a written ordered sequence.
4. From the information gathered reorganize the work to develop the most practical economic and effective method to complete a job.
5. Make the new method a standard practice.

6. By regular checks make the standard practice routine by inspection at intervals to ensure the new method is being maintained.

This only outlines the basic ideas behind work study and further details can be obtained by consulting text books relative to this work. Even so, the good manager will know how to look at his general workshop organization bearing the above points in mind.

It will be appreciated that the use of work study methods in the motor industry can result in the following advantages:

(1)   the best possible use is made of personnel, materials, equipment and buildings;

(2)   costs are reduced;

(3)   there is an increase in productivity, profit, and bonuses;

(4)   fair tasks are established for all personnel;

(5)   achievement is checked against a standard;

(6)   good worker/management relationships are established;

(7)   job security is created.

The relation between the efficiency of an undertaking and its organization is well known, and mention has been made of the difficulty of separating work study from other tools of management.

Work study, including work measurement, which is of general use in management, has rather a bad name in some quarters: it has sometimes been misused in the past in the course of job time-setting, and the resulting tight production schedules have been known to cause labour disputes.

The increase of productivity in the short term (that is, not requiring much, if any, capital expenditure) can be achieved by (1) improving existing methods of using plant and machinery, (2) improving the work-plan and the use of human effort, and (3) increasing the effectiveness of individual employees. Work study therefore embodies two techniques: (1) method study, which is aimed at improving methods of production and (2) work measurement, which assesses the effectiveness of the human unit. Work measurement, involving, as it does, fractional elements, is not entirely applicable to the majority of personnel in a main dealership, and in any case requires long and specialized training of special staff to operate it. It is not proposed therefore to present details of this particular technique.

Method study

The side of work study which is always practicable, method study, can be learned in a fairly short time and its application to the organization need not create any great difficulties as long as the staff are warned beforehand that the study is being undertaken and are told why. Usually, if staff are approached first and taken into the manager's confidence, co-operation will result. It is only where a study is suddenly thrust upon a person or group without notice that objections are raised.

Method study is the critical, systematic investigation and recording of methods and movements necessary to achieve a task. In an industrial plant it is rather an involved process, altogether more complicated than when it is applied to a transport department or service station.

The object of method study is to find better ways of doing things by:

    (i)   revealing and analysing only the true facts of a situation;

    (ii) examining these facts critically;

    (iii) developing the best answer possible from the critical examination of these facts.

The student is advised to (1) Get the facts. (2) Be sure they are the facts. (3) Weigh the facts. (4) Decide on the basis of the facts. (5) Take action. (6) Follow up and check. (7) Modify and adjust as necessary. (8) Put the programme into operation. (9) Exercise control over the programme. By doing this on an organized basis it is possible to:

    (a) get rid of unnecessary work;

    (b) get rid of unavoidable delays;

    (c) get rid of other forms of waste.

Method study procedure

It has already been stated that it is necessary to analyse work.

The techniques of method study should be selected in relation to circumstances and specific situations and may demand the use of operational-procedure and flow process charts and two-handed charts to indicate the activities of an operator's two hands. Multiple activity presentation, flow diagrams, string diagrams, and models are also used. In most of the work done in service organizations it will rarely be necessary to use the refinements of cyclegraphs, chronocyclegraphs, or the more complicated photographic methods, such as time-lapse cameras.

At the most, the following 'instruments' should cover all the applications required for recording studies and adjustments in a workshop, parts department, forecourt, or other area.

Operational procedure charts.

These involve the principal operations and inspection.

Flow process charts.

The activities of men, material, and equipment are recorded on these charts.

Two-handed process charts.

Activities of the two hands are recorded.

Multiple activity time charts and string diagrams.

These are used to show the paths of movement of operatives, materials, or equipment within a limited area over a relatively long period of time. Cord, string, or other material is used on a board to record movements which can then be analysed.

Two- or three-dimensional models.
These are used to illustrate the layout of workshops, parts departments, and so on.

Procedure chart construction

In constructing and interpreting procedure charts, symbols are used which divide and indicate the observed activities by means of a kind of shorthand. There are five of these symbols and they are standard, at least in this country and the United States.

The symbols represent the following functions of activity:

Function symbolized		*Predominant outcome of function*
OPERATION	○	— production, accomplishment, extension of process
TRANSPORTATION	⇨	— travel, movement from one work area to another
INSPECTION	☐	— verification of quantity or quality or both, or of written instruction
DELAY	D	— interference or delay
STORAGE	▽	— holding, depositing, or retaining.

Some examples of activities represented by the respective symbols are indicated in Fig. 2.12.

The procedure chart consists of an analysis of the procedure observed, using the symbols and noting what is done, step by step, what distance is involved, and what amount of time is expended on each step.

In order to illustrate the construction of a procedure chart a very simple procedure within a workshop is taken: it represents a man removing a unit from an engine, cleaning it, adjusting it, and replacing it.

From the flow diagram in Fig. 2.13 it will be seen by reading the symbols and the route lines that the man engages in certain activities at the vehicle, walks into a workshop, engages in more activities there, and then returns to the vehicle where he completes the task. Note that the symbols in the diagram are each numbered consecutively and independently, and that the final number of a particular symbol equals the total on the procedure chart, as indicated in Fig. 2.14.

On reading the 'present' procedure chart Fig. 2.14 it will be noted that, although there is no delay at any point, there are five transportation movements and three inspections. These may be considered high figures in proportion to the ten actual operations.

SYMBOL	EXAMPLES	
Operation ○	Using a screw-driver	Using a vice
Transportation ⇨	Using a small mobile crane	Using a pulley or lifting block
Inspection □	Reading a workshop manual	Examining a tyre tread or component
Delay D	Waiting for vehicle lift or pit	Waiting for materials from the Parts Department
Storage ▽	Filing service or repair documents	Returning a tool to the rack

Fig. 2.12 The standard work study symbols and examples of their use.

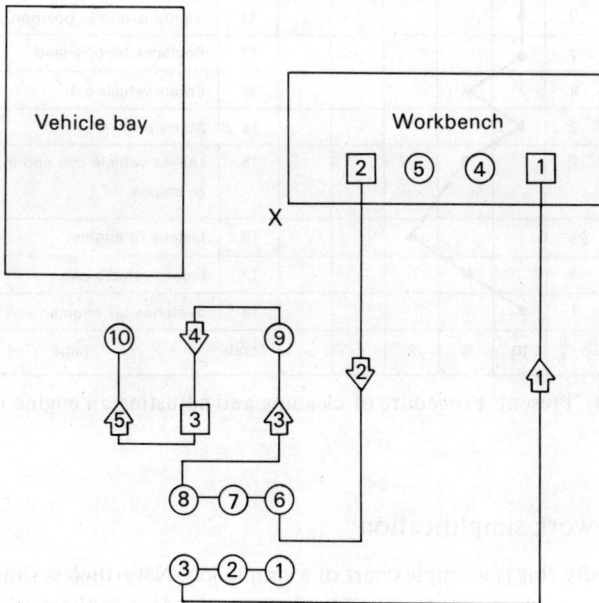

Fig. 2.13 Flow diagram of a typical workshop operation.
Note: 10 Operations
5 Transportations
3 Inspections

PROCEDURE CHART

Present procedure charted: Cleaning and adjusting engine unit.

Chart begins: Removal of unit.   Chart ends: Switching off engine after test

Charted By: Date: 11.2.77

DIST-ANCE (metres)	TIME (sec-onds)	OPERATION ○	⇩	□	D	▽	NO.	STEP
								(excluding opening and closing of bonnet)
	7						1	Removes battery lead.
	8						2	Unscrews unit.
	2						3	Lifts out unit.
8	10						4	Carries unit to workbench.
	16						5	Examines unit.
	14						6	Cleans unit.
	30						7	Adjusts unit.
	15						8	Re-examines unit.
8	10						9	Carries unit to engine.
	2						10	Fits unit.
	9						11	Tightens unit in position.
	7						12	Replaces battery lead.
2	9						13	Enters vehicle cab.
	2						14	Starts engine.
	9						15	Leaves vehicle cab and moves to engine.
	25						16	Listens to engine.
	9						17	Enters vehicle cab.
	1						18	Switches off engine.
TOTALS 22	m s 3 - 5	10	5	3	-	-	Totals	page of pages

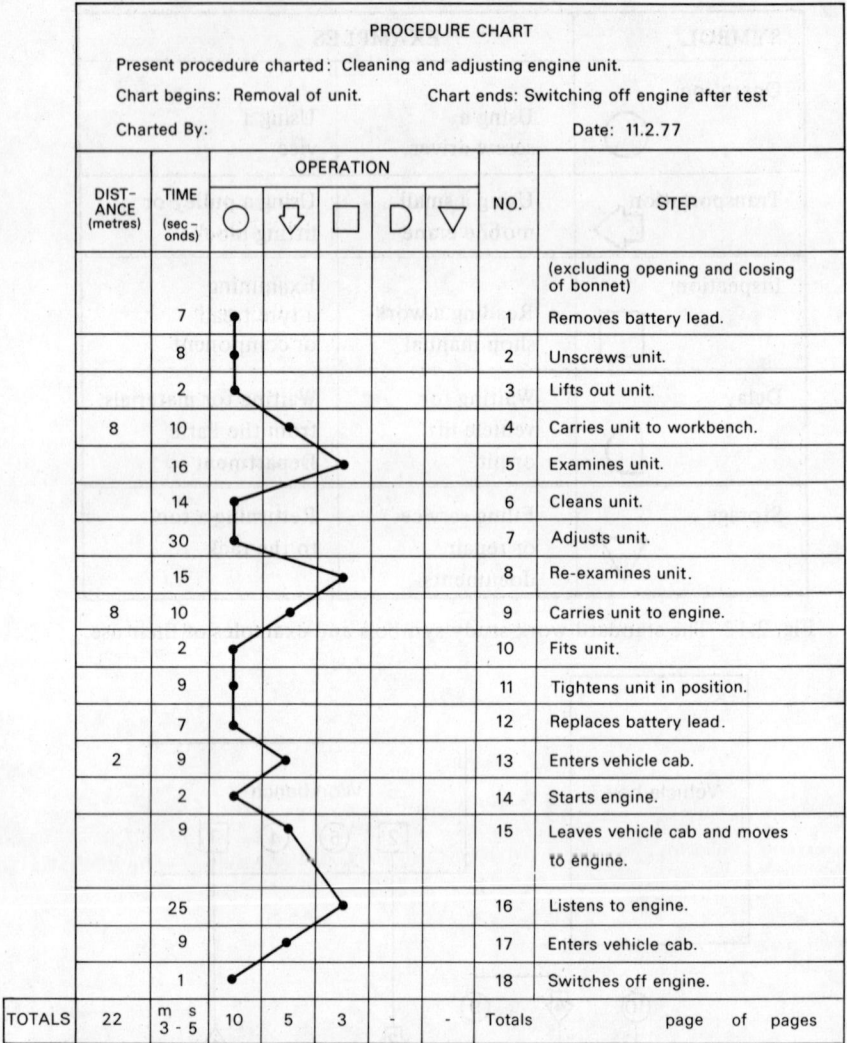

Fig. 2.14 'Present' procedure of cleaning and adjusting an engine unit.

A case of work simplification

Admittedly this is a simple chart of a simple job. Nevertheless simplification of the procedure may be possible. Suppose the door in the workshop was resited at 'X', and suppose the vehicle backed into the bay so that the engine was at 'Y', then the distance between engine and bench would be reduced from 8 metres to 3.5 metres, so that a round trip from engine back to engine would amount to 7 metres instead of 16 metres, with a reduction in the time taken for the return movement from 30 seconds to 12 seconds— savings of 11 metres and 18 seconds per job. This is something, but perhaps the ten 'operation' steps would also stand reduction?

One useful feature of a procedure chart is that it is possible to see at a glance what it would take one some time to realize fully if one were watching a man actually doing the job. The specimen chart throws up the fact that every time a component needs attention it has to be carried and cleaned and adjusted and inspected and carried again. Upon enquiry it may be found that this happens forty or fifty times within a given period. Suppose, then, that a special portable kit of components, already cleaned and adjusted, were available to the mechanic for carrying to the engine. He could then take out the component from the engine, immediately put in another from his kit, and put the extracted component in the kit for cleaning and adjusting at some other time.

This would cut out steps Nos. 4, 5, 6, 7, 8, and 9, and so the revised procedure would appear on the 'proposed' chart as shown in Fig. 2.15. By comparing the two procedure charts one notes a total saving of 11 metres and 1 minute 33 seconds per job, or on 100 jobs, 1100 metres and 2 hours 35 minutes.

The above is a very simple and artificial illustration of the use of procedure charts; but any task may be recorded in a similar fashion.

Incidentally, there would be a further saving of time over-all if the mechanic at the workbench dealt with a number of extracted components taken from the kit as one continuous process: repetition usually improves performance.

Further applications of work study

There are endless applications of work study: for example, in the layout of the parts department, forecourt operations, and so on. With a workshop, the installation of a flow-line for servicing or D.Tp. inspections are excellent examples (see pp. 191–193). Here the application of the methods explained can save a lot of time and money.

Other charts and techniques

As mentioned earlier, work study employs a number of techniques of which the production of flow diagrams and procedure charts is only one. To go further into the intricacies of other techniques it is advisable to read the helpful literature now widely available, or to attend an instructional course on the subject. The R.T.I.T.B., local colleges, and similar establishments offer such courses. Much useful advice can be obtained from the Institute of Work Study Practitioners, (9–10 River Front, Enfield, Middlesex), and the Local Productivity Council or The British Productivity Council, (Vintry

PROCEDURE CHART

Proposed procedure charted: Cleaning and adjusting engine unit

Chart begins; Removal of unit   Chart ends: Switching off engine after test.

Charted by: Date: 11.2.77

DIST-ANCE (metres)	TIME (seconds)	OPERATION ○	⇩	□	D	△	NO.	STEP
								(excluding opening and closing of bonnet)
	7	●					1	Removes battery lead.
	8	●					2	Unscrews unit.
	2	●					3	Lifts out unit.
	4	●					4	Takes replacement unit from kit and fits.
	9	●					5	Tightens unit in position.
	7	●					6	Replaces battery lead.
2	9		●				7	Enters vehicle cab.
	2	●					8	Starts engine.
2	9		●				9	Leaves cab and moves to engine.
	25			●			10	Listens to engine.
2	9		●				11	Enters vehicle cab.
	1	●					12	Switches off engine.
TOTALS 6	m s 1 32	8	3	1	–	–	Totals page of pages	

Fig. 2.15 'Proposed' procedure showing improved method.

House, Queen Street, London E.C.4.) Sawell Publications Ltd., (127 Stanstead Road, London SE23 1JE) issue a monthly journal entitled 'Work Study' (price 50p), and this is well worth reading for up-to-date methods and ideas.

Activity sampling

This deals with identifying sources of lost time. If we consider a workshop and analyse work this could be divided into a number of categories:

(a)   productive work, i.e. work carried out on vehicles.

(b)   supporting work, i.e. work which is necessary to enable the job to be done but does not alter the state of the vehicle. Supporting work includes jobs such as shunting vehicles, carrying parts, tools, materials, etc.

(c)   Not working, i.e. no activity at all, can be the result of such things as waiting for parts, waiting for supervisory approval, personal breaks, tea breaks, rest, lack of work, and many other factors.

At this point it may be useful to refer to a survey carried out by N.E.D.O. in connection with analysis of work in garages in 1968. Many garages were examined and the highest percentage of their time spent by mechanics on productive work was 62 per cent and the lowest 38 per cent, with an average of 54 per cent. Subsequent surveys, e.g. that made in 1974, have revealed little improvement, and illustrate a dismal record of labour utilization.

As already explained, activity sampling is a method used to identify sources of lost time. To do this an observation sheet is used which has headings such as: Activity Sample . . . . Date . . . . The observer, who does not require special training, uses the card to tick times when a mechanic is working or not working. Thus if 100 ticks were recorded e.g. 63 working, 37 not working, this would indicate 63 per cent working time. Of course it is much more useful to detail non-productive time to ascertain if this can be reduced.

In this case the observer goes round to look at each worker in turn and note what activity is taking place at that particular moment. If, say, 10 observations are made of mechanics waiting for parts out of a total of 50 observations then $\dfrac{10 \times 100}{50} = 20\%$ of the mechanic's time is spent waiting for parts. The greater the number of observations made the greater the accuracy of the information obtained. Around 1 000 observations should be made per day, at say 20 to 30 per hour; and they should be made at a time when normal conditions exist. Observations should cover the whole of the working day during the survey, with random checks. This is to prevent misleading of observation patterns such as might occur when a mechanic has a rest at regular intervals and the observer regularly records this, which would suggest that the mechanic wasn't working at all! An activity sample sheet would record the productive work being studied and then have headings under 'Supporting Work' such as: 'search for tools', 'carry tools, parts or materials', 'move vehicles', 'work on equipment', 'plan the job, i.e. use manuals, etc.', 'tidy up', 'use paperwork', 'engage in administration', etc. The number of observations will determine the accuracy of the job being studied. The statistical theory on which activity sampling is based is called attribute sampling. From this a formula has been developed to calculate the accuracy of an activity-sampling study. This formula is:

$$L^2 = \frac{4P\,(100-P)}{N}$$

where $L =$ the limit of error of occurrence of the class being considered, and is expressed as a percentage value;

$P =$ the occurrence of the activity being considered, expressed as a percentage of the total observations (i.e. P is any particular one of the classes of activity defined for the study); and

$N =$ the total number of observations taken for all the classes being studied.

To use the formula the limit of accuracy required is defined. Consider a partsman delivering parts to customers where L is required to be accurate to ± 4 per cent. A pilot study of 100 observations would then be made. If 'delivering' parts to customers' premises took up 30 per cent of a working day then $P =$ 30 per cent and $L = 4$ per cent. We can now calculate the actual number of observations required to obtain our required accuracy.

$$L^2 = \frac{4P\,(100-P)}{N}$$

By transposing the formula to obtain a value for N

$$N = \frac{4P\,(100-P)}{L^2}$$

$$\therefore \quad N = \frac{4 \times 30\,(100-30)}{4 \times 4}$$

$$= \frac{4 \times 30 \times 70}{16}$$

$$= 525 \text{ observations required.}$$

As we have already taken 100 observations in our pilot study we would require a further 425 observations to obtain our desired limit of accuracy.

Other observations of a partsman could include such things as travelling, dealing with customers, loading and waiting to load, arranging route order, meals, clerical work, other work, and non-productive time. A record under the heading of 'not working' would have sub-headings to include such things as 'waiting at stores', 'waiting for supervisor', 'tea break', 'personal break', 'absence for no reason', and 'interference between men (i.b.m.)'. This last occurs when two or more men work on a vehicle and one is prevented from working by another for any reason. The N.E.D.O. survey gave figures for the target losses which should be aimed at for maximum efficiency, and for those which were actually found. These can be summarized as follows:

Lost time activity	Target (per cent)	Actual (per cent)
Carrying tools and waiting for parts	1 – 3	2 – 12
Search for tools	Up to 1	0·5 – 5
Personal breaks and tea breaks	10 – 14	8 – 25
Interference between men	Up to 0·5	0·5 – 6·5
Moving vehicles	Up to 3·4	2 – 10
Paperwork/administration	3 – 4	0·7 – 9.9

The student will appreciate that reducing lost time anywhere in a dealership means that more productive work can be obtained, so that we can produce more profits and higher wage packets. Further details on activity sampling can be obtained from text books dealing exclusively with work study; but from the data given here it is hoped any student or manager would be able to analyse lost time within an organization.

Ergonomics

This involves the influence of working conditions on people. All managers will be aware that the layout of work places is important if operations are to be completed efficiently. Some people tend to fit the worker to the job rather than the job to the worker. It is, of course, difficult to achieve ideal conditions for every job.

Ergonomics has been developed from the biological sciences, and involves the science of fitting the job to the worker. Machines and workplaces should be designed around the capabilities of workers whenever this is possible. With workplaces such as the workshop, parts department, forecourt, body shop, and so on, the following items play a part in the efficiency of personnel:

Temperature:	i.e. heat or cold, humidity, and air movements.
Noise:	Industrial workers commonly lose their hearing because of excessive noise. All kinds of noise can influence productivity and should be kept to acceptable limits for all personnel.
Lighting:	There is a critical lighting level for a given task, and this should be obtained for optimum performance. Glare and dazzle should be avoided.

Vibrations: This is closely associated with noise, and vibration should be kept to a minimum.

Toxic substances: The effect of substances such as carbon monoxide from exhaust gases can affect all workers. Legislation exists about such matters and should be stringently enforced. H.M. Factory Inspectorate will advise on these matters and there are many safety, health, and welfare booklets available from H.M.S.O. e.g. *Carbon Monoxide Poisoning : Causes and Prevention*, price 25p. (1977).

Colours: Correct colours for work areas can influence the accident rates. Red is an accepted colour for danger and can be used accordingly.

Note: There are certain statutory safety, working, and direction notices for commercial establishments, factories, and transport. These can be supplied by Focal Displays Ltd., 33/37 Elm Road, New Malden, Surrey KT3 3AR.

In addition to the items listed, ergonomics also covers anthropometry, i.e. measurement of a person's physical dimensions. Aural and visual capabilities and limitations, the autonomic nerves, and kinaesthetic senses will affect the ability of a person to work. In turn, the placing of machines, lifts, tools, controls, and so on also affects the working environment. People's ages, shift work arrangements and people's expenditure of physical energy are organizational matters which should receive attention to determine how a workplace can best be used; and rest periods should be arranged accordingly.

Just as many commercial vehicles now have cabs designed by ergonomists, so that a minimum of effort is required to look at the instruments and operate the controls, so a workshop supervisor should ensure that by applying basic ergonomic principles, the firm's equipment and tools can be used as effectively as possible.

Cybernetics.

This can be defined as the study of the systems of control and communications in animals and in electrically-operated devices such as calculating machines. It can also be explained as the self-organizing capacity of an animal, a machine or a mechanical brain.

In order to exercise proper control over anything there must be a feedback from the output so that input can be modified to maintain the desired effect of the output. A human body has its own feed-back mechanisms and the senses exist to discharge this function. The nervous system feeds back to the brain. Learning takes place more effectively if the results of progress are fed back to the subject, and this is applied in many ways, e.g. in the progressive assessment testing of apprentices undergoing training.

Progressive assessment testing is a technique which is used to ascertain if apprentices have absorbed their new skills effectively, and the R.T.I.T.B.

have booklets about how to implement such tests. The apprentice is fed back information on his progress and his training is adjusted accordingly. Again, a parts manager can effectively monitor stock levels if he has a continual feedback from a computer, which of course must be fed with data in the first place.

The servo-mechanisms of the human body and of machines are part of the discipline of cybernetics. Human brains and nervous systems are very complex and respond according to the natural make up of individuals. This subject can be referred to in much more depth by studying the measurement of mental processes. In practice all work places should be such that controls for machines and equipment can be safely and effectively used by the personnel involved. Any work being performed by employees under study should measure the activity effectively, so that manning levels for any particular operation can be continually observed and adjusted in the light of figures fed back from report sheets.

Kinetics.

This can be defined as the science of the relations between the motions of bodies and forces acting upon them. It is that branch of dynamics which deals with changes in movements of matter produced by forces. Although not directly concerned with kinetics, a booklet entitled *Safe Loading of Vehicles* price 30p (1977) is available from H.M.S.O. and should be read in conjunction with this work.

The Department of Employment have issued a small booklet entitled *Lifting and Carrying* price 5p. (1977). This booklet describes the practical application of kinetics in the work of lifting and carrying. Within industry, over 40 000 accidents occur each year as a result of the incorrect handling of loads, leaving many people totally disabled. A mechanic off work because of a lifting or handling accident leaves an empty place. Repeat this, and we have a depleted staff and loss of productivity.

Many students will recall from previous work that kinetics is a study of motion in terms of displacement, velocity, speed, and acceleration. The work study practitioner applies these terms to human effort as well as machines. Careful study of kinetics can reduce human effort and help to increase productivity.

All managers must ensure their staff are adequately trained to do the work required. It is very easy to injure one's back by using it in what is described as 'primitive lifting', i.e. manual lifting involving the use of the back. Using the legs in a mechanical lift can be all right provided that they are placed correctly. This type of mechanical handling is quite satisfactory.

By using body weight movement we have what is described as kinetic lifting. To do this it is necessary to have:

(1) a proper hold of the item being lifted;

    (2) a straight back;

    (3) the chin held into the chest;

    (4) correct foot positions, i.e. one foot forward and the feet about 300 mm
        (12 in.) apart;

    (5) arms held in close to the body;

    (6) body weight used in a balance and counter-balance way.

Lifting relies upon the skilful use of the right muscles and not on brute force. Excessive loads should never be attempted; and if the load approaches half the weight of the person lifting the load the risk of injury from possible loss of balance is a real one. Rhythmic action assists limb and back muscles and helps to relieve tension. The work study analyst has special skills when dealing with motion economy. He can also eliminate possible accidents. It is therefore imperative that all personnel involved with lifting should take advantage of courses on this subject and thereby keep their dealership free from lifting and handling accidents. This applies both to physical handling and to the use of all machines for such work. Under the Health and Safety at Work Act 1974 Section 2b states: 'Arrangements for ensuring, so far as is reasonably practicable, safety and absence of risks to health in connection with the use, handling, storage and transport of articles and substances must be made.' Section 2c states that the provision of such information, instruction, training, and supervision as is necessary to ensure, so far as is reasonably practicable, the health and safety at work of all employees must be effected. Managers neglecting or ignoring these instructions place themselves in a very serious position. See also Appendix IV.

Value analysis

This can be defined as an organized approach to an objective appraisal of each element producing a cost, with the object of achieving only that necessary function, and reliability in that function at minimum cost.

Value analysis can be applied to most operations to reduce operational costs. It can result in saving materials, such as oils, split pins, nuts and bolts, body parts, etc.; but it can also eliminate unnecessary effort.

To introduce this a person is elected as a chairman to plan and organize a project, to direct team meetings, to assist in probing and investigating alternative courses of action, and to ensure every idea is brought to finality and implemented. The chairman should be a senior manager and team members should also be senior men from each section of the dealership. The chairman is usually elected full-time and the team men part-time, devoting up to 30 per cent of their time to the project while it is being studied. Costs can usually be cut by a minimum of 5 per cent by the application of value analysis. Early consultation with trade unions and all staff is essential before the project starts. Value analysis operates in the following stages:

(1) Information is obtained from all departments regarding the present cost of operations.

(2) Speculation is then made as to what costs can be reduced.

(3) Investigation into costs is completed to determine accurately where costs can be cut.

(4) Recommendation of all results is then given to the committee and then to higher management.

(5) Implementation of the final agreed cost cuts then takes place, though without impairing reliability and quality.

Value analysis is concerned with materials and things rather than with people; people are a work study matter. It is an analytical investigation of all the elements producing a cost, with a view to reducing the effects of each of them, so far as this is possible.

Critical path analysis

Network Analysis: In a large and complex project the individual operations, with their times, can be recorded on a diagram. This will show up the necessary sequence, with the inevitable delays when one operation cannot begin until another is completed. From this a 'critical path' can be worked out, showing the minimum time for the whole operation, and how subsidiary activities must be fitted in.

This means:

(a) an even flow of work;

(b) reduced waiting time;

(c) reductions in cost;

(d) the provision of better control.

Example	Activity	Time (minutes)
(1)	Disconnect machine from services.	20
(2)	Move machine to new position.	60
(3)	Prepare new position and services.	40
(4)	Install machine in new position.	50
(5)	Connect with services.	20
(6)	Run in and test.	50

DIAGRAM OF ABOVE

①———→②———→③———→④———→⑤———→⑥———→⑦

Note: The arrow line does not correspond with time and the ◯ is a node

We can now add the time

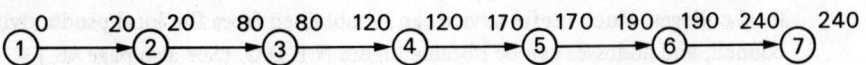

0	20	20	80	80	120	120	170	170	190	190	240	240

①———→②———→③———→④———→⑤———→⑥———→⑦

A close study of the diagram might give the idea that two activities could be carried out at the same time. Once the machine has been disconnected from the services in its existing position, a couple of men could prepare the new position whilst the other men move it across. The diagram would then take the following form:

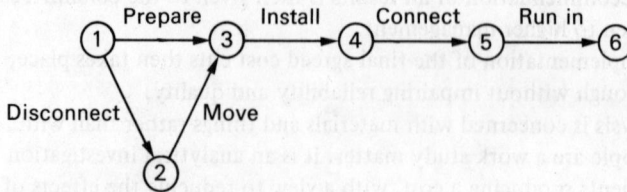

The times would work out as follows:

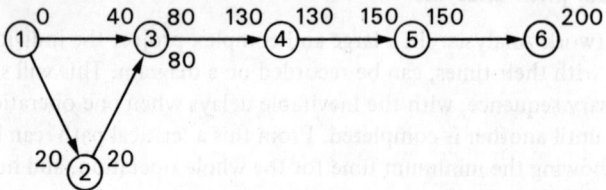

We have now reduced the time from 240 minutes to 200 minutes, enabling the machine to be operated and production of work to start sooner. In complex engineering activities, network analysis can be used to save time and money. Vehicle body building and repairs can utilize such techniques just as well as major repair workshops which undertake engine, gear-box, and rear-axle overhauls on a broad basis involving many units. Students should note that critical path analysis is also known as 'critical path scheduling'.

Work study—summary

The future of all business operations depends upon the efficient use of all personnel. In 1976 a record number of bankruptcies occurred in the United Kingdom. Analytical methods must be used to ensure success. All staff must take part in developing new methods and ideas. Students should analyse small areas of work such as tyre changing, workshop bay layouts, shunting of vehicles, completion of certain tasks in offices, and so on as a means of familiarizing themselves with work analysis methods. Students can make out their own flow charts and procedure charts for this purpose. Where possible, they can also use critical path analysis methods. Managers and supervisors, of course, will need to attend appropriate courses at the R.T.I.T.B. centres or local colleges. Much useful advice can be obtained from the local productivity council, and addesses can be obtained from N.E.D.O. (See also page 86.)

Workshop control systems and workshop loading

It is part of a manager's job to ensure that all his staff has a reasonable amount of work to do and to ensure that the staff complete their work. This does not mean that it is necessary to spy on mechanics who may have stopped to think about the job in hand. It is much better to approach a mechanic in a way that stresses that labour costs must be kept to a minimum rather than with an aggressive 'have you nothing to do?' Any experienced manager will know it is much better to make everyone feel part of the organization and to make everyone understand that wasted time does mean loss for the workshop and, as a result, loss of bonus for the staff.

A service station cannot be run on a hit or miss basis and work must be planned ahead and handled in a systematic manner if it is to function efficiently. Consequently, a service manager must organize his own routine in order that he can organize the work load of other staff. To do this he must list his own duties and how often these need attention.

Daily work

Check all staff present and work is distributed via foreman, deal with correspondence from customers, manufacturers, equipment suppliers. Deal with workshop and staff problems as they arise. Deal with warranty claims and complaints. Ensure training schemes are progressing satisfactory. Check invoices.

Weekly checks

a) *Inspection of premises* to see if any maintenance required e.g. windows broken, toilets clean and working, dirty workshop floor or corners require tidying, white parking lines need re-painting, lighting in good order, lifting equipment and tools satisfactory.

b) *Check all work received* (usually Monday or Tuesday) to see adequate work load for the shop staff and that all repairs and services are proceeding. Use magnetic colour blocks on cars so that a numerical sequence is obtained and any jobs held up can be easily spotted. Complete weekly Labour Analysis Charts.

Monthly checks

c) *Check profit and loss statement* covering repairs and service, the second week of the month is usually the best for this.

d) *Send out special service letters* reminding customers that their cars are due for service or offering some other service such as battery and lighting checks. Appraise current advertising and service promotion ideas.

e) *Take inventory of equipment* being used and check to ensure it is in good order or whether maintenance is required.

f) *Check decoration and painting of premises*—organize cleaning and decorating as required.

Twice monthly checks

g) *Check service follow-up* i.e. customers who have booked a service and failed to appear, likewise follow up truant customers for other work which may have been requested and customer has not turned up.
h) *Sales and works meeting* which can be held every second Tuesday or Wednesday but at a regular time to ensure work and departments are co-operating and running smoothly. Iron out difficulties and disputes.
i) *Annual check*—check very carefully the annual financial report. Any parts not healthy should be considered carefully to see how these can be improved.

Bi-annual checks

j) *Check efficiency of all personnel.* How many staff require re-training or require to be placed on manufacturers' courses to be brought up-to-date? Arrange a rota for staff to go on such courses.
k) *Ensure all Factories Act reports for lifting equipment, compressors, boilers etc.* are filed and any repairs required put into effect.

These are the duties of a service manager. Such duties may be increased or decreased according to the size of the station. In any event a calendar showing these duties should be to hand to serve as a reminder to the manager and could be arranged as follows:

SUN	MON	TUES	WED	THUR	FRI	SAT
			1 h	2	3	4
5	6 a	7 b	8 g	9 c	10 e	11
12	13 a	14 b	15 h	16 f	17	18
19	20 a	21 b	22 g	23	24	25
26	27 a	28 b	29 h	30	31 d	

This calendar covers a monthly work programme which includes daily, weekly, monthly and bi-monthly checks.

The annual report for each firm should be studied when to hand and the yearly diary noted e.g. if the annual report becomes available each January then a date should be allocated to examine the report i.e. 25. Likewise the bi-annual checks should be appended in the diary calendar i.e. the dates these are to be carried out. Thus January 4th and July 4th could be appended as a reminder.

Some manufacturers such as Studebaker use a calendar with symbols such as circles, squares, triangles etc. to indicate job requirements, daily, weekly, monthly and annually.

In addition to these regular checks and inspections a service manager must also allocate time to recruit, interview, select, hire and dismiss personnel, complete R.T.I.T.B. claim forms, meet all vehicle purchasers, maintain good liason with other departmental managers, ensure good contact with insurance companies to maintain good volume of insurance work, supervise used car re-conditioning and new car preparation.

According to the size of station or dealership policy, these duties will be modified but the items listed gives some indication of the total responsibilities of a service manager.

Workshop loadings

Whilst the service manager may deal with workshop loadings the reception engineer will need to know when a job can be completed in the workshop. To load a shop with too much work means a customer is without his car for too long a period whilst too little work means mechanics stand idle. Thus a daily diary should be kept and full details noted of the customers name and address and the job required. If a repair job is needed the customer's car should be checked upon arrival and the job assessed e.g. a customer may assume a differential is at fault when the trouble may be caused by a wheel bearing. Normal servicing jobs are straight forward and time schedules from manu-facturers are available. However, when keeping the diary the reception engin-eer should keep in very close liaison with the foreman to see how jobs are progressing and whether full staff is available or if any are off ill, going on courses and so on. Thus a reception engineer before accepting a job should bear in mind:

a) Number of mechanics in the shop i.e. 10 mechanics 8 hours = 80 hours per day working time (100% efficient—rarely achieved).

b) *Type of job* coming in (repair/service) and length of time required. Manu-facturer's Standard Time Schedules for repair work should be consulted.

c) *Most convenient time* to accept job unless customer can leave a car all day. Rental costs for floor space should always be kept in mind.

d) *If parts are required* approximate length of time required to obtain these and whether they can be ordered before the job comes in: *liaison with store manager* is essential for this part of the work.

e) *Upon arrival of the job* a job card should be made out in duplicate, one for the office, one for the foreman to pass onto the mechanic unless a three or five part job set is used where one copy is the job card.

f) *Some form of indicator* should then be attached to the car to denote arrival time and date. Magnetic coloured holders in numerical order of jobs received are very useful and eye-catching, thus, blue for service work 1, 2, 3, 4 etc., red for repair work 1, 2, 3, 4 etc. When placed on top of a car these magnetic holders serve as a constant reminder that a job is held up for some reason. Colours can be changed daily if required.

The above points are relevant to workshop loading. Service schools in this country and in the U.S.A. stress these points and each have their own workshop loading sheets to keep control of jobs in hand and labour, for it must be remembered that profit on labour sales forms a vital part of every workshop. The full utilization of labour can only be obtained by careful organization and planning which also has its limitations. No one can predict that a customer will not turn up or parts will be excessively delayed resulting in lost time but, all things being equal, the loading of a workshop can be controlled by using a Workshop Loading Chart. These charts which are usually about 50 centimetres (20 in) by 35 centimetres (14 in), are divided into columns to include Repair Order No., Customer's Name, Make and Model of Car, Registration No. of Car, details of Work to be Completed, Hours of Work expected, Collection Date and Time, Mechanic's Name, Name of Tester. A separate sheet is used for each day of each week. A customer telephoning for an appointment can be given a time and date by referring to the Workshop Loading Charts which are made out 7 to 10 days in advance, a new one being completed each day to include on it the day and date, all other details being already given.

In addition to control of labour and jobs in the workshop, the mechanic himself must be constantly reminded of his work load. A Daily Record Card of work done is one method of recording a mechanics' productive work. Leyland use the layout shown in Fig. 2.16. It will be observed that Schedule Time can be recorded either from a Manufacturers' Standard Time Schedule or by separate assessment by the reception engineer if such jobs are not given in the Manufacturers' Schedules. Thus, if a mechanic finishes the work before the stated time, he is credited with the stated time but can commence another job thus obtaining a bonus in 'time saved.' This card serves more than one purpose, not only recording a mechanics total time but also serving as a reminder to him of the work he has actually done. The foreman of the workshop will keep these cards in a suitable tray and complete all recordings necessary. It is the foreman who gives out the work to the mechanics and he is able to keep a check on such allocation using his men to complete work in good time.

The service manager who has overall control of the workshop will receive the job cards from the foreman daily as jobs are completed. From the job cards he will transfer details of the mechanics attendance, overtime at $1\frac{1}{3}$ and $1\frac{1}{2}$ rates, schedule time for the job, non-productive time, internal time spent cleaning tools etc., and finally, assess each day by calculating time saved or lost. Obviously time saved is a vital part of the assessment and if a mechanic

DAILY RECORD CARD

NAME .... No. .... DATE ....

Job No.	Item No.	Item Comp	Sch Time	Productive Hrs.	Non Productive Hrs.		Clockings
						OFF	
						ON	
						OFF	
						ON	
						OFF	
						ON	
						OFF	
						ON	
						OFF	
						ON	
						OFF	
						ON	
						OFF	
						ON	
						OFF	
						ON	
						OFF	
						ON	
						OFF	
						ON	
						OFF	
						ON	
						OFF	
						ON	
						OFF	
						ON	

INCOMPLETED JOBS	C/F	A	B	C	ATTENDANCE	HRS. D
JOB No.	HRS.				(NORMAL) TIME	
		TIME SAVED = A – B			BONUS TIME	
		OVERTIME			@ 1.1/3	
					@ 1.1/2	

N.B.   D – C = B

Fig. 2.16. Mechanics' Daily Record Card

LABOUR SALES RECORD

WEEK ENDING MONTH

COL. 1 = OPERATIVES ATTENDANCE HOURS. COL. 2 = CUSTOMER LABOUR STANDARD HOURS. COL. 3 = INTERNAL LABOUR HOURS. COL. 4 = NON-REVENUE LABOUR HOURS.

SHEET No.

SECTION	OPERATIVE'S NAME	No	Grade	DAY				DAY				DAY				DAY				DAY				DAY				DAY				OPERATIVE'S WEEKLY TOTALS									
				1	2	3	4	1	2	3	4	1	2	3	4	1	2	3	4	1	2	3	4	1	2	3	4	1	2	3	4	1	2	3	4	2&3&4	R.O.F.W	CORRECTED	O TIME	PAY HOURS	OPS No
	TOTALS																																								
	EFFICIENCY %																																								

Fig. 2.17. Labour Sales Analysis Sheet (Standard Triumph)

has a consistent run without time saved the service manager must determine why because 'time saved' means increased profit for the workshop. A Labour Sales Analysis Sheet on a weekly basis is arranged as shown in Fig. 2.17. In connection with 'time saved' and efficiency, the section of this chapter dealing with this should be consulted.

Service records and follow-up schemes

As indicated in the earlier part of this chapter, the hard copy of the 3 or 5 part job set is retained by the service manager for all repairs and services carried out. Keeping these enables a list of customers to be available if work appears to be slackening off, or upon referring to previous work records whether a slack period is anticipated for say, September or October. If this is the case a service manager can send out either service reminder letters or give a special offer of, for example, a braking system overhaul at a reduced price. With regular customers of course, service work can be anticipated. When one service has been done a record is kept in the form of a card diary indicating when the customer should be expected to call in say 3 or 6 months time. If the customer does not call then a reminder letter is sent out to him. Here are two examples:

Reminder for service

Dear Mr. . . . .

Upon referring to our records we note your car is now due for a further service. In case you have overlooked this rather important work, we are taking the liberty of reminding you.

If you would care to telephone or call we should be very pleased to arrange a suitable time and date for your car to receive attention.

Yours sincerely,

SERVICE MANAGER.

Work promotion letter to all past and present customers

Dear Customer,

During the next two weeks we are offering a complete diagnostic analysis of your car's condition for half the usual price!

Our trained technicians, using the latest diagnostic equipment will completely analyse the condition of your car and provide a detailed report. Any repairs which may be required could be carried out at our workshops or elsewhere: we would provide free estimates for such work.

Since we believe it to be in your interest to have your car checked at the reduced price we hope you will be able to call at our Service Department or telephone to arrange an appointment to suit you.

Yours sincerely,

SERVICE MANAGER.

Letters advertising other work might be written in a similar way.

Other service promotion schemes include advertising on local television, local cinema, local football team programmes, local press, posters, circulars, G.P.O. 'yellow pages', signs at the station and roadside, window display and by distributing novelties such as key rings, calendars and so on.

At this point it would be as well to explain that service promotions fall into certain categories:

1. Continuous. Stamp trading comes within this group along with daily or weekly advertising.
2. Semi-continuous promotions usually last up to 20 weeks and embrace some form of 'collecting card' for the customer to complete and redeem the card for some specific item or discount on a car accessory of his own choice.
3. Short-term or 'instant' promotions are usually based on the purchase of a certain gallonage of petrol or oil. With purchase some special gift or discount is given for a limited period of time, e.g. 7 days, 14 days or 28 days only.

All promotions cost money and must be carefully chosen. At the close of any promotion its effect must be evaluated. For example the service manager must ask himself:

(a) What effect did the promotion have on sales?
(b) Did we take full advantage of the selling opportunities opened by the promotion?
(c) Did we achieve our original objectives—if not, why not?
(d) Was it worth the cost?
(e) Could a similar result have been obtained by a cheaper method?

The object of all promotions is to improve profitable sales and to enlarge the scope and prestige of the service station. Consequently when considering a sales promotion scheme the service manager must think well ahead to ensure he is going to market a saleable product at precisely the right time. The seasons of the year, holiday periods, etc., fall at regular intervals and provide a ready-made theme for many promotion activities. Nevertheless, the promotion must be well planned to have the maximum effect. By remembering at all times we are selling service, parts, accessories, new and used vehicles, etc., it is important to bear in mind that we must supply what the customer wants.

With any promotion the following items need to be considered:

1. The method of advertising, (i.e. local press, local television, leaflets, posters, circulars, etc.) is sufficient to achieve the desired object.
2. The cost of advertising will be justified by the increased profit obtained from the sales or services rendered.
3. Your staff are made aware of the promotion and will be able to handle the increased custom expected from the promotion scheme.
4. The promotion will meet the customer's needs at the time it is being offered.
5. Try to make your service station a place attractive enough to make the customer want to call again for service work, petrol or accessory sales.
6. Ensure your promotions are strictly honest and legal. Many motor traders have been convicted in the courts because they have not paid sufficient attention to detail in wording their advertisements. The Trade Descriptions Act 1968 demands strict honesty. If a used car is advertised as 'immaculate' then that is just what it must be.

Warranty procedures and claims

To understand warranty procedures the structure of the retail trade should first be understood. A manufacturer is held responsible for the goods he sells but the retailer of the goods, in our case cars or commercial vehicles, is the person to whom defective goods are returned. The retailer then puts right jobs which the manufacturer authorizes and returns complete units where this is necessary. Therefore, the retailer has some claim on the manufacturer. The rate of reimbursement will be decided between manufacturer and distributor. All new vehicles are sent on order, from the manufacturer to a distributor who holds a franchise. A franchise is a privilege to distribute cars or commercial vehicles by one dealer in a certain area. Manufacturers appoint a distributor in a particular area and the number of distributors depends upon size and population of an area. One large manufacturer has 400 main distributors with a further 1 200 appointed dealers for car sales and 150 truck specialist distributors. The average number of employees for these establishments is 100, the highest being 250, the lowest 50. The larger dealerships can expect to sell some 2 000 cars/light vans a year. Distributors allow locally-appointed dealers to buy cars from them at a suitable discount. The line of distribution in the motor trade is therefore: manufacturer (producer)—wholesaler (distributor)—retailer (dealer)—consumer (customer).

In the event of a claim for defective work this line is reversed. The dealer makes out a Warranty Claim Form and sends this to the distributor who, in turn, sends this to the manufacturer. Sometimes a direct claim is possible from dealer to manufacturer. Also, distributors sell cars and commercials direct to customers as well as selling to dealers.

A warranty Claim Form is shown in Fig. 2.18 and all details must be

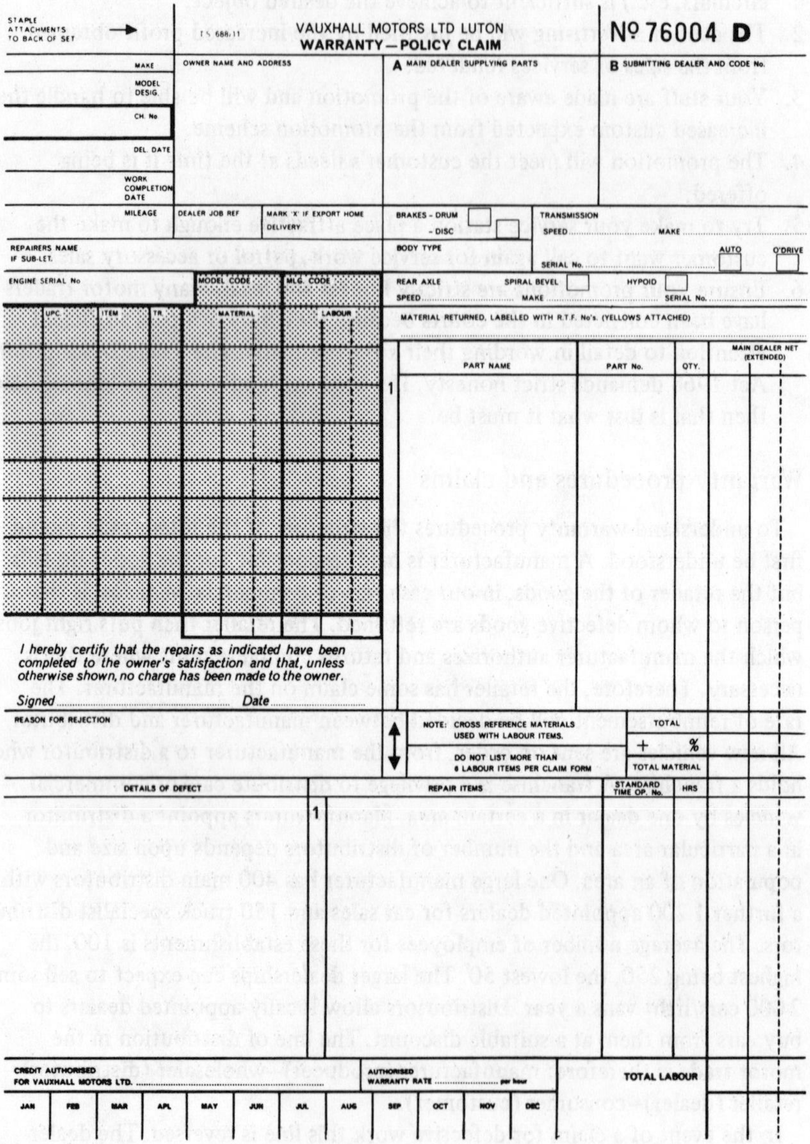

STAPLE ATTACHMENTS TO BACK OF SET →

T.S. 688/11

VAUXHALL MOTORS LTD LUTON
WARRANTY—POLICY CLAIM

Nº 76004 D

MAKE
MODEL DESIG.
CH. No
DEL. DATE
WORK COMPLETION DATE

OWNER NAME AND ADDRESS

A MAIN DEALER SUPPLYING PARTS

B SUBMITTING DEALER AND CODE No.

MILEAGE | DEALER JOB REF | MARK 'X' IF EXPORT HOME DELIVERY

BRAKES - DRUM
- DISC

TRANSMISSION
SPEED .... MAKE ....
SERIAL No. .... AUTO O'DRIVE

REPAIRERS NAME IF SUB-LET.

BODY TYPE

ENGINE SERIAL No | MODEL CODE | MLG. CODE

REAR AXLE SPIRAL BEVEL HYPOID
SPEED .... MAKE .... SERIAL No. ....

MATERIAL RETURNED, LABELLED WITH R.T.F. No's. (YELLOWS ATTACHED)

UPC.	ITEM	TR.	MATERIAL	LABOUR

	PART NAME	PART No.	QTY.	MAIN DEALER NET (EXTENDED)
1				

I hereby certify that the repairs as indicated have been completed to the owner's satisfaction and that, unless otherwise shown, no charge has been made to the owner.

Signed .... *Date* ....

REASON FOR REJECTION

NOTE: CROSS REFERENCE MATERIALS USED WITH LABOUR ITEMS.
DO NOT LIST MORE THAN 6 LABOUR ITEMS PER CLAIM FORM

TOTAL
+ %
TOTAL MATERIAL

DETAILS OF DEFECT		REPAIR ITEMS	STANDARD TIME OP. No.	HRS
	1			

CREDIT AUTHORISED FOR VAUXHALL MOTORS LTD. ....

AUTHORISED WARRANTY RATE .... per hour

TOTAL LABOUR

JAN	FEB	MAR	APL	MAY	JUN	JUL	AUG	SEP	OCT	NOV	DEC

Fig. 2.18 Warranty Claim Form (Note that many warranty claims are now dealt with by computors.)

completed. Some manufacturers expect dealers and distributors to complete minimum warranty work of say, up to £2.00 for labour and materials. If this amount is exceeded then the Warranty Claim Form is made out and sent to the manufacturer's service department. This department besides being responsible for all claims also has to ensure that distributors and dealers 1) receive spare parts 2) receive technical information in the way of service manuals 3) organize refresher courses for mechanics belonging to dealers and distributors 4) provide special service tools as required; service manuals, parts catalogues along with modified sections are continuously sent to dealers from the manufacturer. A service manager should ensure these reach all people concerned by having each department sign on the front of the manual in turn. The manual is then filed in a central position for access as required by all personnel involved. A Warranty Clerk is sometimes appointed at service stations to deal exclusively with this work. This clerk must understand all warranty claims. Certain parts of a vehicle are guaranteed for different lengths of time, for example side and headlamp bulbs for 28 days, radio parts for 3 months and so on. Details of such guarantees are supplied by the manufacturer.

A transport fleet operator who has a number of cars or trucks is usually entitled to special discounts, for example $2\frac{1}{2}\%$ with eleven vehicles or more and 10% on 200 or more vehicles. Percentages will vary between the figures quoted depending on the number of vehicles and these are called 'fleet users terms.' These discounts offer advantages to manufacturer and customer as well as to the dealer who sells and will probably service and repair the vehicles.

Having read this chapter which deals with administration details, students are advised to consult their own employers to ascertain how their systems operate. In addition, colleges who run management courses will generally arrange visits to large efficient dealerships. Students during such·visits would complete the answers, on separate sheets, to a questionnaire similar to that shown below. By this method a student is able to see how theory is put into practice.

Visit to a main dealership—questionnaire

1. What system is employed at reception when a customer arrives with his car?
2. How is workshop loading controlled?
3. If there is a bonus scheme in operation—how does it operate?
4. Outline the flow of job cards in this dealership.
5. What items make up a Profit and Loss Account for the workshop?
6. How are overheads allocated to the workshop?
7. Briefly state the turnover of stock in the stores and how stock checks are made.
8. Sketch to scale, a plan of the workshop area and indicate the position of

all major items of equipment, viz., benches, lifts, pits, brake tester, chassis dynamometer, steering equipment, engine analysers and so on.

Operators' Licensing. The Transport Act 1968 (Section V) requires that repair, service, and vehicle inspection records be filed for at least 15 months. Vehicles which require an Operators' Licence (i.e. certain goods vehicles over 3·5 g.v.w.) must have their records available for D.Tp. inspectors. Consequently, service stations completing repairs and service work for transport operators need to ensure accurate records are kept or passed to the operator in a proper vehicle file folder. The operator has the responsibility for keeping such records but may request the garage to retain the records for inspection. Students should obtain the free booklet 'A Guide to Operators' Licensing' available from the local Traffic Commissioners office.

Questions

1. Describe the best methods of Part Stock Control and Ordering which you know, and which can be applied to a Dealers Part Store to ensure adequate but not excessive stocks at all times. (I.M.I.)
2. A Repair Order Card is a most important document. What information should it give and what procedure should it follow from the time it is completed until the Invoice is made out? (I.M.I.)
3. Modern cars are being designed for much less frequent maintenance periods. This will mean that customers will call at their service stations at larger intervals. Is it considered wise to operate a 'Customer Follow' system under these circumstances and what is the best system you know? (I.M.I.)
4. As a service manager with the stores under your control, what system would you adopt to see that you do not run out of any particular parts? How would you prevent obsolete stock choking your shelves? (I.M.I.)
5. If a service station, during a month, purchases x number of hours from its mechanics, and sells the same number of hours to its customers is said to be 100% efficient. This is a state of affairs rarely, if ever, achieved. What is considered to be a satisfactory percentage of efficiency in a service station, and what steps should be taken to achieve this figure assuming the department was not reaching it? (I.M.I.)
6. State how to assess an hourly rate of charge for work to include not only direct labour charges but also all consumable and processing materials used in a Body Repair Section of a service station. (I.M.I.)
7. Make out a specimen requisition docket for the spares necessary to reline the brakes of a car and decarbonize its engine. Give your reasons for the layout of the form used. (I.M.I.)
8. With labour and other costs continually rising it is essential to ensure that the Workshop or service station is kept as fully employed as possible. Describe any system which you consider is best to fulfill the above requirement. State the number of employees on which your answer is based. (I.M.I.)

9. It has often been said that 'Sales follow Service.' If it were necessary for you to organize an Advertising Campaign to sell Service, how would you do it and how would you evaluate the results compared with the costs of the campaign? (I.M.I.)

10. Imagine you have taken over a workshop with twenty skilled mechanics and, of course, the other workshop personnel. The parts department attached serves both your workshop and over the counter sales, but has not kept up with the growth rate for the area it serves and requires complete reorganization. How would you carry out the necessary reorganization? (I.M.I.)

11. Most dealerships comprise three main departments, viz., sales, service and spares. Each must make its contribution to the profits of the company. As the person in charge of service, what system would you use to make sure that your department was making a profit, or a loss? This is assuming that the overheads allocated to each department are known by the head of the department. (I.M.I.)

12. An inventory of a Parts Department has disclosed a high percentage of slow moving and obsolete material in stock. Suggest how to clear this material and to ensure that in the future this position could not be repeated. (I.M.I.)

13. The way a Warranty or Guarantee Claim is handled can either cement or destroy customer goodwill. Describe how you would handle a major claim from the time the complaint is received to final settlement. (I.M.I.)

14. Much valuable workshop space is often taken up by vehicles waiting for spare parts. In many cases this should not have been necessary. How would you organize your parts stock and your Reception/Workshop/Parts department relations in order to cut this waste to the absolute minimum? (I.M.I.)

15. With costs rising everywhere it is most essential that proper records are kept in order to balance revenue received for Service against the cost of operating the service station. How would you record the production of your mechanics both individually and collectively. (I.M.I.)

16. Your Parts department has a turnover of £50 000 per year, serving both your workshop and the public:
    (1) What should the value of your stock holding be?
    (2) How would you control the stock in order to maintain and probably increase your sales turnover?
    (3) How would you control the issue of parts to your workshop?
    (I.M.I.)

17. Paperwork in a garage is essential for the control of costs. Explain the object of 3 and 5 part job sets which are now used in modern workshops. State what each copy will be used for and where each copy is finally retained. (I.M.I.)

Work study

This is a constantly developing science and certain terms now form part of the 1983 syllabuses. Thus the following explanations need to be known.

Synthetics. In the section dealing with this it will be seen that the elements of a job can be determined, and, from previous time studies, standard times for comparable elements can be achieved. These pre-determined standard times for elements of work are called synthetics. A large number of times studies have to be made before a library of synthetics can be established.

Analytical estimating. One of the problems encountered in the motor industry is the pre-determination of standard times for work on a variety of vehicles, each different make requiring different times for the same type of job. Theoretically the jobs can be broken down into elements and the sybthetic times calculated. Obviously this would involve considerable time and expense. In cases like this synthetic breakdown can be uneconomic and an estimator has to use what accurate synthetic times may be available from jobs already completed. This technique is called 'analytical estimating' which is simple in principle but requires skill in practical application. A supervisor with a sound practical background can be trained as an analytical estimator and eventually be able to estimate target times for most jobs.

Predetermined Motion Time Systems (PMTS). With this system all the movements or motions of the body are reduced to operations which can be described on a card in terms of 400 odd 'motion times'. This then becomes a 'table of motion times'. Time values are related to work factors and unit times established. Movement of fingers, limbs etc. are related to distance to establish analytical units. Actual jobs are also put on the card, motions necessary to do the job are put down in sequence and the analysis of motions can then be made. This type of analysis does require a work study specialist, and, where certain repetition jobs occur either in workshop, offices or other areas it does enable an accurate estimate of a job to be made. A number of recordings have to be made of the same job to ensure detailed accuracy. Standards can be achieved in offices for writing time and for reading or eye-focusing time. In a workshop where repition jobs are completed e.g. overhauling cylinder heads, it is possible to achieve PMTS standards.

From this information accurate estimated job times can be used for calculating the cost of a job for a customer. (See Pages 48–49.)

CHAPTER 3

RECEPTION

Reception engineers (service advisers)

Qualifications and responsibilities

The 'reception engineer' also known as 'service adviser' or 'receptionist', is a most important part of any service station. It is the reception engineer who meets the customer and finally hands back a car when a service or repair has been completed. Consequently, the behaviour and attitude of a reception engineer can reflect an image of a service station to a customer. If this image is poor then it is unlikely a customer will return. On the other hand, a reception engineer who instills confidence into a customer and is pleasing in attitude and appearance will inevitably find such customers returning for further service and repair work. Too often the general public complain—and quite rightly in many cases—that a garage was completely indifferent to a genuine complaint about a new car or about work which has been completed and is incorrect. It would appear to the general public that some service stations are disinterested about their custom. This, of course, is a disastrous state of affairs and can only result in poor profits for the organization as a whole. The reception engineer, then, plays a vital role in attracting customers and keeping them. To do this job he must have certain qualities and the qualifications for the job could be outlined as follows:

1) Good practical background, e.g., a fully-trained mechanic or fitter.
2) Good theoretical background such as indicated by a pass in final C.G.L.I. 381 Motor Vehicle Mechanics' work or, preferably, C.G.L.I. 390, Motor Vehicle Technicians' work. The T.E.C.-O.T.C. is also suitable.
3) In addition to good practical and theoretical knowledge so that he can converse on all aspects of repair work with confidence, a reception engineer must have a pleasing personality. He must be pleasant at all times with customers, dress smartly, have a clean appearance and be able to instil confidence into customers about the work the garage will do.

   Reception engineers should qualify for the designatory letters T.Eng. or Tech. by registration with the Engineers Registration Board (see Appendix I). C.G.L.I. 381-629 Motor Vehicle Service Reception is also a desirable qualification.

Responsibilities of a reception engineer

It has already been stated what the general background of a reception engineer should be. The responsibilities of a reception engineer can be outlined as follows:

1) To meet the customer before and after repair or service work. When meeting the customer he must carefully assess the fault with the car. To do this, he can complete a road test with the car with the customer driving or use equipment which may be available for such work. In any event, the reception engineer will a) decide upon the work to be done b) obtain customer approval for such work c) place an immediate order for parts with the Parts department if required.

2) The reception engineer having obtained approval for repair, will then make out an estimate for the work or will complete a 3 part or 5 part job card set. (These are dealt with in Chapter 2 in detail.) Such estimates or job sets are then sent to the service manager for his approval.

3) Part of the 3 or 5 part job set is a job card for the mechanic. If this system is not used a job card must be made out and passed to the workshop foreman.

4) A record of workshop loading must be kept at reception to ensure that a car or commercial vehicle can be taken at a certain time and date. This must be checked carefully with the workshop foreman each and every day as mechanics can fail to turn up for work because of illness and for other domestic reasons.

5) Depending on the system of costing adapted, it may be necessary for the reception engineer to prepare the invoice or bill for forwarding to the accounts department of the garage. The 3 and 5 part job set uses one of the sheets as an invoice and this then passed to the accounts department.

6) Finally, the reception engineer must hand the car back to the customer, receive payment if an account is not open with the garage and send the customer on his way—content with the repair and the bill for the job. From the customer's point of view he needs to feel he has had a) cheerful reception b) full attention to his instructions c) rapid and accurate service d) reasonable and consistent charges with the bill presented at the proper time i.e. when taking the car away from the workshop or at the end of the month e) that the garage has been honest with all aspects of work completed.

These are the general responsibilities of a reception engineer but there is far more involved in these responsibilities than meets the eye! Complaints do occur even with the best of garages but these can be minimized by careful inspection of work after service or repair. In this connection a reception engineer has not only an obligation to the customer to listen but must also bear in mind his obligations to the car manufacturer and his own employer. Some customers, for example, expect free repairs long after the warranty of a car expires simply because they have only completed a very low mileage. This does involve the handling of complaints which we shall deal with later, in the meantime let us see how many complaints can be avoided by a careful inspection procedure following repair, service or delivery of a new car.

Quality control of workshop repairs, service or sale of new and used cars

It is a distressing thought that many service stations have virtually no inspection of work done and are quite happy to have a high return of cars for correction of faulty work. The worst of these expect 50% of cars serviced, repaired, or a sale of a car, to return for work to be done. Many have a 20% return of work whilst an average is 10%. The aim should be no return of work but accepting only 2%! No matter how this return of work is viewed it still results in mechanics, receptionists and other members of staff having to repeat, for nothing, certain jobs to put the car right. No efficient garage can tolerate such a loss of profits nor the upsetting of a customer who expects good quality work. It is appreciated there always will be human error but so many defects could be corrected before the vehicle leaves the workshop saving time, money and customer dissatisfaction. This can be achieved by checking all work done in the workshops by the mechanics. Whilst a 'tester' is employed in some workshops this work often falls to the reception engineer.

Function of an inspection system

Applied to our trade this could be defined as the means by which a repair or service is checked and certain standards achieved. Inspection is a preventative measure as it seeks to prevent defective work either arising or being allowed to proceed, thus, only acceptable work goes forward either as a new or used car, or as a satisfactory repair. Mechanics commence such inspections for, as skilled men they should be able to execute skilled work without supervision and it should be satisfactory.

However, assuming we are going to quality control all work, the reception engineer or tester must satisfy himself that a car is, as far as can be ascertained, in good order. A road test of 5 miles can normally reveal defects and for certain work is still essential e.g. steering or suspension where equipment is not available to dynamically check such work. Full use of electronic engine tester, 'rolling road', brake tester should be made as these are valuable aids to quality control most types of work. A three or five minute test run on the chassis dynamometer is time well spent if a car does not come back for further attention. Certain chassis dynamometers and brake testers give graphical recordings, thus, a customer can have both before and after results if desired.

From this it will be seen that an area for quality control of all work must be set on one side of all workshops. This is shown in one layout in Chapter 1. From what has been written, to quality control work, the following procedures could be adopted.

Service work

a) Check type of service i.e. 3 000, 6 000, 12 000, etc.
b) An assessment of performance can be made using diagnostic centre or road test. Electronic equipment will reveal work not done—dirty plugs, points incorrectly set etc.
c) Ensure no oil or grease is on the steering wheel, pedals or exterior of the car.

Repair work

a) Check nature of repair e.g. brakes, transmission etc.
b) Complete test for repair only but note any other defects which may be revealed. Test on brakes could be on brake tester and recorded if possible. Whatever repair is completed, it should be checked to ensure it is satisfactory. If not return to mechanic for correction.
c) Ensure car is clean as before.

Sale of new and used cars

Pre-delivery inspection of the car is essential. In addition to mechanical aspects of the car, bodywork, upholstery, door locks, in fact all the car should be completely checked by using a special inspection sheet. Manufacturers of cars rely upon dealers to pick up any minor defects and correct them before a car is delivered. New cars are usually waxed and dewaxing forms part of the pre-delivery work. One of the biggest complaints of customers lies with defects on new cars and this reflects on the manufacturer and the service station who supplies the car. Vehicle salesmen should be trained and educated to meet R.T.I.T.B. requirements and take a suitable educational salesmanship course.

Handling complaints

We have seen that human error will, from time to time, result in a job being returned in spite of an effective inspection system. New parts, which have formed part of a repair will sometimes fail after test and so a customer returns with his car. It can be most annoying to anyone who takes a car from a workshop only to find that the repair fails after a low mileage. Furthermore it can involve considerable expense, for example, a capacitor failure on a motorway or no oil in a repaired rear axle seizing up on a motorway, will involve an expensive tow and could result in a claim against the garage which repaired the car. Hence the need for the quality control of jobs already mentioned. However, the fact remains that the customer will return and the reception engineer will have to deal with him or her. First, the reception engineer must listen to the nature of the complaint and determine that it is a faulty repair, service or broken part for which the garage could be held responsible. In the case of new cars, this would be dealt with under warranty and details are given in Chapter 2. With defective service, for example contact breaker points not set correctly resulting in power loss, then the reception engineer will have to use his judgement to see if this is a bona fide case. Customers have been known to alter adjustments, find such re-adjustments result in poor performance and then are unable to correct such work. It is true to say this applies to a very small minority of customers and, consequently, the reception engineer should show a genuine interest in such complaints. Furthermore, such complaints should receive immediate attention and be promptly rectified. A customer would accept that an error could arise but it should always be stressed that inspection of all cars is made. An apology for inconvenience never goes astray and providing the customer is made to feel his complaint has been handled with courtesy and has received attention he will be pleased to return to the workshop again. No customer should be kept waiting because it is 'a complaint' only as this can antagonize anyone. 'The customer is always right' is an old maxim but a valuable one.

Inevitably, the odd customer will return and swear something has gone wrong following a repair which has had no bearing on it whatsoever. Here, the invoice, which has detailed the exact repair is a vital aid on the part of the service station. The need for correct invoicing is essential and is stressed in Chapter 2. However, if we assume a customer has had a new clutch and 4 weeks later a universal joint becomes defective, he may fully expect rectification free of charge as he might not realize that two entirely different jobs are involved. This is where the invoice and the reception engineer's necessary qualifications are used to his and the garage's benefit. He must tactfully but firmly explain the position without insulting the customer. The service manager can always assist if required or asked for his opinion by the customer.

To summarize, it can be stated that angry, emotional customers must be brought to a level where they can be reasoned with. A number of things will enable a reception engineer or manager to achieve this state of affairs. For example:

    (a)   He or she must be a good listener.

    (b)   The customer must be allowed to 'let off steam' and get the anger out of his or her system.

    (c)   A genuine interest in the complaint must be shown.

    (d)   A customer should not be contradicted.

    (e)   The person dealing with the customer must not lose his or her temper, otherwise all will be lost.

Having got the customer in a better frame of mind by courteous attention it will then be necessary to put right the complaint. The customer could be offered a cup of tea or coffee whilst investigation takes place. The procedure to adopt might be as follows:

    (1)   Obtain all the facts about the work completed by getting all the facts from records such as job cards, invoices, and so on.

    (2)   Road test or quality-control check the vehicle in the workshop to ascertain the precise nature of the complaint.

(3)   Determine what can be done to satisfy the customer. Never make a customer fight for something to which he or she is entitled.

(4)   Take action by being specific. Explain and demonstrate that you are going to do something to put right the complaint.

(5)   Follow up the completed work by contacting the customer in two to three weeks' time to ensure he or she is satisfied. A genuine effort must be made if a customer is to be retained. By showing a genuine interest in keeping a person as a customer the reputation and prestige of the service station will be retained. There is no substitute for personal interest in all instances.

At frequent intervals a manager would be well advised to check that his or her customers are securing the attention they deserve. A typical check list on customer satisfaction is shown in Fig. 3.1.

The items listed below are those which affect customer satisfaction and dealership image. A service department can be rated on these items. Of course, wherever the rating is unsatisfactory every effort should be made to correct the condition in order to improve the business.

		Yes	No
1.	Are my customers greeted promptly?		
2.	Are my customers waited on promptly?		
3.	Is our work done completely the first time?		
4.	Do we pay attention to minor details?		
5.	Do I keep promises?		
6.	Do I avoid overselling and underselling?		
7.	Do I phone about unexpected extras before proceeding with the work?		
8.	Are cars ready when promised?		
9.	Are repair bills ready without delay?		
10.	Does the cashier handle customers in a courteous, friendly manner?		
11.	Do my customers receive a clear and intelligible statement of charges?		
12.	Are completed cars returned to my customers in a clean condition?		
13.	Are all my employees courteous?		
14.	Are my employees understanding?		
15.	Do my employees receive continuous training in customer relations?		

Fig. 3.1. Customer Satisfaction

Service and sales

The selling of used cars is normally one of the functions of a dealership.
Used cars always need attention of some kind and, the car sales department
will call upon the workshop to execute the repairs needed. The *car sales* allow
for repairs in part exchange allowances and the cost of such repairs must be
paid for by the car sales department. In making a profit and loss account for
each department a workshop must pay its way and make a profit. All departments must do the same. Thus, when a car comes into the workshop for
complete renovation each job must be carefully estimated and costed as if
it was a customer's car in for repair. The car sales department will then pay
the cost of such repairs and the workshop will be credited with the repair
work. Cases have arisen where a car sales department of a garage have found
their own workshop prices far too high and they have had work done outside
their own organization: an incredible situation! Obviously something is wrong
since car sales departments and the workshop must work together to get the
maximum gain from all trading of cars. Some unimportant jobs could be left—
for example a small upholstery tear—depending just how old the car is and its
cost. No car can be allowed to be sold which is unsafe in any way. By liaison
with the car sales, precise repair bills can be agreed upon and, where necessary,
a warranty for a used car given. Here, use of the quality control bay will be
essential so that car sales do not get a bad name, nor, in turn, the workshop.

Service can be sold with a car and in this way help not only car sales department but the repair shop also if such work is costed correctly. A *free* service
of a new or used car can help each department to support one another. In
advertising new and used cars, special services can also be sold to the public.
Service Weeks have been advertised and operated successfully. Such weeks are
used to offer a service at a reduced price to attract custom, similarly car sales
might offer *special reductions*. These *weeks* are organized when business is
likely to be slack to help keep all staff fully employed. It is, of course, always
possible to become so deluged with work as a result that it becomes impossible
to cope and thus a certain disadvantage is developed by not being able to live
up to what is advertised. On the other hand such arrangements can attract new
business and staff could be requested to work overtime prior to the week in
question so that all work could be completed in time.

Non-technical receptionist.

The duties of a reception engineer have been listed earlier in the chapter.
The R.T.I.T.B. in their booklet *Motor Vehicle Service Reception* detail a
job description of a receptionist. Responsibilities include receiving customers; discussing, identifying and processing routine service and repair requirements; advising specialists where technical assistance is required; and

promoting the sale of service and accessories within the limits of his or her technical ability.

The reception engineer's duties include:

(1) Promoting and maintaining good customer relations;
(2) discussing and identifying routine service and repair requirements with customers, and obtaining detailed background information to assist specialist personnel in diagnosis/testing/inspecting;
(3) recording in detail customer requests for workshop action and obtaining authority to proceed;
(4) being aware of the workshop loading situation and the progress of work, and advising customers of delays or additional work required;
(5) dealing efficiently with customer complaints, referring to management or specialist assistance according to policy;
(6) finalizing job cards for invoicing and accepting payments for work according to company policy;
(7) ensuring vehicles are clean and correctly presented to customers on collection or delivery;
(8) maintaining adequate customer/workshop records;
(9) promoting and effecting the sale of workshop repair and service facilities, and knowing the facilities offered by other departments;
(10) Being aware of the legal implications of reception duties.

The additional duties for a technical receptionist include:

(11) utilizing diagnostic and test facilities as necessary;
(12) preparing detailed test/diagnosis reports for quotations, estimates, or job card development;
(13) carrying out final testing and inspection.

Closing a sale

All personnel involved with selling, i.e. receptionists, partsmen, vehicle salesmen, and so on must be well trained to ensure good sales. An aptitude for selling is the most important asset of any salesman and he or she must be quick to recognize 'closing' hints from customers. It is similar to scoring a goal in football—if the opportunity arises, score! Signs which herald an opportunity to sell are questions from customers such as:

(1) How long will delivery take?
(2) What after sales service is there?
(3) Can you deliver it for me?
(4) What colours are available?
(5) Do you have a particular model?

Whenever a buyer shows an extension of interest in a car, product, or service the salesman should realize the opportunity to sell has probably arisen and he could ask for an order, e.g. 'Can I order one for you, sir/madam?' If the indications are not so precise a 'trial close' can be made. A trial close is one to be

used where the buyer implies that he will buy, but not directly. Thus a salesman will use phrases such as:

(1)   What car will be best for your work or leisure?
(2)   Which colour do you prefer?
(3)   This service is on special offer for four weeks.
(4)   When would you require deliver?

Techniques will vary according to the circumstances, but once a salesman has
established any key issue he can use this to close a sale and obtain an order.
Having satisfied a buyer's need, it should not be difficult to take positive
action to obtain an order. Thus we could summarize the sequence of all sales
interviews by stating that closing the deal depends upon preparation, approaching the customer, demonstration, and presentation. Knowing a customer in
detail i.e. classifying the customer, his interests, needs, status in business and
social life, personality and character, organization of a buyer's business, etc.,
is the method to adopt to ensure successful sales.

Questions

1. A dealer organization comprises a sales, parts, service and accounts department each being to a large degree dependent upon the other. Describe
   briefly how the service department can help each of these, and what assistance they can expect in return. (I.M.I.)
2. Complaints of inefficiency are sometimes made against repair shops because
   of lack of co-operation between customer, receptionist, mechanic and
   tester. How would you ensure that such complaints were reduced to a
   minimum? (I.M.I.)
3. A customer of some years standing with a certain service station, demands
   that the necessary repairs and adjustments to his car be completed by a
   certain mechanic. How should a service manager, faced with this problem,
   reply to that customer's demands? If unable to agree, what reasons should
   be given? (I.M.I.)
4. With operating costs continually rising, discuss whether servicing costs
   could be reduced without reducing the standard of workmanship and without reducing wages. (I.M.I.)
5. Describe a system of inspection to ensure the highest possible standard of
   work being maintained in a service department. (I.M.I.)
6. There are many ways in which a service department may charge the sales
   department for work done. Which system do you prefer and why? (I.M.I.)
7. With most mechanics to-day working on an Incentive Bonus scheme, it is
   more essential than ever to see that only the best quality work leaves your
   workshop. What system would you employ to see that faulty work was
   reduced to the absolute minimum? (I.M.I.)
8. It is common practice to hold service weeks:
   (a) What are the objects of such weeks?

(b) How and when would you organize one?

(c) What are the advantages or disadvantages of them? (I.M.I.)

9. In order to operate a workshop successfully the amount Rectification of Faulty Work must be kept down to an absolute minimum. How would you achieve this object in a workshop under your control? (I.M.I.)

10. Explain how you would deal with the following situation:
Your workshop has appraised a used vehicle for the sales department and said the vehicle wants x pounds spent on it. The sales department complete the sale, then come back to you and say the deal was so tight that they can only afford to spend half the amount you have quoted. (I.M.I.)

11. As it is most important to recruit the right personnel for staff positions such as reception engineers or shop foremen, state what characteristics you would look for and what questions you would ask when interviewing an applicant for either of the two posts mentioned. (I.M.I.)

12. A customer's reaction to a service station is mainly based on the quality of work carried out on his car. State the supervision and inspection necessary to ensure satisfactory results in this direction. (I.M.I.)

13. Your Department has a Workshop Foreman, a Controller, a Tester and a Receptionist.
(a) Name the basic functions of each.
(b) Assume that each has a reasonable basic salary. What form of bonus incentive scheme would you apply in each case? Justify. (I.M.I.)

14. Bearing in mind the statutory requirements of the E.E.C. (January 1st, 1973) and V.A.T. (April 1st, 1973) what minimum information must a customer's repair order contain? There are 17, list not less than 10. (I.M.I.)

15. (a) The Receptionist is said to be one of the most important members of the Service Department's team. Why?
(b) What are the personal qualifications required to do this job well?
(c) A modern trend is to introduce women into this job function. Name the advantages, and if any, disadvantages of this inclusion. (I.M.I.)

16. What information should service records (vehicle history) contain? Name *three* important uses that can be made of this information. (I.M.I.)

17. A customer's Repair Order contains a request that you fit a Part which is not in stock and cannot be obtained and fitted prior to the customer collecting his car. Describe the procedures . . . through Mechanic to Parts Department to customer . . . that you would adopt in this event. (I.M.I.)

CHAPTER 4

COLLISION REPAIR

Accident repair work

One of the greatest tragedies associated with the motor vehicle retail and repair trades is the terrible accident rate involving motor vehicles. In 1958, 237 265 vehicles were in collision on roads in the United Kingdom. The number of serious collisions in 1968 had increased to 291 275 and in 1982 the total collisions had exceeded over 350 000. The loss of life and limb is a tragedy in itself and the material loss in damage amounts to millions of pounds. Repairing the damaged vehicles forms a vital part of the profits for a lot of garages but, like all other aspects of repair work, it must be done efficiently to obtain maximum profits.

Most collision damage is covered by insurance. All vehicles must have a minimum of third party cover whilst a large amount of vehicles have fully comprehensive insurance cover. This means that work coming into a body repair shop is paid for either by the customer direct or by an insurance company. Consequently, when a vehicle arrives for repair work, the first thing a workshop manager must do is to determine who is going to pay the bill. If a customer is to pay the bill then an estimate is prepared for the customer but we will consider this later.

Where a vehicle is involved in a collision the insured, that is the customer, will make out an accident claim form obtained from his insurance company. This will detail the nature of the accident and where the vehicle has been taken for repair. Some companies authorize work to proceed immediately but in any case body repairers usually prefer to have their work authorized in writing before commencing any work on the damaged vehicle. This is the best method to adopt from the body repairers view as it does eliminate any argument.

Assuming the repair is to be covered by insurance then the first stage of the repair work is to make out an estimate for the damage and then to contact the insurance company so that their assessor, or engineer as he is also called, can visit the workshop to examine the damaged vehicle and consider the estimate. A typical form of estimate is shown in Fig. 4.1. The actual number of copies of the estimate to be prepared will depend upon the system adopted by the

ESTIMATE   No............................

CHARLES H. ALLEN (BODIES) LTD.

Works:
JUTSUMS LANE,
ROMFORD, ESSEX.

Registered Office
17 LONDON ROAD · ROMFORD · ESSEX

Telephones : ROMFORD 45091 (8 Lines)

⌐ Mr. R. Smith   ⌐
200, Victor Avenue,
BARKING. ESSEX.

Telegrams : "MOTORS, ROMFORD."

L   ⌐

DATE

Vehicle: FORD CORTINA MK 11		Mileage. 46362
Chassis No.: BA 98GE 12345 Reg. No.: ABC 123 A		Policy No.:

Remove frontbumper, bumper irons, headlamps, front flasher lamps, grille, bonnet, radiator. O/side front door, horns and battery. Cut away O/Side fender, bonnet closure panel. front lower apron panel, and O/side headlamp panel. Reshape O/Side engine valence N/Side fender and O/side radiator mounting panel. Weld in and metal finish new O/Side fender, bonnet closure panel, front lower apron panel, O/side headlamp panel and front body re-inforcement panel Re-hang O/side front door and new bonnet panel, adjust clearances and seal all joints. Re-paint front end of vehicle from door to door, re-assemble vehicle replacing listed parts.		
LABOUR	75	75
Supply PARTS TO BE CHARGED AT MANUFACTURERS CURRENT LIST PRICE		
Bonnet. Bonnet moulding Front bumper (exchange) Grille. O/side headlamp bezel N/S headlamp bezel P/side flasher lamps Front lower apron panel Bonnet closure panel O/side fender O/Side headlamp panel. Front body re-inforcement panel assy. Radiator bottom hose.		
Plus Sundries as required.		

Above subject to addition of V.A.T. at the current rate.

Customers' cars are only driven by our staff at
customers' own risk and responsibility

Fig. 4.1 Estimate of Repair Work

workshop manager. For example some workshops find it convenient to type out six copies and these are distributed as follows: 1) stores for ordering spares as required, 2) workshop for full details of job to be done, 3) costing for accurate assessment of the final bill, 4) office for retention by the workshop manager to enable him to keep a check on the job, 5) assessor for his retention, 6) spare copy for customer or assessor if required. Needless to say, the number of copies can be reduced if the organization is small, For example, costing and office copies could be both completed or used as one. Likewise the stores and workshop copies could be completed together. Nevertheless, for the price of copies of the estimate, each section having individual copies can avoid hold up of work and allows paper-work to flow smoothly.

On the estimate it will be observed that the present method is to include labour prices which are current at the time. Parts' prices change from week to week and insurance companies are quite prepared to accept the current prices as per manufacturers' catalogue when the work is completed.

To prepare the estimate a detailed knowledge of body repair work is essential. This knowledge can only come through an apprenticeship in the trade. Thus, an estimator in a body repair shop will have served his apprenticeship in the trade and will have an appropriate City and Guilds of London Institute certificate such as T.E.C.–O.T.C. or 385 Vehicle Body Work courses or similar qualifications such as intermediate section of I.M.I. examinations dealing with body construction and repair.

However, having made out the estimate form, the insurance assessor will now visit the workshop and approve or amend the work to be done. Insurance companies are not charity organizations and they will only want to pay for the accident damage and not other body work requiring attention because of rusting and so on. The insurance assessor is usually a trained and qualified engineer and will know exactly what is a fair price for the actual collision repair. On visiting the repair firm the assessor will verify repairs required and at the same time state if the customer is liable for the first £10, £20, £50 and so on. These are known as policy excess payments also referred to as endorsements for policies. In any event, where these exist, the customer will have to pay this amount and the workshop manager will get approval and a signature from the customer to proceed with the work. In a similar manner approval will also be obtained from the insurance assessor. It cannot be stressed too strongly that all estimates should detail all the work required. A very careful examination of the vehicle should be made to ensure that nothing is omitted.

At this point it is as well to mention that insurance companies have endorsements and condition clauses written into some of their motor insurance policies. For example, a spares endorsement could indicate that the company would be liable to replace the cost of a part as stated in the manufacturers' catalogue. Whilst this may be obvious and fair, cases have arisen where parts were not available and a new part has to be made at many times the cost of a part from the manufacturers. Such cases arise with old vehicles or vehicles made abroad where shipment of parts creates difficulties. In a similar way, the insurance company which writes into its policies 'the car can be removed to the repairers and instructions given for reasonable and necessary repairs to be commenced subject to a detailed estimate being obtained as soon as possible and sent forthwith to the Company' is operating a conditional clause.

Having obtained approval all round, the repair work can now proceed.

A good body repair shop needs to have highly-skilled workmen and good tools for body-repair work. Workshop equipment is mentioned in Chapter 1 but for a body repair shop the essential equipment could be listed as follows:

1. A well planned layout operating on a flow line principle if possible. Whilst each and every repair presents individual difficulties it is possible to have repairs organized so that major work is completed in one area, minor work in another, sanding and flatting in another and finally painting.
2. Alignment jigs for body and chassis checks.
3. Portable sanders. Air-operated sanders are preferred for safety, finish and as a means of deterring theft of the tools (air-operated tools are useless unless a good air supply is available).
4. Pullers and Dozers to pull out or push in damaged sections.
5. Sheet-metal cutting and forming tools such as guillotines, folders, light presses, air-operated chisels.
6. Comprehensive panel beating tools viz. dollies, spoons, hammers etc.
7. Welding equipment to include oxyacetylene, metallic-arc, resistance welding machines (spot welders) and/or CO_2 welding machines.
8. A well planned spray booth adjacent to a suitable low-bake oven for drying purposes.
9. Fire-fighting equipment.

As stated in Chapter 1, a list of suppliers of equipment can be found in trade journals but much valuable information in connection with bodywork equipment will be obtained from A.R.O. Machinery Co. Ltd., 190 Castelnau, London, SW13 9DJ.

Safety in or near any paint spraying operations is vital. Strict observation of No Smoking signs, clean floor, use of masks, fire extinguishers prominently displayed and always ready for use, should be enforced.

Estimate forms, invoices, etc. for collision repair work can be obtained from the V.B.R.A. and M.A.A. (see Appendix II for addresses).

The Completion Note

Having gone through the repair shop, the finished vehicle is brought back for the customer to collect. The customer will inspect the work and if satisfied will sign a completion note, (sometimes referred to as a Satisfaction Note), stating the work has been done satisfactorily. The completion note is part of every accident insurance repair job and is required by the insurance company so that a client is unlikely to come back several months later complaining that something was not done or something else has arisen as the result of the previous accident. Consequently, it is the responsibility of the customer to indicate satisfaction. This does not mean a customer cannot return with defective paintwork or other faulty work which has been done as part of the repair. Most body repair shops would always correct such faulty workmanship but would not be prepared to do work not connected with the original estimate. It is in everyones interest that the completion note is signed by the customer and the vehicle should not be allowed out of the workshop until a signature is obtained.

This outlines the operation of a body repair workshop. As recommended in other chapters, a visit organized by a college (by arrangement with the proprietors) to a well-organized and equipped body repair workshop would prove to be a valuable aid to all students. A typical questionnaire to be answered during the visit might be as follows:

1. When a damaged vehicle comes to the workshop who makes out an estimate and what does this involve?
2. When an accident to a car is covered by insurance what must the manager of the workshop do before commencing work?
3. Explain the importance of a conditional clause and spares endorsement in a policy and explain how these can affect this workshop.
4. Sketch to scale a layout of the repair workshop and show where all major items are located, e.g. paint booth, alignment jigs, welding equipment, finishing equipment, quality control.
5. Make a line diagram of the flow of a job through this workshop.
6. State all the methods of welding employed and explain which jobs each method is suitable for giving a clear example.
7. Itemize all safety precautions enforced in the workshop.
8. Before a vehicle leaves the workshop a completion note is signed by the customer. Who obtains this signature and why is it important? Has a customer any redress once the note has been signed?

In 1976 the V.B.R.A., in consultation with the Office of Fair Trading, introduced a Code of Practice for Vehicle Body Repair (Motor Car and Caravan Sector). The aims of the code are as follows:

1. To ensure that the public receives the best possible service from V.B.R.A. members.
2. To maintain and enhance the reputation, standing, and good name of the Association and its members.
3. To ensure that the public interest shall predominate in all consideration of the standards of competitive trading between V.B.R.A. members.
4. To offer a guarantee in respect of all repair work undertaken;
5. To resolve complaints by users on any aspect of repair work and provide a procedure for conciliation or simple arbitration when complaints cannot be settled directly between a member and his customer.
6. To encourage initiative and enterprise in the belief that properly regulated competitive trading by and between V.B.R.A. members will best serve the

public interest and the well-being of the repair industry.

7. To encourage the growth and development of the body repair industry consistently with the above aims.

From these aims it will be seen that good-quality work is essential from all points of view. A copy of the Code of Practice can be obtained from the V.B.R.A.

The Motor Insurance Repair Research Centre, (M.I.R.R.C.) Calthrop Lane, Thatcham, Berkshire RG13 4NP was founded in the early 1970s by leading insurance companies in the United Kingdom. With very high repair costs, research carried out at the centre has been centred on achieving more economic repairs through increased efficiency. Other research is carried out both in body repairs, design, and paintwork techniques. Standard repair times have been established for the replacement of most car body panels; and a manual for this and one for paintwork have been produced. Most body repairers will have copies of these for reference, because insurance assessors do use them as a guide for vehicle repair times. The manuals can be purchased from the British Insurance Association, P.O. Box No. 538, Aldermary Hourse, Queen Street, London EC4P 4JD.

Role of the automobile assessor

The prime function of an assessor is to ensure his company are paying only for accident damage and not for 'betterment' of a vehicle. An example of 'betterment' is improving a vehicle that has been involved in a collision. If it has sustained damage to one area and this has been resprayed it may now look very slightly different from other areas. As a result of this, a customer may demand a complete re-spray which is not really required to put the accident damage right. An automobile assessor must then:

(a)   ensure his company is getting a fair deal. This will entail close scrutiny of a customer's insurance policy to note any excess payments due or special endorsements. This information is usually supplied by the insurance company itself. It will also involve a close inspection of the vehicle to ensure it was roadworthy at the time of the accident. An unroadworthy vehicle, e.g. one with bald tyres, could make an insurance policy void.

(b)   Ensure the customer is satisfied with all completed repairs.

(c)   Obtain a satisfaction note for the complete job.

(d)   Maintain close liaison with body repairers in his area to ensure that vehicles are repaired in premises suitably equipped for such work.

(e)   Arrange regular visits to body repairers whenever possible to obtain a routine so that jobs in hand can be checked.

(f)   Keep up to date with M.I.R.R.C. developments.

There is an Institute of Automobile Assessors which enables suitably qualified personnel to register as members. Their current address can be obtained from any major insurance company. It is, of course, very important that companies dealing with assessors appreciate that a lot of custom can be obtained by keeping close contact with insurance company assessors and independent 'free-lance' assessors.

Licensing of Body Repair Premises

The highly specialised body repair industry demands great skill and knowledge. It is with this in mind the V.B.R.A. have been pressing the D. Tp. for only licensed repaireres to repair damaged vehicles. Although not yet ratified (1983) it is expected that a two tier system will operate, e.g.:

1. Licensed Repairers would be permitted to restore structural damage and all other bodywork. With suitable premises, equipment and qualified staff at all levels a licence would be granted.
2. Non-licensed Repairers would be encouraged to meet the above requirements but, until they did, such repairers would only be permitted to carry out cosmetic work including panel replacement and similar work which does not affect the safety structure of the car.

   Such licensing has been a legal requirement in many countries for many year. Surely the near future will see this requirement met in the United Kingdom?

Questions

1. As a service manager, you are proposing to set up a body repair section and also a paint shop. Describe what equipment you would require and what safety precautions must be maintained in each section. (I.M.I.)
2. Insurance repairs has been the subject of some criticism recently for length of time from accident to completion, and for cost. Explain how you would deal with such a repair bearing both the above points in mind. (I.M.I.)
3. In connection with insurance repairs explain the following terms and give an example of the application of each term:
   (a) Completion note   (c) Endorsement
   (b) Conditional clause   (d) Excess payment. (I.M.I.)
4. A popular front engine, rear-wheel drive saloon car (1750 cc.) was involved in a collision with a commercial vehicle. The body damage sustained was mainly on the off-side front end but the steering and suspension were also affected.
   (a) Describe the procedure which should be followed in dealing with the repair of the vehicle under an insurance claim.
      Make reference to
      (i) the claim form,
      (ii) the detailed estimate,
      (iii) the authority to repair,
      (iv) the satisfaction note or clearance certificate.
   (b) Prepare a typical estimate to cover the cost of repairs, and include a list of replacement parts which are considered necessary.

CHAPTER 5

STAFFING

Staffing a service station

A service station needs a wide variety of staff with varying degrees of skill and knowledge. As the size of service stations vary considerably, the type and number of staff will differ to meet the requirements of individual stations. From the very small garages employing 6 to 10 staff, we have large organizations employing up to 300 personnel. Future garages will have to be fairly big in order to justify the investment of capital for equipment needed to service modern cars and commercial vehicles; the staff required will also be large in number.

The staff required to operate a service station will normally consist of the following:
Directors including managing director, service manager, parts department manager, car sales manager, forecourt manager, receptionists (service advisers), workshop foreman, chargehands, mechanics, semi-skilled mechanics, apprentices, office staff, cleaners, labourers.

This is a general layout and their order within the structure of a garage is shown in Fig. 5.1. A variation of a staff layout is shown in Fig. 5.2.

Each member of staff shown in the organization chart will require to have a certain knowledge and skill. Perhaps the most important of all selection commences with apprentices, for here a considerable amount of time and money is invested in the hope that a young man will eventually become a skilled mechanic, technician engineer, body builder/repairer etc. It is, therefore, vital that wastage be avoided by using some means of selection. Ideally, every apprentice coming into the trade should have received a good basic education with four or five G.C.E. 'O' levels (or C.S.E.) with mathematics, science, technical drawing, English and metalwork amongst the subjects passed. If a prospective apprentice has these 'O' levels or C.S.E. passes, he is well on the way to proving his suitability for an apprenticeship. Academic attainment, however, is only part of the requirements of an apprentice, as we shall see later on in this chapter, but before we consider these other attributes, let us consider the young enthusiastic boy approaching a service manager for an apprenticeship when the boy has no 'O' levels at all. Should he be turned down

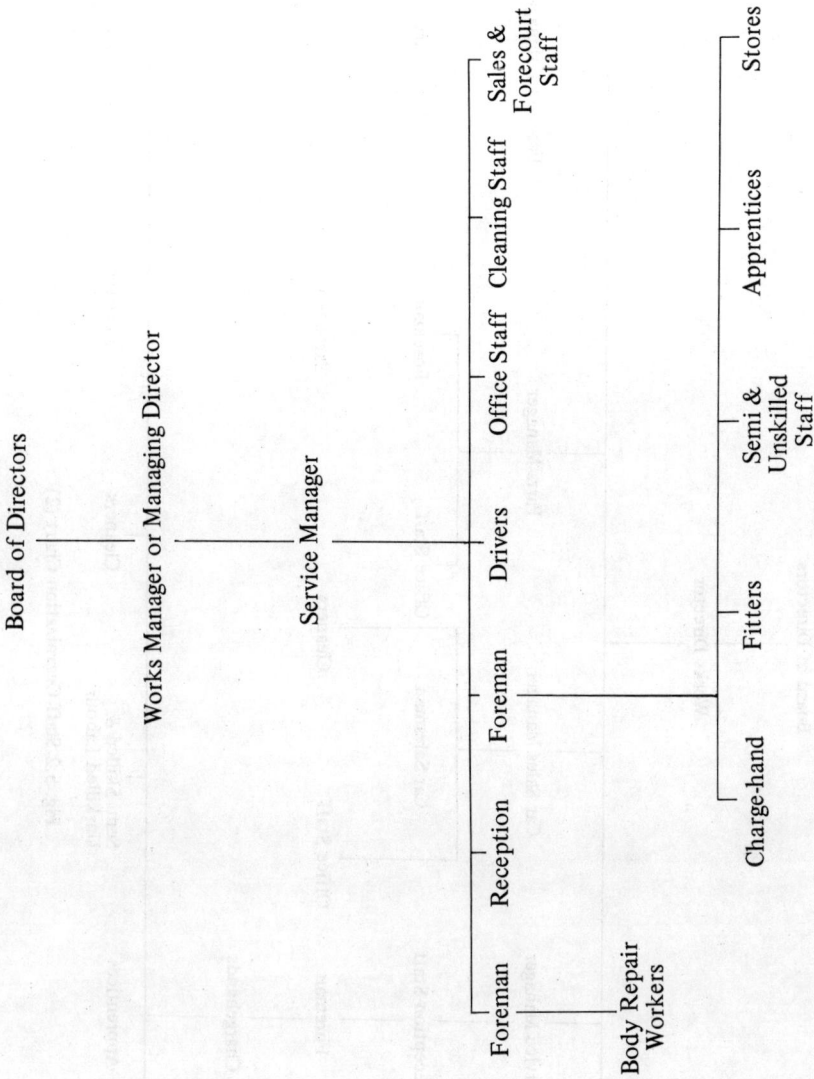

Fig. 5.1 Staff Organization Chart (1)

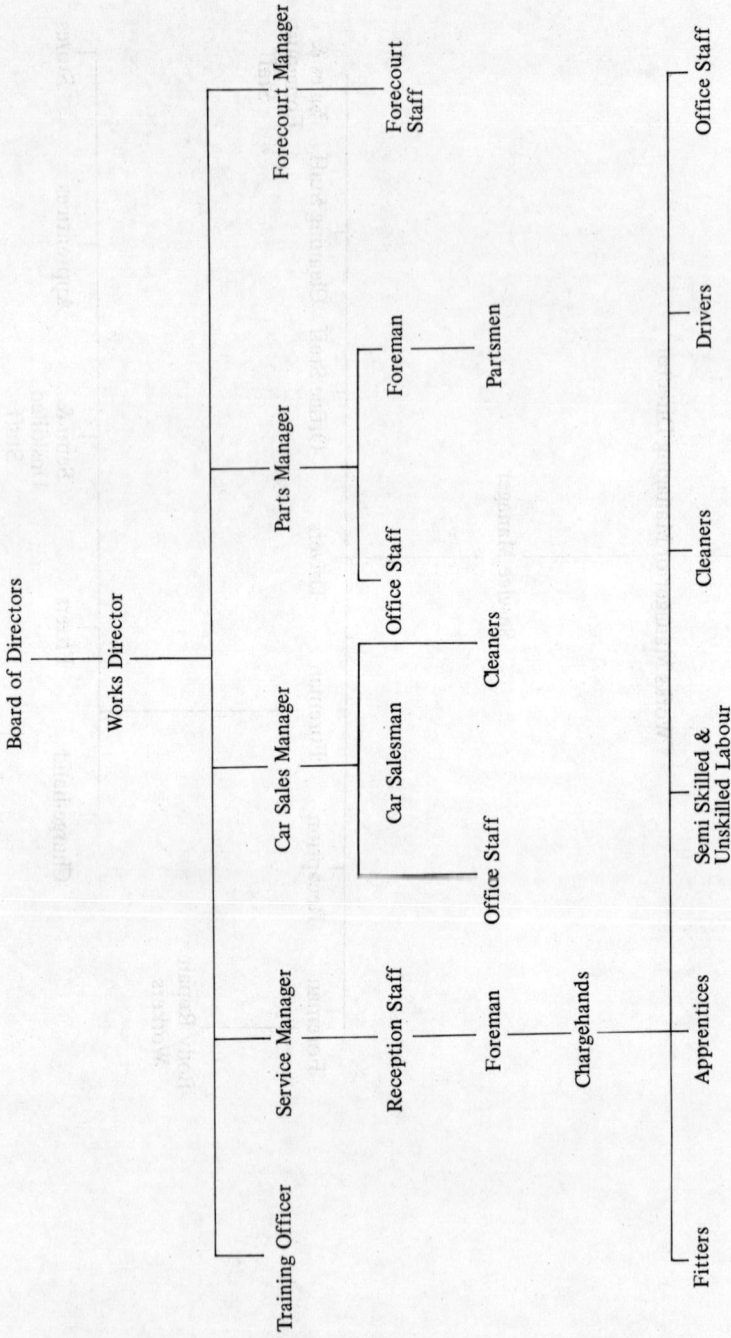

Fig. 5.2 Staff Organization Chart (2)

without consideration? Is it fair for a service manager to appoint or reject an applicant for an apprenticeship because the manager likes the look of a boy or, conversely, he doesn't look the right type? This haphazard method of choice sometimes does work, but it can be unfair and unjust to both employer and employee. Before a boy commences any apprenticeship he must have a reasonable intelligence in order that he can absorb the wealth of detailed knowledge required by all skilled personnel in the motor vehicle trades. If a boy does not have the necessary intelligence, it is surely unfair to ask him to try to do something beyond his capabilities. So how can we assess an eager young man who could prove to be a good tradesman even though he may not possess 'O' levels or equivalent C.S.E. passes?

Many service managers make full use of local technical colleges where trained lecturers can give selection tests to determine the suitability of a boy for a particular motor vehicle trade. Some garages employ a training officer to administer such tests, but, because of the specialized nature of such selective tests, most garages will request the assistance of local technical colleges.

Academically, a boy must have a reasonable attainment in arithmetic and certainly must have mechanical comprehension of a good level if he is to have the basic requirements of a good mechanic or fitter. It is possible that a boy may have disliked school simply because he was not allowed to apply his knowledge to practical matters that held his interest such as mathematics to measuring cylinder bores or crankshaft journal wear using Mercer gauges and micrometers. Nevertheless, unless a young man has a mechanical comprehension of a certain level and an arithmetic ability of a reasonable standard, he can never hope to become a skilled fitter who needs a high degree of knowledge and skill involving mathematics, mechanisms, electrical theory and manual dexterity as a basis for the maintenance of complicated and fast modern cars and commercial vehicles. It can therefore be concluded that before any boy is signed on for an apprenticeship he must be tested at a local college or by a training officer—unless of course he does possess proof of his academic ability by having 'O' levels or suitable C.S.E. passes. Having assessed the academic side of the young man's ability, other aspects which will affect his apprenticeship must also be considered.

The R.T.I.T.B. in their booklet *Recommendations for Training Apprentices* state the following requirements for apprentice selection. How these attributes can be determined are given alongside the requirement.

1. *A mechanical aptitude.* This can be ascertained by two methods. (a) a timed simple exercise in stripping down and reassembling a mechanical fuel pump, distributor or similar component in correct order. (b) a mechanical comprehension test which lasts 30 minutes or so and is completed by a technical college. This method is more scientific and gives a clear assessment.

With the first method, a practice adopted is to give the job to an experienced mechanic who, for example, completes dismantling and assembling in 15 minutes. Allowing twice this time, a candidate should complete the task in 30 minutes and the state of the finished job can give some idea of the mechanical aptitude of the boy.

The second method is used nationally and internationally. A candidate reaching a given level can be placed on a course to suit his ability.

2. *An inquiring mind.* The application form will reveal the nature of the boy's hobbies and recreation. Curiosity will be revealed if for example a boy goes kart-racing, motor cycling, caving—finding out things or showing a lively mind in the form of a hobby.

3. *Desire to become a skilled mechanic.* Whilst a boy might have ability he must be told of the dirt and hard work required to become a highly-skilled mechanic. Today's dream of white overalls and racing cars is a far cry from the reality of the underside of heavy commercial vehicles covered in dirt, oil and grease!

4. *Course of study.* This must be stressed. It is essential for a boy to attend technical college to have theoretical training in order that he can understand thoroughly his practical work. Normally attendance at a college forms part of the condition of employment of apprentices.

5. *Physical ability.* A boys health must be good to withstand some of the rigours of motor vehicle workshops. He should be fit, reasonably strong and not suffer from colour blindness if he wished to become an electrician which would mean coloured wires could not be identified correctly.

6. *Stable mentality and disposition.* This involves an assessment of a boy's personality—a complex subject. One of the best assessments of a boy's ability to mix and work with other people is his last report from school. The headmaster should be able to give a valuable assessment of a boy's character, especially if the boy has attended his last school for many years. In any event, a headmaster will generally be pleased to state how a boy has behaved. During the interview, it will become fairly obvious if a boy is egotistical or modest. Certain aspects of a boy's mentality and disposition are difficult to assess completely without stringent personality tests at a college or by a training officer. However, as workshop staff work as a team, a boy should be alert, responsive to questioning and a hard worker. Hot tempered, aggressive boys can cause a good deal of upset in a workshop and these should not be encouraged to join an existing harmonious team of workers. Punctuality is very important and whether a boy can get to work on time should be ascertained from the school report or during the interview.

Now, having completed selection tests and an application form, the next step is an interview. With all details before him, the service manager can now determine a boy's general attitude, which the application form cannot reveal. For example, in reply to further questions or in outlining the work the young man will be involved with, the service manager can determine whether the boy is aggressive, cheeky, insolent, cheerful, asks reasonable questions in return, quiet and so on, bearing in mind the boy must be part of a team and therefore must be able to mix and work with other people without causing unnecessary upset.

It is the responsibility of the service manager, personnel officer or training officer of the firm to complete the process of personnel selection which in the case of apprentices is based on (a) academic suitability, (b) completion of employment application form, and (c) interview: from this a boy is either accepted or rejected.

Assuming appointment is made, the boy's future career with the firm should be carefully explained to him. For example, his training will probably start with a full-time basic motor vehicle engineering course at a local technical college, followed by further periods of training at work and at the local college for theoretical education. A chart similar to that shown in Fig. 5.4 could be used to show academic advancement and at the same time, indicate where his future lies with the firm using charts similar to Fig. 5.1 and Fig. 5.2. During the interview the R.T.I.T.B. recommend that emphasis is placed on the following items:

1. *Length of training.* This is usually 3 or 4 years and this should be explained to the boy using the R.T.I.T.B. programme shown in Fig. 5.3 to show how he will progress.

2. *Wages on starting.* The wages paid are normally determined by National Joint Industrial Council agreement. Apprentices when starting do not always share in bonus schemes and this should be explained to the newcomer if necessary so that he clearly understands what his rates of pay will be.

3. *Explanation of future prospects.* Once again, the R.T.I.T.B. programme shown in Fig. 5.3 can be used to explain prospects. In addition success in the final examinations of the City and Guilds of London Institute, courses 381 Part 1 Motor Vehicle Craft Studies and 381 Light or Heavy Vehicle Mechanic, Part II, Motor Vehicle Technician, 384 Vehicle Parts Personnel and other related subjects can lead to supervisory jobs. Success in the final examinations of the Institute of the Motor Industry, it can be explained, often is a means of climbing up the ladder within a firm. Thus, succession and prospects could be: apprentice, fully-skilled fitter, chargehand, foreman, reception engineer, management: all depending on work done and success in examinations. Before interviewing the boy, the parents or guardian can be consulted and all details of employment explained to them. With the parents' co-operation the firm is likely to get the best out of the boy during apprenticeship and afterwards. The apprentice is then fully aware of his future working conditions and prospects.

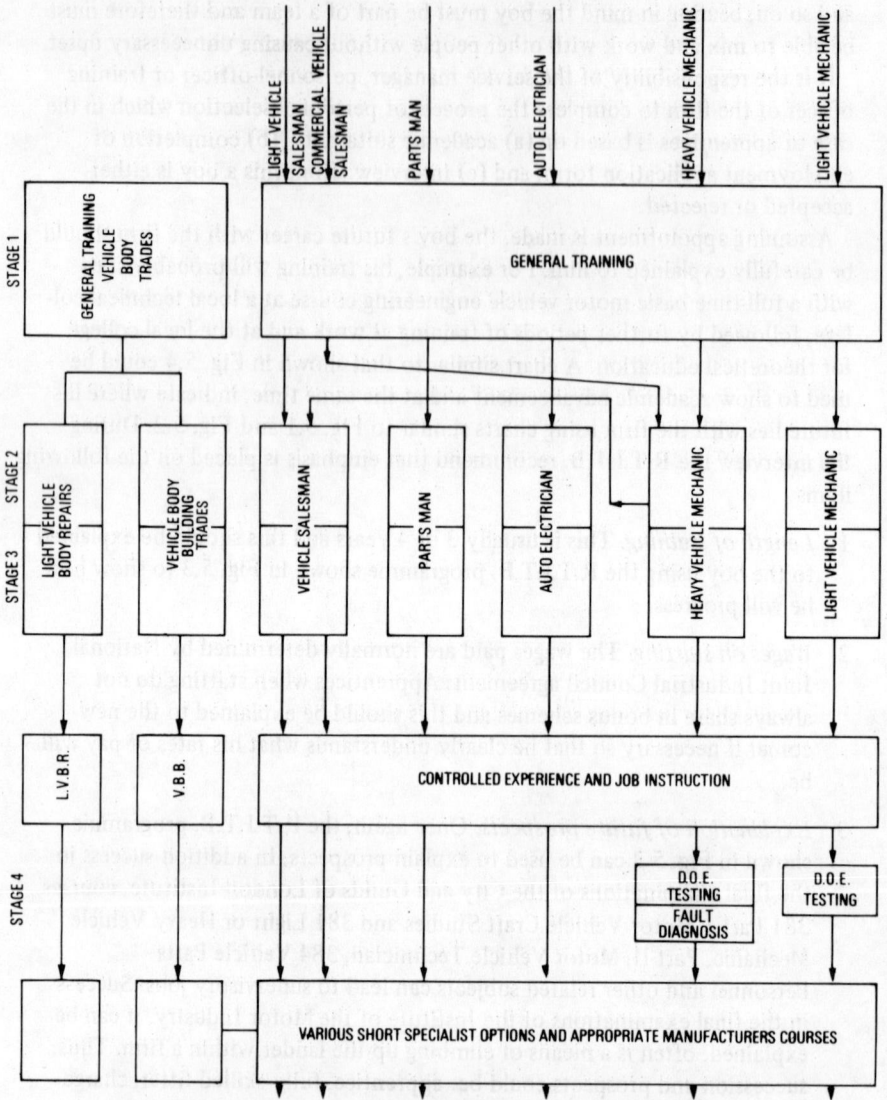

Fig. 5.3 R.T.I.T.B. Training Programme for Apprentices. Note that some employers now have three-year apprentice schemes–stage 4 being completed during stage 3 training. Some employers favour training by modules. As number of modules attained increases so does status, e.g. operative, semi-skilled, skilled.

AUTOMOBILE ENGINEERING PRACTICE
City and Guilds of London Institute Courses
Schemes for Motor Vehicle Mechanics, Motor Vehicle Technicians and Parts Department Personnel

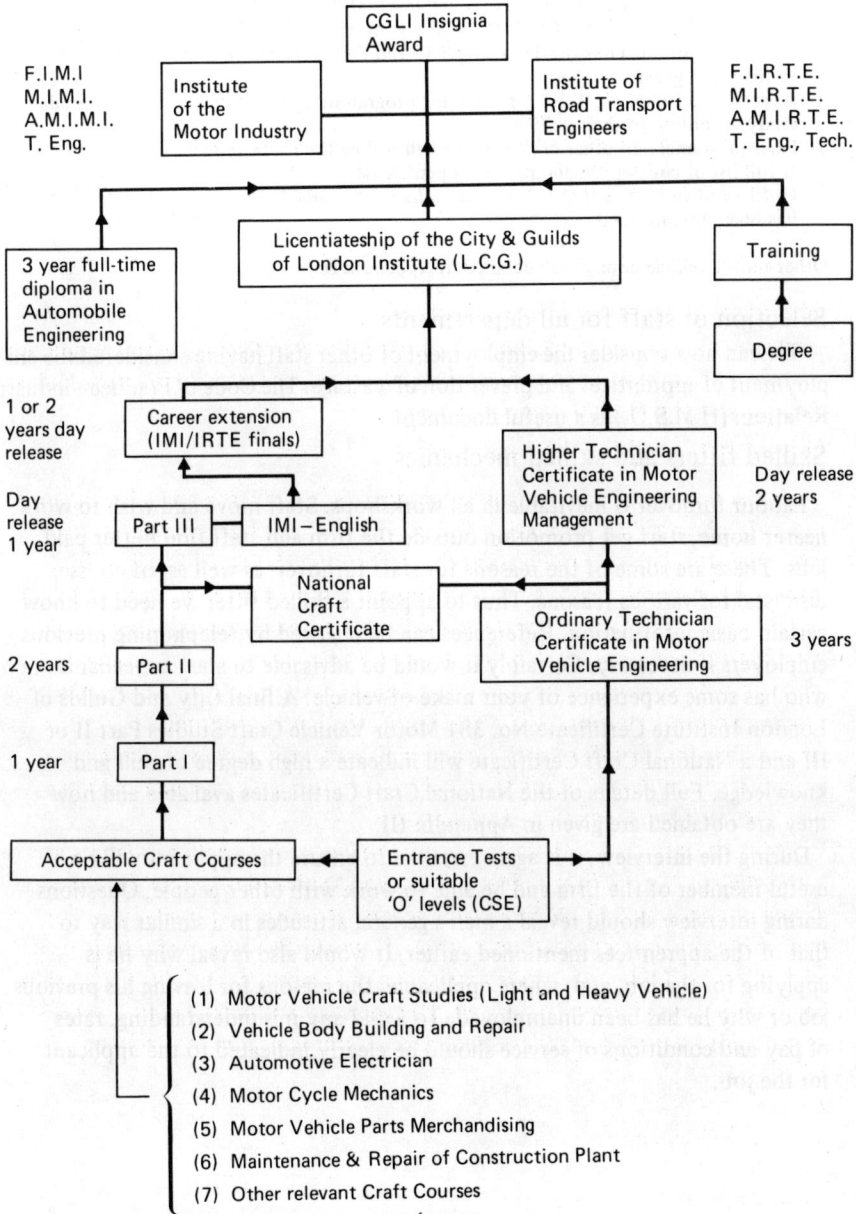

CGLI Insignia Award

F.I.M.I
M.I.M.I.
A.M.I.M.I.
T. Eng.

Institute of the Motor Industry

Institute of Road Transport Engineers

F.I.R.T.E.
M.I.R.T.E.
A.M.I.R.T.E.
T. Eng., Tech.

Licentiateship of the City & Guilds of London Institute (L.C.G.)

Training

3 year full-time diploma in Automobile Engineering

Degree

1 or 2 years day release

Career extension (IMI/IRTE finals)

Higher Technician Certificate in Motor Vehicle Engineering Management

Day release 2 years

Day release 1 year

Part III

IMI – English

National Craft Certificate

Ordinary Technician Certificate in Motor Vehicle Engineering

3 years

2 years

Part II

1 year

Part I

Acceptable Craft Courses

Entrance Tests or suitable 'O' levels (CSE)

(1) Motor Vehicle Craft Studies (Light and Heavy Vehicle)
(2) Vehicle Body Building and Repair
(3) Automotive Electrician
(4) Motor Cycle Mechanics
(5) Motor Vehicle Parts Merchandising
(6) Maintenance & Repair of Construction Plant
(7) Other relevant Craft Courses

Fig. 5.4 Routes to the top in the Motor Industry

For notes see overleaf

Notes for Fig. 5.4

1. Entance to the Technicians' course is usually gained by having suitable 'O' levels at grade 'C' or CSE's with grades 1 to 3. 'O' levels at 'C' grade (CSE. 1) will give exemption from certain TEC-OTC units e.g. mathematics, physics, technical drawing, english and so on. Thus the T.E.C.-O.T.C. can be completed in 2 years day release instead of 3 years.
2. Apprentices following R.T.I.T.B. training programmes or modules will follow academic study according to their ability.
3. Parts personnel and other craft persons will follow the route shown.
4. A full list of courses are detailed in Appendix III.
5. Until 1978 an M.A.A./I.M.I. Diploma course was available for mature students but has been discontinued.

Other motor vehicle courses are detailed in Appendix II.

Selection of staff for all departments

We can now consider the employment of other staff having considered the employment of apprentices and prevention of wastage. The Code of Practice—industrial Relations (H.M.S.O.) is a useful document.

Skilled fitters and skilled mechanics

Labour turnover is inevitable in all workshops. Staff move and wish to work nearer home, staff get promotion outside the firm and staff find better paid jobs. These are some of the reasons for staff turnover, as well as, of course, dismissal for various reasons. Thus to appoint a skilled fitter we need to know certain basic information. References can be checked by telephoning previous employers if necessary. Certainly it would be advisable to start a mechanic who has some experience of your make of vehicle. A final City and Guilds of London Institute Certificate No. 381 Motor Vehicle Craft Studies Part II or III and a National Craft Certificate will indicate a high degree of skill and knowledge. Full details of the National Craft Certificates available and how they are obtained are given in Appendix III.

During the interview, it is again essential to ensure the applicant will be a useful member of the firm and be able to work with other people. Questions during interview should reveal a man's general attitudes in a similar way to that of the apprentices mentioned earlier. It would also reveal why he is applying for the job, and, where applicable, the reasons for leaving his previous job or why he has been unemployed. To avoid any misunderstanding, rates of pay and conditions of service should be clearly indicated to the applicant for the job.

Semi-skilled mechanics

People of this type require some supervision on repair work. Such workers will not normally have any academic qualifications, but would have achieved some practical skill by working with skilled personnel. Appointment of such men will require some form of testimonial from a previous employer. Promotion of labourers to semi-skilled workers within a workshop can be usefully arranged, where this is warranted.

Charge-hands and foremen

It is well known that a skilled fitter who may be a first class tradesman may not necessarily make a good charge-hand or foreman. A skilled fitter can be defined as a man able to execute all repair work on a motor vehicle without supervision. Thus, a man who has had suitable training will be well able to complete this work and do it well. However, when a man is asked to take on the responsibilities of managing men and things, it requires more than the ability to execute skilled repair work, although this knowledge is an essential basic requirement of any charge-hand or foreman.

Appointment of charge-hands and foremen is almost invariably done from within a firm. An apprentice who becomes a skilled fitter and stays with the firm for a number of years will soon be noticed for his ability to execute repairs well, his punctuality, co-operative attitude, ability to work with other personnel, persistance to sort out difficult repair jobs, ability to remain cool and calm when a job demands maximum skill, patience and knowledge. All these are the attributes of a good foreman or charge-hand. When dealing with men it is vital for a foreman or charge-hand to be fair and firm at all times. During the running of any workshop, problems constantly arise: problems of a technical nature and personal problems e.g. which fitters can best do a particular job such as steering overhaul, diesel engine overhaul, gear-box or rear-axle overhaul and so on. A foreman must decide where to pass the work and the charge-hand must liaise with the foreman to ensure a smooth running of the workshop. However, let us itemize the requirements of any workshop supervisor. At this stage we can now state the essential differences between charge-hand and foreman. The foreman has overall control of the workshop including shop loading for work to be completed whilst a charge-hand will handle a small group of men, receiving work from the foreman. To ensure adequate work loads for all personnel, liaison between charge-hands and the foremen is absolutely vital. Charge-hands and foremen both manage men and offer advice to fitters and apprentices where and when required, and both need the following basic requirements:

1. A good practical background, (e.g. an apprentice-trained fitter with a minimum 3 years practical experience as a skilled fitter).
2. A good theoretical knowledge, preferably with a final City and Guilds of London Institute 381 Parts II and III, 390 Final or T.E.C.-O.T.C.

3. The ability to control men and work loads. To do this he must be a good organizer and have the attributes previously discussed such as pleasing personality, fairness, persistance and so on.

Before actually taking over a supervisory post it is advantageous for a potential supervisor to attend a manufacturers' course for supervisors or one organized by the R.T.I.T.B. or local technical college.

Service managers

The modern service manager needs a large amount of technical and managerial knowledge. The R.T.I.T.B. have stated the requirements of a service manager as follows:

(a)   A good practical background, i.e. an apprentice-trained mechanic or fitter.
(b)   Theoretical achievements to include a final 381 Part II and 390 City and Guilds of London Institute Certificates plus a pass in the final examination of the Institute of the Motor Industry. An H.T.C. or H.T.D. is suitable.

Equivalent certificates approved by the Department of Education and Science can be accepted in lieu of those mentioned. For example passes in the Institute of Motor Industry Part 1 or Institute of Road Transport Engineers can be accepted in place of City and Guilds of London Institute 381 Part II or 390. Likewise, the M.A.A./I.M.I. Management Diploma in lieu of the final I.M.I. examinations and so on. It is, however, vital that a potential manager has a good practical and theoretical background to enable him to meet the needs and demands of a modern service station. The service manager is the hub of the station and it is upon him that success or failure will result. He must be able to motivate all staff to work together as a team. To arouse and maintain enthusiasm for the jobs in hand, to deal fairly with personnel and customers to ensure bills are delivered and paid promptly, to see that service follow-up procedures are completed are but a few of the requirements of a service manager. A detailed list of inspection duties (Vauxhall Motors Service School) and a job description form (R.T.I.T.B.) are shown in Figs 5.5 and 5.6. However, in addition to the basic theoretical knowledge required by service managers what else will go to make up an ideal service manager? Certain characteristics are essential and these can be outlined as follows:

Honesty. A service manager is in a position of trust and must therefore be honest with his employers, customers and employees. This applies to all financial aspects as well as the general approach to problems and difficulties. References from previous employers will determine this characteristic or if a service manager is appointed within a firm, his previous records should assist.

Integrity. This requirement is another vital aspect of a service manager's build-up. The way in which people at all levels are treated can make or break a firm. If a man is treated fairly even when he is wrong, he will respond much better

Date . . . .

Area	Condition			Action Taken	Responsibility	Frequency of Inspection
	Bad	Fair	Good			
S/S Approach						
Entrance						
Reception Area						
Car Wash						
Lubrication Bay						
Parts Department						
Waiting Room						
Service Mgrs. Office						
Toilets, Men						
Toilets, Ladies						
Floors						
Walls						
Windows						
Ceilings						
Work Areas						
Tool Room						
Cloak Room						
Canteen						
Lights						
Signs						
Advertising						
Personnel						
Remarks						

Fig. 5.5 Good Housekeeping Appearance and Check and Assignment Form (Vauxhall)

MANAGEMENT JOB DESCRIPTION FORM

Job Title   Service Manager

Job Location   XYZ Garage Limited,
High Street, Uxminster

Department   Service

1 MAIN PURPOSE OF THE JOB

To achieve an agreed return on the Company's investment in its workshop facilities.

To promote customer satisfaction by providing high quality service and workmanship.

To increase turnover.

2 RELATIONSHIPS

Directly responsible to –   Garage Manager

Functionally responsible to   Garage Manager

Others with whom there are regular but
direct working relationships –

Parts Manager
Office Manager
Vehicle Sales Manager
Forecourt Supervisor

Subordinates directly supervised –

1 Workshop Controller
3 Foremen
3 Reception Engineers

Others with whom there are regular but
indirect working relationships –

Vehicle and other manufacturers
Specialist repairers
Insurance company assessors
R.T.I.T.B. Officers

3 SCOPE

The object of this section is to get into perspective the manager's main responsibilities, for example

a) Numbers Employed

Supervisors	7
Semi-skilled	10
Clerk	1
Shunter	1
Skilled staff	26
Apprentices	12
Cleaner	1

Total 58

b) Assets (e.g. vehicles, stock) if any, with indicative costs

Stock/Materials	£55,000
Equipment	£30,000
Recovery vehicles	£ 5,000

c) Any Other Responsibilities

All paperwork to be cleared weekly
Monthly check of work in progress
Preparation of new and used vehicles for retail jobs
Technical advice to Commercial and Fleet operators
Weekly check of apprentices' 'on-the-job' training programme

4 MAJOR RESPONSIBILITIES FOR RESULTS – for example

a) Costs

To improve efficiency by monthly examination of labour and other direct costs within his control against agreed targets.

To ensure that all customer service accounts are despatched within 3 days of job completion.

To prepare a list of consumable workshop tools and materials with an estimated monthly itemised list.

b) Improved Profitability (return on capital employed)

Hours sold to be not less than 80% of productive capacity.

Gross profit percentage on labour sale to be not less than 70%.

c) Improved Job Satisfaction (to those employed)

To improve efficiency by the provision of better workshop conditions, modern equipment and tools and more opportunities for training and development.

5 LIMITS OF AUTHORITY

Financial –

All requirements to Garage Manager.

No authority to grant Credit or Discount facilities

Personnel –

Engagement and dismissal of staff – up to but not including foremen.

Operational –

As limited by Garage Manager

6 DESIRABLE QUALIFICATIONS, EXPERIENCE AND TRAINING

a) A sound and up-to-date knowledge of motor vehicles, including legislation and trade practices, preferably supported by documentary evidence of a National Certificate or other recognised qualifications such as Associate Member I.M.I./or M.A.A./I.M.I. Diploma. *Note: It is desirable that Service Managers be registered with the E.R.B.*

b) An ability for administration, organisation and leadership.

Signed ....

Date ....

Fig. 5.6 R.T.I.T.B. Service Manager Job Description

when he knows this treatment could have been expected by any member of
staff who had made the same mistake.

Personality. This covers a wide range of a man's build-up. Passivity, aggression,
vitality, enthusiasm, pessimist, are some of the characteristics which go to
build up the personality of a man. A service manager needs to be pleasing in
appearance and in speech, enthusiastic, and calm in the face of difficulties.

Ability. This has already been defined, but whilst academic attainment is vital,
the other factors, honesty, integrity and personality also form a large part of
a service manager's make-up. Once having been trained, a manager must be
able to use his theoretical knowledge in a practical way to run a service station
efficiently. The monthly Profit and Loss Account will soon determine this
factor. Consequently, a manufacturers' course such as those run by Vauxhall
Motors, Ford Marketing Institute and Leyland will be extremely valuable aids
to train a man to meet the needs of his particular products. The R.T.I.T.B. and
local technical colleges also run short courses to assist potential managers,
but these do not replace the detailed and required knowledge of the final
examinations of the I.M.I., M.A.A., or I.R.T.E.

Parts managers, forecourt managers, car sales managers

Having considered in some detail the requirements of a service manager, the
requirements of other managers will be similar, but with ability slanted in their
particular direction. For example, a parts department manager must have had
a good practical parts training and attained an Advanced Pardic Certificate, a
forecourt manager will require a similar background to a car sales manager who,
in turn, must have passed the appropriate sections of the I.M.I. final syllabuses.
Again, courses by manufacturers and the R.T.I.T.B. are very useful aids to
managers specializing in a particular field.

Reception engineers (service advisers)

The responsibilities of a reception engineer also referred to in some garages
as service adviser, are discussed in Chapter 3. Qualifications for such posts
should include (a) good practical workshop background (b) theoretical
attainment to final City and Guilds of London Institute 381 Part III, T.E.C.-
O.T.C. or 390 Parts II and III. Remembering that receptionists meet the
customer and consequently represent the garage, a vital part of any reception
engineer is a pleasing personality. Customers can be very difficult sometimes
and frequently give obscure instructions. A service adviser must, therefore,
have the ability to mix and meet all kinds of people and have a personality
similar to that of a good foreman.

Office staff

Office staff will be appointed according to the needs of the garage. A qualified accountant will run all the firms accounts and also be responsible for ensuring suitable staff are appointed to meet the special skills of office work, e.g. typists, clerks, computer operators, etc.

Cleaners

For workshops and other areas cleaners need no special skills, but they do need to feel they are an essential part of the service station operations. No special forms are needed, but essential basic details must be taken such as full name and address, age, health. Rates of pay must be clearly indicated and any profit-sharing schemes explained. It is vital that cleaners do understand the importance of clean workshop floors as an aid to accident prevention and here the service manager appointing can use his personality to motivate a cleaner to work with the minimum of supervision. Similarly, the ability of a cleaner to work with people and not against them is essential and should be stressed. The actual duties of a cleaner, as with other posts, should be very clearly defined to avoid jobs not being done or repeated, and prevent misunderstandings and loss of work output.

A similar technique must be adopted for labourers in the workshop and other areas.

Interview techniques

This chapter has dealt with selection of staff for different posts and the needs of each job have been outlined. Before any interview takes place to appoint any person for a job, basic information and more detailed information where required is obtained. The object of the interview is to assess parts of a persons character and personality which an application form can not.

For positions up to foreman, service advisers, chargehands, mechanics, apprentices and cleaners, the service manager will generally appoint, but he may have the assistance of another manager so that two will sit on the employers side to interview the applicant. Obviously, questions will be pre-written on a separate sheet with blank spaces for the service manager to write in the applicant's verbal replies. Questions will be framed to bring out special knowledge or attitudes. For example, in the appointment of a foreman, a question to determine an applicant's attitude upon discovering a mistake could be as follows: 'You have found an oil filter has not been changed and the car has been allowed out of the workshop. What action would you take against the mechanic?' An immediate 'sack him' would obviously reveal a lack of ability or interest to obtain details of why the filter change was missed. If it had been done deliberately, obviously a mechanic would have to have a severe warning at least because of the serious position in which he had placed the company. The reply would reveal many of the personality traits referred to earlier in the chapter. Therefore, when interviewing, questions must be written with an object in mind but the applicant should be given time to ask for any further details about the post so that he knows fully what his duties will be.

Committee interviews. Usually these are reserved for management posts. At least two or three senior members of a firm will interview candidates in turn, usually alphabetically so that discrimination is avoided. Depending on the importance of the post, for example, a senior service manager, could expect an interview to last at least 30 minutes. Candidates would be shown around the workshops and a general assessment of bearing, speech, dress, attitudes etc., made during this period of time. Finally, the successful candidate will be brought back to the interview room and appointed. There are many reasons for this interview technique, but basically it is to obtain the right man for the job. So many things are revealed: for example the man who must loudly proclaim what he has done is not likely to be any better than the quiet man who has achieved exactly the same but with increased efficiency and without upsetting the entire staff. Appointment of senior posts, it may be mentioned here, can be from within a firm or from outside. From within a worthy man should be considered, but not from length of service only. A man from outside can inject new ideas, prevent stagnation and has the advantage of not being known on a personal level to the people he is to manage.

Training programmes: road transport industry training board

Training programmes and the R.T.I.T.B. must be mentioned together, for it is the Board who have instituted, recommended and generally brought about excellent training programmes for all members of the staff of all service stations. Unless suitable training programmes are instituted and trained competent staff obtained, service stations must surely go out of existence. The general public expect a good service but have, unfortunately, received very poor service from many. Not all service stations should be labelled as such because some have been very progressive indeed having training programmes for all staff before the R.T.I.T.B. came into existence in 1966/7. No progressive person can dispute that good training must result in better personnel and, in turn, more efficiency with resulting increased profitability for the service station. So it now is a fact that apprentices undergo training which is properly planned, laid out in correct and detailed form, and the employer and apprentice has an Apprentice Log Book issued and inspected by Training Officers of the R.T.I.T.B. Details of apprentice training recommended by the R.T.I.T.B. can be found in the Boards booklet *Training Recommendations for Motor Vehicle Mechanics.* Similarly, training recommendations and requirements for all other staff can be found in the R.T.I.T.B. booklets.

To obtain grants from the R.T.I.T.B. to which all employers pay a levy according to the size of the wage bill, training programmes must be strictly adhered to, that is a certain part of training must be completed within a certain period of time. Technical colleges are operating workshops for basic training facilities within their own workshops to meet the R.T.I.T.B. requirements.

Training Officers from the Board are always willing to offer expert advice about any aspect of training.

Manufacturers of cars and commercial vehicles have and still are providing first class training programmes for special aspects of motor vehicle trades. For example, engine overhaul, automatic transmission, parts department procedures, service managers' courses, body repair course, brake system overhaul, car sales course, in fact almost every aspect of car repair and subsequent sales is covered by the car manufacturers in this country. Application to attend such courses must be made to the manufacturer concerned. As all such courses are invariably recommended and approved by the R.T.I.T.B. full grants are paid to employers sending employees on such courses. As vehicle manufacturing processes change resulting in better vehicles each year, employees must from time to time attend refresher courses in order to bring themselves up to date and retain their efficiency as employees of a firm. The service manager or training officer of a firm must arrange attendance on such courses by employees who need such training.

N.I.I.P. seven-point plan.

A seven-point plan for the selection of staff was introduced by the National Institute of Industrial Psychology (N.I.I.P.) many years ago. This plan applies to all staff. Correct selection of staff is now extremely important as the Employment Protection Act 1975 gives employees considerable protection against wrongful dismissal. The Department of Employment have issued six separate leaflets dealing with this act, and every manager should obtain these and study them in detail. Quite recently an employer dismissed a third-year apprentice because he was not responding to training. The apprentice went to the appropriate industrial tribunal which ruled that he must be reinstated. As the employer was responsible for appointing the apprentice he should have known the capabilities of that person. Thus analytical means of selection are vital. The N.I.I.P. seven-point plan does much to eliminate guesswork in appointing staff. The plan highlights the following areas:

(1) *Physique*. This deals with a person's health. Is the candidate's general health good? Are there any special fitness requirements for his particular job? Colour blindness, for example, would affect the appointment of an automobile electrician.

(2) *Attainments*. For certain jobs special qualifications are needed. A potential apprentice with 'O' levels or C.S.E. requirements in mathematics, science, etc. has attainments which will enable him to absorb the training and education he will receive.

(3) *General Intelligence*. A rather debatable item, as this is difficult to define. It is however true that certain jobs demand high intellectual ability. Apprentices should have what is referred to as an 'average intelligence quotient', while higher posts demand higher ability.

(4) *Special aptitudes*. Does the job require manual dexterity, mechanical aptitude, and so on?

(5) *Interests.* How far does the job require real interest in certain areas, e.g. solving problems, construction, etc? Does the person have practical constructive hobbies or a lively interest in any particular subject?

(6) *Disposition.* This is an indicator of whether a person will work well as part of a team. Important characteristics are a person's acceptability within a group, self reliance, aggression, dependability, persistence, and so on.

(7) *Circumstances.* A number of factors enter into this area, e.g. mobility—can he/she get to work on time? Is a certain age range required? etc.

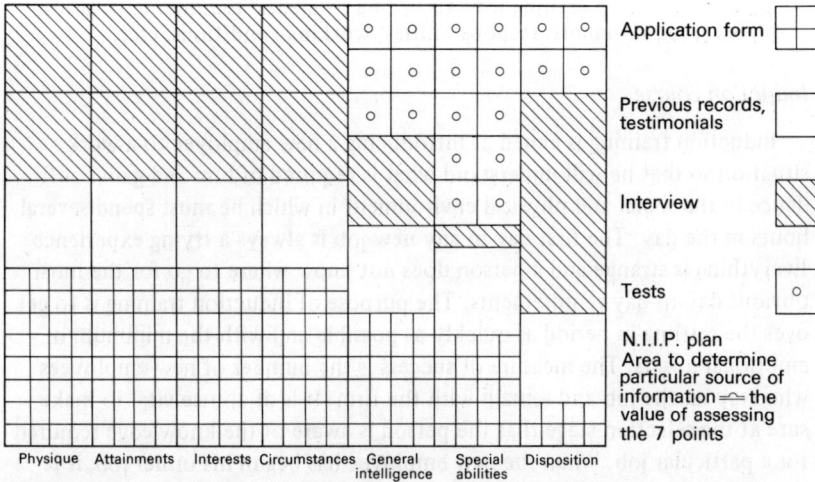

Fig. 5.7 Outline of N.I.I.P. seven-point plan assessment for appointment of new staff

How these seven points are assessed is outlined in Fig. 5.7. Bearing this in mind, the sequence of a staff appointment should, for most jobs, be completed by adopting the following procedure: (1) a job description is written out, followed by job specification to ensure that it is clear in everyone's mind what the job entails and what type of person is needed; (2) the post is then advertised; (3) applicants are sent application forms, which are considered when they are returned; (4) suitable applicants are asked for interview (an objective interview appraisal form is made where required so that answers by the applicants can be given a points rating); (5) the best candidate is then appointed. This, of course, must be considered with other relevant items dealt with in this chapter. Some personnel departments now use a five-point plan which embraces all the items listed. Analytical methods should be applied to all areas of personnel management and the student should study textbooks dealing with this particular subject. The student should however note the following important definitions:

Staff appraisal form. This is a form which enables an honest and analytical appraisal of a person's performance at his job. It highlights his strengths and weaknesses. It can be used as a means for promotion to other work or re-training. Suitable items, such as trade ability, punctuality, dependability, etc. are examined—usually once a year.

Job analysis is the process of studying the job, its methods, and equipment which leads to:

Job description or an account, in greater or lesser detail, of the actual content of the job and from this we derive:

Job specification which sets out the personal qualities required in the man or woman who will do the job to the standards set.

Job evaluation is a means of working out the relative value of jobs in a logical manner by grading jobs according to mental requirements, skills, physical requirements, responsibilities, working conditions, etc.

Induction course

Induction training is aimed at introducing a new employee to a work situation so that he will understand what is required of him and gain confidence in the social and physical environment in which he must spend several hours in the day. The first day in any new job is always a trying experience. Everything is strange and a person does not know where to go for the most obvious day-to-day requirements. The purpose of induction training is to get over the settling-in period as quickly as possible and with the minimum of emotional upsets. The measure of success is the number of new employees who stay on the job and remain with the firm. It is of course vital to make sure at the selection stage that the person is aware of the knowledge required for a particular job. When the new employee has begun his or her job, it is then the duty of the general manager, service manager, training officer, or other appointed person to ensure that sufficient time is given to helping the new employee to become familiar with his surroundings and with the people with whom he will be working. New apprentices should meet the general manager, who should give an outline of the company's operations and where the apprentice fits into the work situation. The apprentice then needs to have a conducted tour of the working environment and meet the people in charge. In the case of a main dealership this would involve (1) service workshops, (2) vehicle sales, (3) parts department, (4) offices, (5) reception, (6) forecourt, (7) canteen, (8) rest rooms, (9) first aid, and (10) any other areas. This could take a full day or even longer. Having completed the tour, he would then be introduced to the manager of the workshop, the foreman, the chargehand, and the mechanic he will work with. The training officer would have outlined his training programme when the apprentice was appointed. When he actually commences work it will be essential for him to know (1) Whom he must approach for advice, e.g. a supervisor, (2) where to report for first aid, (3) fire drill and procedure, (4) meal break times, (5) canteen facilities, (6) laundry facilities, (7) safety requirements, e.g.

protective clothing, goggles, axle stands, safe driving of vehicles and age restrictions, precautions against fire risks with petrol and other substances, clean floors free of oil/grease, tidy and clean work areas, safe working loads of machines and tackle, etc. and the penalties he could expect for failing to observe the procedures laid down (all these items, and others if necessary, could be suitable titles for safety lectures to new apprentices), (8) trade union representatives, (9) sickness procedures, and (10) holiday procedures.

The immediate supervisor of any new apprentice or other person must take full control of any work or training activity. A carefully planned induction training programme would last for five days or so, depending on the size of the firm. The personnel department arranges the course so that personnel wastage is avoided; new people know whom to ask for advice and where they can be found, a sense of belonging and job security is established; safety is observed and accidents prevented. Having trained and contented staff results in greater work output.

The induction course could be modified for other personnel depending on their experience and knowledge.

Personal record form

An example of a form used to record basic data is shown in Fig. 5.8 and is self-explanatory. All personnel should know the purpose of such forms and why the information is required. The form can be modified to suit the particular requirements of any company.

Legislation and employees

A host of laws in connection with employees surround an employer. It is impossible in a book of this size to list all the legal pitfalls, as this is a subject in its own right. Readers are however urged to make themselves aware of the following Acts:

>   Employment Protection Act 1975 and Employment Protection
>   (Consolidation) Act 1978 (also subsequent employment legislation)
>   Redundancy Payments Act 1965
>   Equal Pay Act 1970
>   Contracts of Employment Act 1972
>   Health and Safety at Work Act 1974
>   Trade Unions and Labour Relations Act 1975
>   Sex Discrimination Act 1975
>   Race Relations Act 1976

'Guides' to the operation of most government Acts are available from H.M.S.O. and other sources. The 'guides' explain simply the basic observations necessary to comply with legal requirements.

The Commission on Industrial Relations (140 Gower Street, London WC1E 6HT) aims to solve problems of unions and management and to en-

PERSONAL RECORD FORM

COMPLETE IN BLOCK CAPITALS

Surname . . . . Christian names . . . .

. . . .

Present job . . . .

Home address . . . .

. . . .

National Insurance number . . . .

Religion. . . . . .Nationality. . . . .

Age. . . . .

Name of next of kin (Parent/Guardian/Wife/Husband/Other)

. . . .

Address of next of kin . . . .

. . . .

Home telephone Number . . . .

(or No. for emergency use) . . . .

Name of own doctor . . . .

Address of own Doctor. . . . .

. . . .

Telephone number of doctor (Give STD Code) . . . .

To be completed by trainees/apprentices/skilled craftsmen and other
personnel who require protective clothing

Height. . . . . Chest measurement . . . .

Inside leg measurement. . . . . .Approximate weight . . . .

Size of shoes. . . . . Head Size for helmet/cap . . . .

Your signature . . . .

Date . . . .

Fig. 5.8.

courage a sounder basis for industrial relations. Many reports are available such as *Shop Stewards' Facilities, Communications in Bargaining*, and so on. Full details can be obtained from the Commission.

A good manager will always remember that he can motivate most staff to work with the organization instead of against it as long as he understands their needs, such as job satisfaction, recognizes their abilities, gives them opportunities to develop whenever possible, creates job security, gives fair treatment to all staff without exception, shows them respect and recognizes employees knowledge. Reasonable employee benefits and good working conditions with good tools and equipment will also help employers to motivate staff so that maximum productivity is obtained.

By the same token, customers will be motivated to return to a dealership which recognizes their needs. Fig. 3.1. should be studied in this connection.

Safety

From Fig. 5.5 it will be seen that the good housekeeping chart is also a safety check form. The Health and Safety at Work Act 1974 places a heavy responsibility upon all personnel to ensure they are working in a safe manner. A booklet entitled *Protecting People at Work* is available from the Department of Employment and should be carefully studied as it outlines the scope of the Act. The Health and Safety Commission issue eight booklets in connection with the 1974 Act and readers are strongly advised to obtain these. A full list of safety booklets may be obtained from H.M.S.O. (the address is given in the appendix). By ensuring that all employees are adequately trained in their jobs, managers will be giving themselves reasonable protection against prosecution if a serious accident should occur. Using safety practices check forms like the one illustrated in Chapter I is an essential part of a manager's duties.

Fire is one of the greatest hazards in a motor vehicle workshop. Petrol is an extremely dangerous liquid and special precautions are always necessary when draining tanks or repairing fuel systems. All staff should know how to use fire extinguishers. It is important to remember that wherever we have heat or people there is a fire risk. Local fire officers should be consulted for inspection of premises and their recommendations implemented. A useful booklet entitled *Fire-fighting in Factories* is available from H.M.S.O., price 12½p, (1977). Fires have been classified according to various factors and suitable extinguishants recommended. The following table should be noted:

Classification of Fire and Suitable Extinguishing Agents

B.S.4547 (1972) EN2 Classification of Fire	Typical Fires and Locations	Suitable Extinguishing Agents
CLASS A Fires involving solid materials, usually of organic nature, in which combustion normally takes place with the formation of glowing embers.	Burning wood, paper, cloth, Rubber, plastic, etc. Found in homes, offices, stores, work-shops, shops, caravans, hotels, hospitals, etc.	Water and water/foam solutions which will prevent the embers from igniting. General purpose powder is also effective.
CLASS B Fires involving liquids and liquifiable solids.	Petrol, oil, grease, fat, paint, solvents, inks, etc. Found in garages, facto-ries, stores, offices, vehicles, boats, hospitals, hotels, etc.	B.C.F., CO_2 Regular Dry Powder and Foam are all effective. Halon 1211 and CO_2 leave no mess.
CLASS C Fires involving gases (in this section we in-clude fires in-clude fires involving live electrical equipment).	1. Butane, propane, town gas, oxygen, acetylene etc. Found in garages, boats, caravans, homes, factories, stores, shops, hospitals, etc.	B.C.F., CO_2 are effective. Regular Dry Powder can also be used.
	2. Television sets, generators, trans-formers, switchgear, lighting, wiring, com-puters. Found in factories, homes, hos-pitals, shops, offices.	B.C.F. and CO_2 are safe up to 100 000 volts and will not harm electronic equipment.
CLASS D Fires involving metals.	Magnesium, sodium, potassium, titanium, etc. Found in fac-tories, some vehicle body-building and repair workshops etc.	Special Purpose Dry Powder.

B.C.F. = Bromochlorodifluro Methane which is a liquefied gas which kills fires by interfering chemically with the chain reaction of combustion. It does not conduct electricity, has low toxity, and is non-corrosive. B.C.F. is also known as 'Halon 1211'.

CO_2 = Carbon dioxide, usually in powder form.

In connection with all fires

DO . . .

(1)   Specify the correct extinguisher for the risk. There won't be time to pick and choose in a fire!

(2)   Minimize the variety of extinguishers available. Most people who have access to an extinguisher have never used one.

(3)   Train personnel in the use of appliances. An appliance could save a business, stock, home, or even lives.

(4)   Keep spare extinguishers on stand-by while others are being serviced after use.

(5)   Have extinguishers inspected regularly. An inspection and maintenance service is available from most suppliers.

(6)   In the event of fire, call the fire brigade first, then do what you can about the fire yourself, but remember a hand extinguisher is only a first aid appliance.

(7)   Have regular practices to ensure that all staff know the fire drill.

DON'T . . .

(1)   Use the wrong extinguisher for the type of fire. For example, water is taboo on live electrical equipment, the extinguisher, and you, could become live!! Combustible metals such as magnesium, titanium, zirconium, sodium, potassium, etc. will explode if a cooling agent such as CO_2, water, or B.C.F. is used. These require special-purpose powders, which are available on special order.

(2)   Use pressurized extinguishers on fat fires or other contained liquids, as splashing can result and cause the fire to spread, unless the extinguishers used by a skilled operator. A fire blanket is preferable here.

Progressive assessment testing

While apprentices proceed with their training, it is necessary to test them to ascertain if new skills have really been absorbed. To do this a check list is made out by a training officer, instructor, or supervisor who has been trained to execute such tests. A specific task is named, e.g. using a torque wrench to tighten cylinder-head bolts to the correct setting. A time is allotted for the job on a basis realistic for apprentices. The apprentice will then be set at ease and some prepared questions asked, e.g. What is the purpose of a torque wrench? How is the correct loading indicated when a torque wrench is used? The apprentice should give clear answers and then he will be told how he will be assessed. Assessment could be made as follows:

Assessment items	Maximum score	Marks deducted
(1) Condition and use of tools:		
(a) Uses worn or damaged tool.	5	
(b) Does not set torque wrench correctly.	20	
(c) Does not use wrench correctly.	20	
(2) Workmanship:		
(a) Does not work systematically when tightening head bolts.	20	
(b) Damages any part.	20	
(c) Does not ensure bolts or nuts are free before tightening.	20	
(3) Cleanliness of work:		
(a) Does not ensure all tools and finished job are left clean and tidy.	10	
(4) Answering of questions: Deduct marks objectively for incorrect answers to all questions set. Question No. 1. What is the purpose of a torque wrench?	5	
Question No. 2. How is the correct loading indicated when a torque wrench is used?	5	
(5) Time taken to complete the job, say, 10 minutes. (N.B. a realistic time must be given and extra time taken should only carry a low penalty for first-stage apprentices.) For every minute taken over time allowed deduct one mark.	10	
Total:	135	

Usually an apprentice will pass his assessment if he scores more than half the total marks obtainable. His assessment sheet, duly signed and dated, is then placed in his file.

All the important areas of training should be tested in this manner. The case for skills assessment is really simple—it should ensure an apprentice has absorbed his training and can complete a job correctly. If not, he will require further training before he is allowed to do certain tasks alone, e.g. setting tappets, relining brakes, fitting a clutch plate, etc. The R.T.I.T.B. have an excellent booklet available on this subject and is a very useful source of information on P.A.T. The R.T.I.T.B. also have booklets which describe managament appraisal and these are worthy of study.

Wages structures

The law of supply and demand causes wages to vary throughout the country, just as the cost of living varies, e.g. it is much more expensive to live in central London than say in Liverpool or Manchester.

A basic wage scale is arranged for apprentices and tradesmen by negotiation between employers and employees. The National Joint Council for the Motor Vehicle Retail and Repair Industry produces each year a Memorandum of Agreement on the Pay, Classification, and Working Conditions of Skilled and other Employees. Sick pay and bereavement leave is included in the document.

The council members are as follows:

The Motor Agents' Association Limited and the Scottish Motor Trade Association Limited represent employers, and the Trade Unions are represented by the Vehicle Building and Automotive Group of the Transport and General Workers Union, the Amalgamated Union of Engineering Workers Engineering Section, the General Municipal Boiler Makers and Allied Trade Union, the Electrical Electronic and Telecommunications Union-Plumbing Trades Union, and the National Union of Sheet Metal Workers, Coppersmiths, and Heating and Domestic Engineers.

The memorandum covers pay; guaranteed pay; suspension of guarantee; notice of termination of employment; hours of work, including shift working; overtime; emergency call pay; outworking and subsistence allowances; customary holidays; annual holidays; general items, such as higher basic rates of pay above those within the agreement; amendment and termination of agreement; job classifications; and agreed rates of pay for the classified jobs.

It is most important for any manager to have a copy of the current memorandum and to be familiar with it. The document costs 25p (1977) for the first copy and 8p for subsequent copies (post free).

Job titles coming within the scope of this document are motor mechanic (general), light vehicle mechanic, heavy vehicle mechanic, motor cycle mechanic, automobile electrician, body repairer, and partsman. Semi-skilled and unskilled workers' rates of pay are also listed. As the document can be amended annually, readers should obtain a current document to ascertain up to date rates of pay, etc. Important definitions include such things as Group 1 A: skilled employees who are qualified by appropriate training and can complete skilled work without detailed supervision; and Group 1 B: skilled employees who also have additional skills such as the ability to do electronic engine analysis diagnostic work, to prepare estimates, to inspect and test repaired vehicles or to determine what repair work may be required. Consequently Group 1 B has a rate of pay of £2.35 per hour, and Group 1 A £2.19 per hour minimum (1983). The other groups, i.e. 2, 3, and 4, have rates of pay to suit their skills. Indentured apprentices commence at 42–50p per hour and rise to the skilled rate in suitable increments over four years. At present, when an apprentice obtains his National Craft Certificate he is entitled to

to full skilled rate, regardless of his age. Without this certificate, he is entitled
to full rate at the age of 20 years, providing he has completed his skilled
training and education to satisfactory standards. Any supplements which may
be paid are added to the basic rates of pay.

Other staff within a dealership are paid according to the responsibility and
skills required. For example we could have rates similar to the following:

Let x = mechanics' weekly rate	Minimum rates	Possible rates
Skilled mechanic	$£x$	$£1.25x$
Charge-hand	$£1.1x$	$£1.4x$
Foreman	$£1.25x$	$£1.6x$
Reception engineer	$£1.25x$	$£1.6x$
Service manager	$£1.75x$	$£2.5x$

In some dealerships foremen, reception engineers, service or other managers
are regarded as staff positions and will therefore have an annual rate quoted
e.g. service ($£2.5x$)52 per year. Payment during sickness is usually automatic
for such posts. A service manager in charge of 15 staff will obviously not be
paid the same rate as a man controlling 150 staff. As service work becomes
more streamlined, e.g. flow line servicing, use of sophisticated testing machines and so on, it is quite possible for mechanics to have a flat rate much
higher than at present, with service managers commanding a salary in excess
of ($£4x$)52 a year for top posts.

The National Joint Council referred to earlier issue an agreement on the
Procedure for the Avoidance of Disputes and Related Matters (25p for one
to five copies, 5p for subsequent copies) and this should be obtained and
studied. A number of booklets are available which deal with industrial relations
and, for current details, the N.A.A. and the Sewell organisation should be
contacted. (See Appendix II for addresses.)

To conclude this section it is important for students to know that procedures, once agreed, must be followed. There are many national joint councils
and wages councils in the United Kingdom. A council for vehicle body trades
exists and has the following title: United Kingdom Joint Wages Board of
Employees for the Vehicle Building Industry. Members of this board include
the National Federation of Vehicle Trades, Vehicle Builders and Repairers'
Association for the employers, and The Vehicle Building and Automotive
Group, the Transport and General Workers Union, the Furniture, Timber, and
Allied Trades Union, the National Union of Sheet Metal Workers, Coppersmiths, Heating and Domestic Engineers and the Electrical, Electronic, and
Telecommunications union, and Plumbing Trades Union, on behalf of the
trade unions. This board agrees rates of pay, etc. for all vehicle building
trades and vehicle body repairers. Copies of agreements can be obtained
from the members forming the board. The V.B.R.A. address is given in the
appendix of this book.

The Memorandum of Agreement on Wages and Conditions covers wages, training, the ratio of apprentices to craftsmen, e.g. up to 3 craftsmen: 1 apprentice; 4–6 craftsmen: 2 apprentices; 7–9 craftsmen: 3 apprentices; and so on. Also included in the code are explanations of the working week, nightshifts, meal breaks, the guaranteed week, notice of termination of employment, payment for overtime, overtime on short working week, payment for Sunday and holiday work, annual holidays, public holidays, systems of payment by results, procedure for the avoidance of disputes, the position of shop stewards, and special provisions relating to the employment of electricians.

It is interesting to note that at the beginning of 1977 apprentices' wages were calculated as follows:

> 16–17 years 42½% of craftsman's rate
> 17–18 years 57½% of craftsman's rate
> 18–19 years 67½% of craftsman's rate
> 19–20 years 80% of craftsman's rate

Skilled rate is applied at 20 years of age, when apprenticeships commence at 16 years of age. The skilled rate is paid later where apprenticeships are taken up later. Readers are strongly recommended to obtain current codes and memoranda from the V.B.R.A.

Recommended conditions of service forms for employees are also available from the V.B.R.A. The M.A.A. also issue such forms. As they are a legal requirement under recent legislation e.g. the Employment Protection Act 1975, etc., students should obtain and study these documents. Procedures for dismissals should be studied in detail.

Incentive schemes

The basic rates of pay require some means of reward to improve productivity. Most workshops now use the basic hourly rates for jobs, arranged by manufacturers by time and motion study methods, as a means of payment of incentive money. For example, a service job requiring 3 hours work, completed in 2 hours by a mechanic means 1 hour saved. Thus, a mechanic gets 3 hours pay for 2 hours work and immediately starts on another job. The customer of course pays for 3 hours work and the workshop must profit from time saved. In fact, many workshops now expect mechanics to be earning a minimum of 10 hours bonus per week as this increases profit from the workshop.

Overtime rates are agreed as per basic rates and incentive bonus operates the same.

Tool-kits can be supplied to mechanics at trade prices or less as an incentive for completing so many bonus hours or for any other reason which a firm may decide upon such as so many weeks without being late or absent. Such schemes are called *financial* incentive schemes. Free holidays for the most work output have also been financial incentive schemes tried successfully.

Profit sharing schemes. These have now become a very popular means of financial incentive awards. Part of the total profit for a workshop is proportioned out to all employees from cleaners, labourers, mechanics and so on in relation to their rate of pay. Everyone is made to feel part of a team knowing that the quicker a job is completed and completed well the more money is going to be in their pay packet. Wastage of split-pins, nuts and bolts, oils etc., is kept to a minimum because employees are made aware that such items will be costed against the workshop operation and result in less profit and less money in the pay packet.

Non-financial incentive schemes. Such schemes are those in which money is not directly involved. Under this heading comes free overalls laundered twice a week, free tea breaks, social outings, use of sports and social club amenities, free transport to and from work to mention a few.

Financial and non-financial schemes must assist in keeping staff, providing they are fairly operated, which is the direct responsibility of management. Mismanagement of such schemes must result in disgruntled staff with poor work output and large staff turnover which reduces profits because of the extra advertising costs and training costs involved.

Formulating an incentive scheme for mechanics and other personnel

We have seen that as an aid to productivity a scheme has to be devised to encourage personnel to work hard and efficiently. To enable a fair system to operate so that all personnel are treated the same some garages have a card which details many characteristics of a man's ability to get an all round picture of a man's productivity. A number of points are given for each attribute, and, depending upon the number of points a man obtains, a rate of pay is subsequently awarded. Let us itemize some of the attributes which go to make up a good worker and allocate a number of points for each of these characteristics:

(a)	Ability in his trade	120
(b)	Productivity and effiency	40
(c)	Reliability	40
(d)	Cleanliness	40
(e)	Timekeeping	20
(f)	Knowledge of vehicles	40
(g)	Extra trades ability	40
(h)	Driving ability	20
(i)	Academic qualifications	40
	Maximum total possible points	400

Now these items can be put on a card with a space underneath to award the actual points for a particular asset as shown in Fig. 5.9. The service manager will record the actual marks scored (probably on a 3 or 6 monthly basis) so that a rate of pay can be established.

When scoring the card a mechanic could score points on the following lines:

(a) *Ability in trade*
    (1) Able to complete all repairs without supervision and conversant with modern equipment for diagnosing and rectifying faults.
                            Score = maximum points i.e. 120
    (2) Requires some supervision. Deduct 20 points.   Score = 100
    (3) Has reasonable skill but requires more training and experience. Deduct 30 points.   Score = 90
    (4) Semi-skilled and needs supervision. Deduct 40 points.   Score = 80

(b) *Productivity and efficiency*
    (1) Productivity record over the past 3 months is in excess of 100%. Does not waste time and is always looking for extra work. Looks for better methods for completing repairs.   Score = maximum points i.e. 40
    (2) Has 90% plus productivity record over the past 3 months and looks for extra work. Deduct 6 points.   Score = 34
    (3) Below 90% productivity record over the past 3 months and continually requires supervision to get work done. Deduct 14 points.   Score = 26

(c) *Reliability*
    (1) Faulty work not known. Will report any extra work needed on a vehicle on his own initiative.   Score = maximum points i.e. 40
    (2) Work returned occasionally for correction. Deduct 6 points.   Score = 34
    (3) Work returned for correction several times and does not report extra work needed on a vehicle unless asked. Deduct 20 points.   Score = 20

(d) *Cleanliness*
    (1) Always clean and tidy in appearance. Keeps work areas clean and tidy. Uses seat, wing and steering wheel covers.   Score = maximum points i.e. 40
    (2) Always clean in personal appearance but tends to leave tools and parts in untidy state. Uses covers to protect vehicles. Deduct 10 points.   Score = 30
    (3) Requires constant reminding about cleanliness and importance of safety with oil not cleaned from floor, etc. Parts left about and tools not cleaned properly. Deduct 25 points.   Score = 15

(e) *Timekeeping*

    (1) Always on time and ready to start work.

                                  Score = maximum points i.e. 20

    (2) Arrives on time but starts work after time.

        Deduct 5 points.   Score = 15

    (3) Generally on time but has a number of late starts during a month.

        Deduct 10 points.   Score = 10

(f) *Knowledge of vehicles*

    (1) Good up-to-date knowledge of vehicles which he is working on e.g. Vauxhall, Leyland, Ford, etc. Has obtained good passes in Factory Courses which he has attended say 6 in last 3 years (2 each year)

                                    Score = maximum points i.e. 40

    (2) A fairly good knowledge of vehicles with passes in Factory Courses attended.

        Deduct 10 points.   Score = 30

    (3) Requires pressing to read up-to-date literature on vehicle repairs and needs improving generally.

        Deduct 20 points.   Score = 20

(g) *Extra trades ability*

    (1) Can do extra work such as good quality repair welding, fit body trims, etc.

                                    Score = maximum points i.e. 40

    (2) Can do extra work under supervision.

        Deduct 15 points.   Score = 25

(h) *Driving ability*

    (1) Good driver—no accidents over past 12 months. Ability to use driving knowledge in diagnosing faults.

                                    Score = maximum points i.e. 20

    (2) As above except 6 months accident free record.

        Deduct 6 points.   Score = 14

    (3) Has driving licence but cannot use his ability in road test diagnostic work owing to lack of experience.

        Deduct 10 points.   Score = 10

(i) *Academic qualifications*

    (1) Holds C.G.L.I. 390 Final or Full Technological Certificate or T.E.C.-O.T.C.

                                    Score = maximum points i.e. 40

    (2) Holds C.G.L.I. 381 Part II Final and National Crafts Certificate

        Deduct 12 points   Score = 28

Name of Mechanic: For Month: Year:

Ability with trade	Productivity and efficiency	Reliability	Cleanliness
Max. 120	Max. 40	Max. 40	Max. 40
Actual	Actual	Actual	Actual
Timekeeping	Knowledge of vehicles	Extra trades ability	Driving ability
Max. 20	Max. 40	Max. 40	Max. 20
Actual	Actual	Actual	Actual
Academic qualifications			
Max. 40			
Actual			

Total max. = 400

Actual =

Hourly rate of pay =

Signed . . . . SERVICE MANAGER

Date . . . .

Fig. 5.7 Incentive Scheme Card

(3) Holds C.G.L.I. 381 Part III.
   Deduct 20 points.   Score = 20
(4) Holds Factory Certificates—4 points for each to maximum
   of 20 points.

By breaking down an incentive scheme in this way a fair system of incentive can be awarded to mechanics and disputes avoided. Depending upon the number of points obtained a mechanic's rate of pay will be determined. For example a rate of pay on the merit points gained could be as follows:

Pay scales for mechanics

Points	380–400	360–379	340–359	320–339	300–319	
Pay per hour	£1	£0.97	£0.95	£0.93	£0.90	
Points	290–299	280–289	270–279	260–269	250–259	Below 250
Pay per hour	£0.89	£0.87	£0.86	£0.85	£0.84	£0.80

The mechanic will be presented with a card similar to that shown in Fig. 5.6 and his rate of pay indicated.

Whilst this system does involve a lot of initial work, once it has been established a fair system of incentive pay will operate especially where a large number of mechanics are employed. The special needs of each garage could be included in such a scheme and items not considered essential deleted. It will be the responsibility of the service manager to decide finally what will make up his incentive scheme in order to improve and maintain efficiency in his workshops and other departments.

Whatever scheme is devised the basic essentials of a good incentive wage plan are:

1. A guaranteed minimum wage must be ensured.
2. The plan must be fair and just to employer and employee.
3. Employees and employer must support the plan.
4. All standards set must be based on a time study or, alternatively, on realistic attributes of personnel.
5. The plan must be as simple as possible so that an employee can determine his potential earnings.
6. The incentive must be correct in detail; if the standard set is high, the reward must be generous.
7. No restriction on earnings should be imposed.
8. The plan must assist good work and, if possible, aid team work.
9. Costing of the plan should be as simple as possible.
10. Any standards set must be guaranteed against change unless methods alter.

In implementing any plan a student should remember that it is easy to lose money and be popular. The incentive scheme used must result in greater productivity in the workshop which, in turn, means higher wage packets and higher profits for the service station.

It will be appreciated where any new schemes are to be introduced, staff, trade unions and other personnel involved must be consulted if industrial relations are to remain satisfactory. In implementing payment by results bonus schemes it must be remembered certain advantages and disadvantages occur, e.g.:

Advantages
1. Lower costs of production and higher earnings for the workers.
2. Enhances efficiency, eliminates lost time.
3. Labour costs can be estimated more accurately in advance.
4. Output levels can mean less direct supervision.

Disadvantages
1. Tendency for quality to deteriorate unless inspections/checks are made.
2. Clerical work increased.
3. Some workers can overwork and harm their health.
4. Slow workers can resent faster workers who can earn more.
5. Payment by results may lead to opposition or restriction of output when new machines and methods are proposed or introduced. This is due to fear that a job may be restudied and earnings reduced.

Questions

1. Most manufacturers issue standard times for service work. Some issue standard charges. How would you ensure that these times and charges are kept and what action would you take when you find that the time has been grossly exceeded. (I.M.I.)
2. In some establishments a lot of time is spent in obtaining material from the parts department. How would you operate your workshop to cut this time down to a reasonable minimum, bearing in mind that there must be a proper record of all parts issued? (I.M.I.)
3. It is now a well established principle to pay an incentive bonus to all repair-shop personnel. As a service manager, what type of scheme would you employ. (I.M.I.)
4. As it is most important to recruit the right personnel for staff positions such as reception engineers or shop foremen, state what characteristics you would look for and what questions you would ask when interviewing an applicant for either of the two posts mentioned. (I.M.I.)
5. Many firms have clearly printed forms showing the conditions of service. As a service manager say what you consider such conditions should be. (I.M.I.)

6. Discuss the following from the point of view of retaining skilled labour.
   (a) Direct payment—higher rates of pay.
   (b) Financial incentives, i.e. bonus or similar schemes.
   (c) Non-financial incentives. (I.M.I.)
7. Describe any 'Bonus Scheme', 'Merit Pay' or any other 'production incentive' which you know as being fair to all concerned, i.e. customer, the employer and the employee. (I.M.I.)
8. Large organizations frequently appoint a personnel officer, one of whose duties is to help employees with their problems. In smaller organizations this usually falls on the manager's shoulders. Do you consider it is a good policy to render welfare assistance to employees and state your reasons whether yes or no. (I.M.I.)
9. Selection of personnel for a particular job is extremely important. State the requirements you would expect when appointing—
   (a) An apprentice mechanic
   (b) A skilled fitter
   (c) A foreman
   (d) A service manager. (I.M.I.)
10. Skilled mechanics are still in short supply in the retail motor trade. Semi-skilled mechanics are a little easier to obtain. Suggest a practical method through which semi-skilled men can gain the necessary experience and knowledge to qualify for higher grading while remaining in employment. (I.M.I.)
11. The National Joint Council for the Motor Vehicle Retail and Repair Industry agree the Wages and Conditions of certain classes of employees in the industry.
    (a) Who on the Council represents employees?
    (b) Who on the Council represents the employers?
    (c) Under the current agreement, in what circumstances is an apprentice entitled to be paid the skilled rate?
    (d) There are now two groups of 'skilled employee', Group 1 A and Group 1 B. What are the qualifications necessary to be graded under each of these heads? (I.M.I.)
12. (a) State FOUR aims of the Health and Safety at Work Act 1974.
    (b) List
       (i) FOUR general duties of employers to their employees under the Act.
       (ii) TWO of the duties of employees under the Act.
    (c) Outline the action which is necessary on the part of the garage manager to carry out the duties laid on him by the Act (I.M.I.).

CHAPTER 6

FORECOURT WORK

Forecourt management

The forecourt area of any service station is one which must attract the attention of potential customers. It is essential to arrange that the forecourt is cleaned every day, petrol pumps and oil pumps are wiped clean, windows are cleaned, advertisements are kept clean and up-to-date, accessories are well displayed, customers have good access to the forecourt, toilet signs are displayed clearly and staff are trained for their jobs. Forecourts usually are concerned with petrol, oil and accessory sales and it is these with which we shall concern ourselves. As the staff to operate a forecourt are of prime importance, we can consider this aspect first.

Forecourt manager

As explained in Chapter 5 any manager needs to have a good background for his particular area of operation. The sale of parts, accessories, petrol and oil demands a thorough knowledge of parts mechandising and management techniques. Thus, a forecourt manager would possess a relevant management qualification. In addition he would also require the personal qualities of honesty, integrity, ability and have a pleasing personality. His personality should be such as to motivate his staff to keep the forecourt and accesssory area in first class condition. It is the manager who will make out his profit and loss account and he will depend a great deal on his staff to ensure a profit is made. Staff must, therefore, be made aware that spillage of oil, breakage of accessories and so on all mean loss. Profit sharing schemes help to achieve the right attitude and can be very usefully employed.

Forecourt staff

Manning the petrol pumps and accessory shops on a service station forecourt is an important job. This job has traditionally been regarded as unskilled and, therefore, anyone is allowed to sell petrol and parts. The result of this negative thinking has been a very high staff changeover rate: it is difficult to retain people for over 3 months.

According to a published survey, forecourt staff were rated—'50% lazy, 40% dishonest, 10% useless': no praise at all for anyone who had been employed! Most forecourt staff had a combined tendency of laziness *and* dishonesty: what a sad picture! Who should be blamed for this state of affairs? Well, who appointed them and arranged the conditions of service?—managers of course! When conditions of service are poor what kind of staff is the job likely to attract? In any event, conditions and payment should be made attractive so that reasonable staff will be obtained and profits will increase. The customer has a right to good service for his money and he will certainly go where his custom is appreciated. *If* the right staff are recruited a forecourt can prove to be a highly profitably area, but the right staff must first be obtained. What are the requirements of a member of the forecourt staff? Would he be useful if he attended the Vehicle Partsmen's Craft Studies Part II City and Guilds of London Institute Course No. 381 at technical college? The size of the station and the parts department would enable a man to decide if attendance for such a course would be justified. Mostly, forecourt staff don't need such detailed knowledge as is required by the parts department staff, but forecourt staff need to know:

1. How to operate petrol pumps and oil pumps.
2. How to unlock various types of bonnets.
3. The positions of dipsticks in various engines, correct oil levels, grades of oil.
4. Correct water levels for radiators and batteries, correct dilutions of anti-freeze and water mixtures for anti-corrosion purposes and prevention of frost damage.
5. The types of radial and cross-ply tyres available, the air pressures for different cars, and how to use air pressure equipment safely.
6. The range of accessories available in the forecourt shop.
7. How to complete money addition quickly and accurately.
8. How to use fire extinguishers for fire control: a working knowledge of first aid would also be a valuable asset.

This basic list could be added to or reduced to suit individual cases. In any event the duties of the staff can be listed and, whilst they are not very demanding in skill, it is essential for all staff to be able to satisfactorily deal with the points covered. Thus, suitable training must be given and a course of instruction is available at the M.O.T.E.C. establishment in Shropshire, which is operated by the R.T.I.T.B. Some technical colleges also provide similar courses.

In addition to the knowledge required:

1. Staff must be punctual and understand shift work rotas for days off.
2. They must be smart and clean in appearance. This is in part accomplished by the manager supplying fresh overalls every 2 days or so.
3. Staff must be tidy and keep the forecourt tidy. The forecourt area must be kept clean and free from obstructions at all times to avoid accidents and give a good impression to customers.

4. Customers must be served in correct rotation as quickly and courteously as possible.
5. Staff must remain pleasant at all times and preserve good customer relationships by a friendly approach. A smile and a courteous 'good morning' or 'good afternoon' can help a great deal.

Given a knowledgeable and friendly approach to customers, a good forecourt salesman can easily assist profitability. A new accessory can be mentioned in passing and always a 'thank you' for any sale, whether it is petrol, oil or accessory should be automatic.

Cleaners

Where cleaners are employed, they should have clear instructions about their duties. The concrete floor of the forecourt for example will need to be washed down every morning. Pumps should be wiped down and polished. Toilets should be kept scrupulously clean and stocked. Windows should be polished and cleaned each day. Cleaners should be encouraged so that they are aware of the importance of their part in the profitability of the station. A dirty and untidy forecourt can turn customers away and cleaners should be reminded of the fact.

Cashiers

Some petrol forecourts—especially the self service type—employ a cashier who handles money only. As the automated pumps record the amount delivered on the console in the office, the cashier takes the money from the customer and hands him a receipt if required. The cashier usually gives trading stamps, gifts and so on according to the amount of petrol purchased so she must be fully aware of these arrangements. The ability to handle money well is essential. An efficient manager will be able to tabulate at any given moment all petrol sales and cross-check money in the till. Some stations make the cashier responsible for all shortages and the cashier has this amount deducted from his or her wages.

Control and costing of petrol sales

As with all other departments a Profit and Loss account must be made to ensure this part of the station is making adequate profits. There are a number of factors to be considered when making up the account. The cost of running this department would be made up as follows:

(1) rates and rent for building and land,
(2) electricity used for pumps and lighting,
(3) wages for all staff,
(4) purchase of petrol, oil accesories,
(5) advertising and printing costs,
(6) cost of trading stamps and gifts (if any),
(7) maintenance of pumps and buildings,
(8) evaporation losses of petrol (maximum = 0.5%).

On the credit side would be the sale of petrol, oil and accessories. Petrol profits are not high and great care and control must be exercised over the staff. For example, when the delivery of petrol takes place, the tanker should stand for 15 minutes before a dip reading is taken so that the fuel is not turbulent and giving a high reading resulting in a loss during delivery. The station tanks should be checked before and after delivery, the latter only after the petrol has settled in the tanks. Some tankers now have a metered system which can be checked. Besides the practice of checking actual delivery, the station tanks must be able to take the proposed load of petrol and the tanker driver will demand a signature to this effect—e.g. 'No. 1 tank 500 gallons'—hence the need to check the station tanks before delivery.

Actual delivery of fuel through the pumps can be checked daily by the meters. Each pump checked along with cash taken means a good control of all sales.

Where an account is at the petrol station, sales are recorded on an account form and total sales added up at the end of the month. A very useful account sheet available from Kalamazoo Ltd., and is shown in Fig. 6.1. Keeping these forms in alphabetical order in the office provides an accurate check of petrol, oil and accessories sales, along with the customer's signature. At the end of the month the second or duplicate copy is sent to the customer as a bill and payment is then made.

Self-service petrol stations

A fairly recent innovation has been customers serving themselves with petrol. This has certain advantages to the customer and the garage. For the garage it offers:
1. Reduction in staff
2. Increased custom, with increase in petrol, oil and accessory sales.
For the customer self-service offers:
1. Cheaper petrol in the form of trading stamps and gifts or some form of discount
2. Speedy service.
Self-service disadvantages for the station are nil unless, of course, initial training of customers to use the pumps to obtain correct octane and amount of fuel could be considered. For the customer, the smell of petrol on his hands, especially if he is going out and is not dressed for such work, having to get out of the car, complexity of instructions on pump operation, absence of friendly personal attention, are the price of cheaper fuel, increased speed. However, the general public have taken well to such stations and the layout of some of these is now described.

Layout of self-service petrol stations

This is best considered from the ergonomic point of view, a) the customer must fill his own tank, b) more than one customer may want to do so at once.

Petrol pumps can still be found standing very close together on conventional stations which means that access can be gained to one pump only, and, at the same time, the adjacent pump is rendered useless as another car cannot get

Invoice / Statement

Date (Tax Point)	Reg. No.	Fuel		Oil	@	Amount	Accessories	Amount	Signature
Kalamazoo BUSINESS SYSTEMS P-19Y-647121-96						(Tax inclusive)			Total £

SALE

The TOTAL is made up of | VAT £ | | Value £ |

Fig. 6.1 Customer's Petrol Account

near to it. This is illustrated in Fig. 6.2. Self-service stations have well set-out forecourts with access for a car on either side of a pump. A typical layout is shown in Fig. 6.3. Adequate room is allowed in each lane for cars to move along and obtain a flow of cars by having one direction only and not the confused situation of cars entering from both sides, creating blockages and a danger of accidents. Thus, with the pump islands spaced as shown along with one way traffic, a flow-line of petrol fill-up is obtained. With high density of traffic this type of station can be very profitable and, indeed, essential in some cases for the station to exist with the fierce competition in this field.

Whilst operating on the same principle, self-service stations now exist where the pump islands have been removed with the intention of reducing the possibility of accidents. It has been found that vehicle flow has increased by having overhead pump nozzles which are lowered electrically and can be lowered manually in the event of a power failure. The ground surrounding the nozzle area is clearly marked in coloured paint to indicate octane and grades of petrol. This type of arrangement has been very effective in other countries, Japan for example, has over 2 000 such installations.

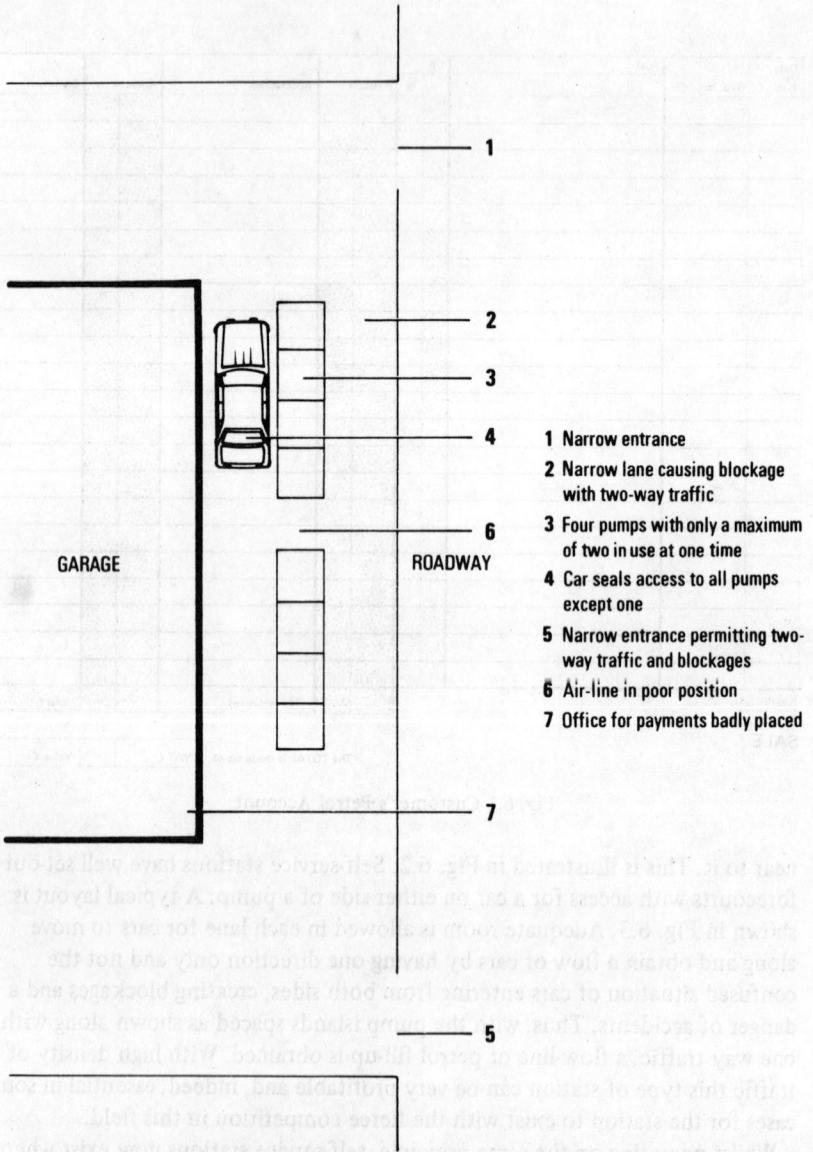

1 Narrow entrance

2 Narrow lane causing blockage with two-way traffic

3 Four pumps with only a maximum of two in use at one time

4 Car seals access to all pumps except one

5 Narrow entrance permitting two-way traffic and blockages

6 Air-line in poor position

7 Office for payments badly placed

Fig. 6.2 Poor Layout of a Petrol Station Forecourt

GOOD SELF-SERVICE PETROL LAYOUT

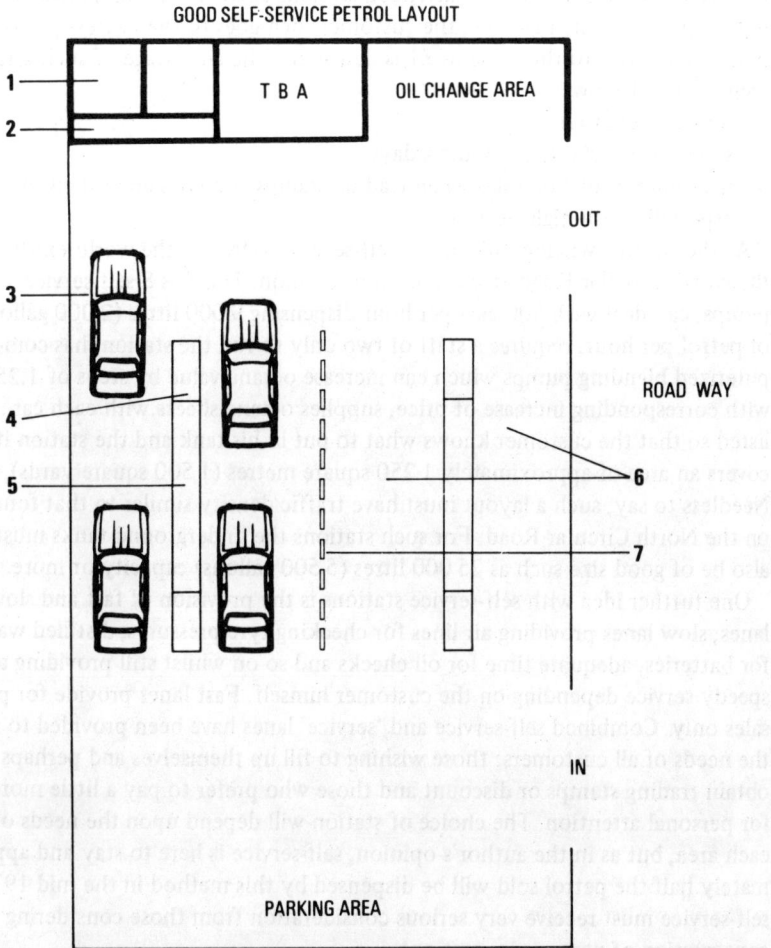

1 Office with master switch
2 Console to record gallonage and price
3 Cars with access to a single or double pump from either side
4 Blender pump to deliver up to 50 litres (11 gallons) per minute
5 Island holding central air line - accessible to all cars
6 Clear lanes at least 2 metres (6·56 feet) wide
7 Painted white line to indicate lane

One way traffic arrangement to speed flow and prevent blockages Petrol tanks with capacity
up to 55000 litres (2000 gallons) are encased in concrete below ground A canopy will normally
cover the filling up area Water for radiators and batteries will be available on the pump islands
T B A shop provides useful addition to profit of station Fire fighting apparatus should be placed
at points recommended by local fire station officer

Fig. 6.3 Layout of a Self-Service Petrol Station Forecourt

Unattended self-service stations have been installed throughout Britain. At the present time about 200 unattended stations exist. To obtain petrol, a £1 note is placed in the machine, the customer then goes to the nearest petrol pump and petrol to the value of £1 is delivered. The advantage of such arrangements are as follows:

1. no staff required,
2. service can operate 24 hours a day,
3. maximum profit on sales when trading stamps and gifts are not given—especially with night service.

At the time of writing, the largest self-service station in the world exists on the North Circular Road at Edmonton in London. This has 8 self-service pumps, can deal with 500 cars per hour dispensing 9 000 litres (2 000 gallons) of petrol per hour, requires a staff of two only to run the station, has computerized blending pumps which can increase octane value by steps of 1.25 with corresponding increase of price, supplies octane sheets with each car listed so that the customer knows what to put in his tank and the station itself covers an area of approximately 1 250 square metres (1 500 square yards). Needless to say, such a layout must have traffic density similar to that found on the North Circular Road. For such stations the underground tanks must also be of good size such as 25 000 litres (5 500 gallons) capacity or more.

One further idea with self-service stations is the provision of fast and slow lanes, slow lanes providing air lines for checking tyre pressures, distilled water for batteries, adequate time for oil checks and so on whilst still providing a speedy service depending on the customer himself. Fast lanes provide for petrol sales only. Combined self-service and 'service' lanes have been provided to meet the needs of all customers: those wishing to fill up themselves and perhaps obtain trading stamps or discount and those who prefer to pay a little more for personal attention. The choice of station will depend upon the needs of each area, but as in the author's opinion, self-service is here to stay and approximately half the petrol sold will be dispensed by this method in the mid 1970's, self-service must receive very serious consideration from those considering the construction of new service stations.

The law and the forecourt (See also Appendix IV)

It is not intended to detail the law affecting the forecourt, but as the running of a forecourt can be seriously affect by old and recent legislation, a brief survey of important aspects of the law must be considered.

Petroleum (Regulations Acts 1928 and 1936)

All managers must have a detailed knowledge of these regulations with up-to-date amendments, which can be obtained from H.M.S.O. Some special points from these regulations are as follows:

1. No petrol is to be served in containers other than steel cans painted red

and marked clearly with the word 'Petrol'.

2. A master switch inaccessible to the public should be provided in a suitable position so that supplies can be cut-off instantly.

3. No stop must be fitted on the nozzle which would enable the valve to be kept fully open without manual control.

4. Power connections to the pumps should be to the satisfaction of the local authorities and all metal enclosures to the pumps should be efficiently earthed.

5. Each pump should have a fuse or circuit breaker for its electrical circuit and such fuses or circuit breakers should be outside the pump-equipment housing.

6. The maximum delivery of petrol where the public have access should at one delivery not exceed 50 litres (11 gallons). Up to 136.5 litres (30 gallons) for one delivery is allowed on premises where the public have no access.

7. In normal installations, maximum pump delivery pressure should not exceed 0.206 N/mm^2 (30 lbf/in^2) and, where sight glasses are provided, these should be capable of withstanding a hydrostatic pressure of 0.512 N/m (75 lbf/in^2).

8. Enclosure of pump motors should be flameproof, likewise all switches and relays.

9. Lighting fittings mounted on the outside of pumps should be sealed to prevent the ingress of petrol vapour.

10. All cables should be enclosed in heavy gauge galvanized solid drawn steel conduit and all joints treated to prevent ingress of water.

11. A 'no smoking' sign, to conform with the petroleum regulation requirements for size and colour, should be prominently displayed.

12. Staff should not wear steel-tipped shoes or boots.

13. Adequate fire-fighting apparatus must be available on site and be approved by the local fire station officer. Local licensing authorities have their own local requirements and they should be consulted for advice and for details of any local restrictions. For example, it is illegal in some areas for tankers to discharge their load whilst parked under the canopy of the station. As stated previously, tanker drivers must also get a certificate signed before they discharge their load, stating that the tank can take the load they are about to deliver. All managers should have a copy of the petroleum regulations and be conversant with local requirements of the licensing authority.

Weights and Measures Act (1963)

Each pump is inspected periodically by local officers from the weights and measures department of the local council. Pumps are checked for delivery and duly sealed by the officers. Interference with such seals will result in prosecution. The Measuring Instruments (Liquid Fuel and Lubricants) Regulations 1979 state that with brand new pumps delivery of 2 or more litres have to be accurate to ± 0.5%. Once used, pumps have then got to be accurate to ± 1% of indicated minimum delivery. This came into effect from 1st March 1980. With the imperial gallon on older pumps delivery must be within −0.3% to +1.25%. The current regulations gives full details on all measures.

Trade Descriptions Act (1968)

This Act deals with the honesty of a trader. Any advertisement or offer of sale or service must be strictly correct. If not, prosecution could result. For example, if a certain oil is offered at 20p per 5 litres (9 pints) below retail price, then it must be exactly 20p below the price. Very careful scrutiny of all advertising must be made to ensure it is a true and honest statement.

Town and Country Planning Act (Control of Advertisements amendment 1970)

Hitherto, advertisements on forecourts has been virtually unrestricted. In many cases the result has been a tendency towards garish and distasteful forecourt frontages. The control of advertisements has now been made a legal requirement and this Act generally deals basically with taste. Restriction on size and quantity of advertising is now controlled by local council officers who will advise on the advertising permissible for any forecourt area.

A voluntary agreement had been arranged between the M.A.A. and the Office of Fair Trading in connection with advertising on forecourts. A leaflet was available from these organizations which explained how the agreement should be implemented. Briefly this was as follows (see also Appendix IV):

1. Price reduction claims
1(a) When petrol is promoted by a claim that its selling price has been reduced or is less than the posted pump price, the following price information should be displayed so as to be clearly visible to the motorist from inside the car before entering the forecourt: either
   (i) the price per gallon payable by the cash customer, taking account of any reduction claimed; or
   (ii) the higher price per gallon from which the reduction is claimed.
(b) The nature of whichever of these two prices is displayed should be made clear and the information should be given for the following grades:
   (i) four star grade (whether or not it is covered by any claimed price reduction); and
   (ii) if the reduction claim covers other grades, at least one of these grades.
(c) Where the price reduction depends on buying a minimum quantity, this should be made clear both in the wording of the claim and adjacent to the above price information.

(d) This information should also be given when the motorist is offered a choice between a price reduction and some other promotional offer.

2. Displays of prices or promotional offers

In displays of petrol prices or promotional offers:

(a) The price or promotional offer should be clearly and prominently stated.

(b) Any figures used should be clear, and any fractional figures and decimals should not be less than half the size of the main figures.

(c) Any restrictions, e.g. about the method of payment, or the purchase of complete gallons or a minimum quantity, should be unambiguous and prominently displayed.

(d) Indications of a minimum price for petrol (e.g. 'from x p') should be accompanied by a clear and prominent indication of the grade (or grades) to which the minimum price relates.

3. Planning considerations

The implementation of the above provisions shall be subject to the Regulations on Control of Advertisements and any other central or local government controls relevant to the display of the material in question.

As many retailers did not respond to this voluntary code, legislation was introduced in mid-1977 to enforce it. Consequently it is now illegal to advertise in other ways than that required by the law. The legislation also includes grades of petrol other than four-star grade. Students should obtain a current copy of the 1977 law. Failure to observe the law can be very costly, e.g. fines up to £400. See also Appendix IV.

Much more detailed information in connection with advertising can be obtained from the Advertising Authority, 15-17, Ridgmount Street. London WC1E 7AW. The A.S.A. has a Code of Practice which seeks to ensure that advertisements don't mislead or offend. Complaints referred to the A.S.A. will be investigated. The voluntary code applied to press, posters, or any other printed advertising matter. The Office of Fair Trading have issued a small booklet entitled *Fair Deal* and readers are strongly advised to obtain a copy as it details many legal Acts which protect the consumer.

To conclude this chapter it is essential to remember that many petrol stations are owned by major oil and petrol companies. A great deal of useful advice can be obtained from the oil companies when considering all aspects of forecourt design and management.

Having read the theory of operation of a forecourt, students would assist themselves a great deal by visiting a successful station by arrangement with the proprietors to find out how theory is put into practice. Before the visit a student could make out a questionnaire similar to the following:

1. Detail the checks made by the weights and measures departments when they visit this station.

2. Itemize the costs of running a petrol station.
3. The Petroleum Regulations govern the sale of petrol. List the regulations which this station consider imperative.
4. What gallonage will each pump give at one operation and how many octanes are available?
5. Detail the normal running of a petrol station on a day for day basis. What checks are made on petrol sales and how are shifts arranged?
6. Sketch a layout of the station indicating distances between pumps and lanes and state why this layout was chosen.
7. Name ten accessories sold at this forecourt and state which items have the most rapid turnover.

Before a visit is made to any forecourt a review of the text is important. The legislation indicated in the text should be noted. Changing laws do affect retailing of petrol. One example is the Petroleum Spirit (Plastic Containers) Regulations which came into force on June 4th 1982. This regulation permitted storing and selling of petrol in plastic containers with a nominal capacity not exceeding 5 litres. Such containers however must comply to SI 1982/630 and this must be marked on the vessel along with the words 'Petrol–highly flammable!'. Only 2 containers should be kept for private use.

The licence to trade with petroleum spirit is given by the local fire officer under the Petroleum (Consolidation) Act 1982.

It is possible the Health and Safety Executive will become involved with site installations in the future.

Obviously a manager who does not keep abreast of such changes can easily create serious problems for a dealership.

Questions

1. Assume petrol sales have slumped in your garage.
   (a) Give possible reasons for this.
   (b) List possible ideas to attract custom. (I.M.I.)
2. 'Self-service' petrol stations have become a reality. Explain, with the aid of a sketch, how a self service petrol station is arranged and list the advantages of such a station over a conventional petrol station. (I.M.I.)
3. Detail the costs of running a petrol station and explain in detail how petrol costs can be controlled. (I.M.I.)
4. The Petroleum (Regulations) Acts closely govern the dispensing of petrol. Name 6 important parts of the regulations and state how you would ensure each of these was carried out. (I.M.I.)
5. List the basic knowledge which every forecourt attendant needs to know and state how you would ensure he was efficient at his job. (I.M.I.)
6. Cash and Credit are part of Petrol Sales. Explain how you would control each of these arrangements. (I.M.I.)
7. Name four important legal acts which govern the sales on a petrol forecourt. Briefly describe how each act can affect the forecourt and how you would ensure you were operating within the law in each case. (I.M.I.)

CHAPTER 7

VEHICLE SALES

New and used car sales

All departments add to the profitability of the service station. Car sales are very important. As with other sections, the car sales section must be run efficiently. Salesmen must be well trained and R.T.I.T.B. recommend 380 Basic M.V. course followed by 382 Vehicle Salesmanship course. A young man would start his career in the Car Sales office learning about the following documentation involved.

(a) Hire purchase agreements and arrangements, warranties, used vehicle guarantees, service voucher books, vehicle licence forms, insurance certificates, D.Tp. certificates, refund applications, Hire Purchase Information checks—re outstanding finance on 'trade in' cars, invoicing, allocation of registration numbers, self-drive hire facilities and procedures, contract hire, and letter writing.

(b) Purchase, control, and sale of new and used vehicles. New cars through manufacturers create few problems. Purchase of used cars require an excellent knowledge of car operation. Glass's guide is a guide only. A test run of all used cars with critical analysis of mechanical work and bodywork required plus upholstery, etc. can determine a final allowance for a 'trade in' price. The number of vehicles on the premises at any one time depends upon:

(i) size of storage space,

(ii) capital available,

(iii) types of vehicles sold, e.g. if 20% of sales represent a certain make then a balance of 20% of that particular make should be aimed for at all times.

The MAA New Car Order Form is shown in Figs. 7.1 and 7.2 and has been designed to ensure the sale of Goods (Implied Terms) Act 1973 has not been infringed. The Department of Trade and Industry issue a very useful free leaflet about the 1973 Act. Also see Appendix IV and pages 176–180.

(c) Glass's Guide issued every month details the value of all vehicles on a minimum and maximum basis. An annual charge is made for a comprehensive guide with subsequent issues at a reduced price. Note: Two guides are issued one to give values, the other to give registration numbers, chassis numbers, etc. along with dates issued.

NEW CAR ORDER FORM

(Revised March 1973)

TRADE DESCRIPTIONS ACT 1968
This Order Form may be used only by members of the Motor Agents' Association or the Scottish Motor Trade Association. Use by non-members of these Associations is a contravention of Section 14 (1) of the Trade Descriptions Act 1968, and, as such, makes unauthorised use of the forms liable to action by the Weights and Measures Inspectorate under the above Act.

Copyright of the Motor Agents Association Ltd.

FOR OFFICE USE ONLY

Chassis No.	
Engine No.	
Registration No.	
Invoice No.	
Salesman	
Passed by	

To ....

(hereinafter described as the "Seller")

I/We hereby agree to purchase from you SUBJECT TO THE TERMS AND CONDITIONS HEREOF (including those printed overleaf) the undermentioned vehicle, extras and accessories, hereinafter called the goods:

		£ p	£ p	VAT £ p
DESCRIPTION OF VEHICLE	Upholstery			
Make	Type			
Colour	PRICE			
MANUFACTURERS' OPTIONAL EXTRAS fitted ex works				
	CAR TAX* *(or purchase tax if applicable)*			
ACCESSORIES fitted subsequently				
	Number Plates			
	Delivery Charge			
TAX FREE EXTRAS	Insurance			
Licence: From .... to				
PLACE OF DELIVERY				
ESTIMATED DELIVERY DATE	VAT brought down			
DEDUCT: Allowance (Subject to Condition 8) for Used Motor Vehicle which I/We certify conforms to the following description:	TOTAL CASH PRICE			
Make .... c.c.	Type			
Type of Body	Registered No.			
Chassis No.	Engine No.			
Date first registered	Date of last M.O.T. Test			
Licensed to	Recorded Mileage			
	DEDUCT: Allowance			
Is the Part Exchange Vehicle subject to a Hire Purchase Agreement, or other encumbrance? YES/NO				
If YES, state name of Hire Purchase Company:	ADD: Hire Purchase Balance outstanding (if any) under condition 8 (a)(ii) as notified by H.P. Co. concerned			
NOTE. *This final balance should be completed only when settlement figure, if any, is known.* ▶	FINAL BALANCE			

This document contains the terms of a contract. Sign it only if you wish to be legally bound by them.

I/WE AGREE to deposit the sum of £ .... forthwith and to pay the balance (see clause 10) as soon as the goods have been completed for delivery and notification thereof given to me/us by post at the following address

....

I certify that I am 18 years of age or over (where the Purchaser is an individual)

Signature .... Date ....

IN FULL AND IN BLOCK LETTERS

Name of purchaser ....
Address ....

I/We accept and confirm the above order and undertake to supply the said goods upon and subject to the terms and conditions referred to herein.

Signature of seller ....

Date ....

Fig. 7.1 New car order form

1 — This order and any allowance in respect of a used motor vehicle offered by the Purchaser are subject to acceptance and confirmation in writing by the Seller.

2 (a) — The Seller will endeavour to secure delivery of the goods by the estimated delivery date (if any) but does not guarantee the time of delivery and shall not be liable for any damages or claims of any kind in respect of delay in delivery. (The Seller shall not be obliged to fulfil orders in the sequence in which they are placed.)

(b) — If the Seller shall fail to deliver the goods within 21 days of the estimated date of delivery stated in this contract the Purchaser may by notice in writing to the Seller require delivery of the goods within 7 days of receipt of such notice. If the goods shall not be delivered to the Purchaser within the said 7 days the contract shall be cancelled.

3 — If the goods to be supplied by the Seller are new, the following provisions shall have effect:

(a) — this agreement and the delivery of the goods shall be subject to any terms and conditions which the Manufacturer or Concessionaire may from time to time lawfully attach to the supply of the goods or the re-sale of such goods by the Seller, and the Seller shall not be liable for any failure to deliver the goods occasioned by his inability to obtain them from the Manufacturer or Concessionaire or by his compliance with such terms or conditions. A copy of the terms and conditions currently so attached by the Manufacturer or Concessionaire may be inspected at the Seller's Office;

(b) — the Seller undertakes that he will ensure that the pre-delivery work specified by the Manufacturer or Concessionaire is performed and that he will use his best endeavours to obtain for the Purchaser from the Manufacturer or Concessionaire the benefit of any warranty or guarantee given by him to the Seller or to the Purchaser in respect of the goods;

(c) — notwithstanding the sum for Car Tax specified in the order, the sum payable by the purchaser in respect thereof shall be such sum as the seller has legally had to pay or becomes legally bound to pay for Car Tax in respect of the goods and notwithstanding also the sum for Value Added Tax specified in the order, the sum payable by the purchaser in respect thereof shall be such sum as the seller becomes legally liable for at the time the taxable supply occurs;

(d) — if after the date of this order and before delivery of the goods to the Purchaser the Manufacturer's or Concessionaire's recommended price for any of the goods shall be altered, the Seller shall give notice of any such alteration to the Purchaser, and

(i) — in the event of the Manufacturer's or Concessionaire's recommended price for the goods being increased the amount of such increase which the Seller intends to pass to the Purchaser shall be notified to the Purchaser. The Purchaser shall have the right to cancel the contract within 14 days of the receipt of such notice. If the Purchaser does not give such notice as aforesaid the increase in price shall be added to and become part of the contract price;

(ii) — in the event of the recommended price being reduced the amount of such reduction, if any, which the Seller intends to allow to the Purchaser shall be notified to the Purchaser. If the amount allowed is not the same as the reduction of the recommended price the Purchaser shall have the right to cancel the contract within 14 days of the receipt of such notice;

(e) — in the event of the Manufacturer of the goods described in the order ceasing to make goods of that type, the Seller may (whether the estimated delivery date has arrived or not) by notice in writing to the Purchaser, cancel the contract.

4 — If the contract be cancelled under the provisions of clauses 2 or 3 hereof the deposit shall be returned to the Purchaser and the Seller shall be under no further liability.

5 — If the Purchaser shall fail to take and pay for the goods within 14 days of notification that the goods have been completed for delivery, the Seller shall be at liberty to treat the contract as repudiated by the Purchaser and thereupon the deposit shall be forfeited without prejudice to the Seller's right to recover from the Purchaser by way of damages any loss or expense which the Seller may suffer or incur by reason of the Purchaser's default.

6 — The goods shall remain the property of the Seller until the price has been discharged in full. A cheque given by the Purchaser in payment shall not be treated as a discharge until the same has been cleared.

7 — Where the Seller agrees to allow part of the price of the goods to be discharged by the Purchaser delivering a used motor vehicle to the Seller, such allowance is hereby agreed to be given and received and such used vehicle is hereby agreed to be delivered and accepted, as part of the sale and purchase of the goods and upon the following further conditions:

(a) (i) — that such used vehicle is the absolute property of the Purchaser and is free from all encumbrances;

or (ii) — that such used vehicle is the subject of a hire purchase agreement or other emcumbrance capable of cash settlement by the Seller, in which case the allowance shall be reduced by the amount required to be paid by the Seller in settlement thereof;

(b) — that if the Seller has examined the said used vehicle prior to his confirmation and acceptance of this order, the said used vehicle shall be delivered to him in the same condition as at the date of such examination (fair wear and tear excepted);

(c) — that such used vehicle shall be delivered to the Seller on or before delivery of the goods to be supplied by him hereunder, and the property in the said used vehicle shall thereupon pass to the Seller absolutely;

(d) — that without prejudice to (c) above such used vehicle shall be delivered to the Seller within 14 days of notification to the Purchaser that the goods to be supplied by the Seller have been completed for delivery;

(e) — that if the goods to be delivered by the Seller through no default on the part of the Seller shall not be delivered to the Purchaser within 30 days after the date of this order or the estimated delivery date, where that is later, the allowance on the said used vehicle shall be subject to reduction by an amount not exceeding 2½% for each completed period of 30 days from the date of the expiry of the first mentioned 30 days, to the date of delivery to the Purchaser of the goods.

In the event of the non-fulfilment of any of the foregoing conditions, other than (e) the Seller shall be discharged from any obligation to accept the said used vehicle or to make any allowance in respect thereof, and the Purchaser shall discharge in cash the full price of the goods to be supplied by the Seller.

8 — Any notice given hereunder must be in writing and sent by post to the residence or place of business of the person to whom it is addressed and shall be deemed to have been received in due course of post.

9 — Notwithstanding the provisions of this agreement the Purchaser shall be at liberty before the expiry of 7 days after notification to him that the goods have been completed for delivery to arrange for a finance company to purchase the goods from the Seller at the price payable hereunder. Upon the purchase of the goods by such finance company, the preceding clauses of this agreement shall cease to have effect, but any used vehicle for which an allowance was thereunder agreed to be made to the Purchaser shall be bought by the Seller at a price equal to such allowance, upon the conditions set forth in clause 8 above (save that in (c), (d) and (e) thereof all references to "delivery" or "delivered" in relation to "the goods" shall be construed as meaning delivery or delivered by the Seller to or to the order of the finance company) and the Seller shall be accountable to the finance company on behalf of the Purchaser for the said price and any deposit paid by him under this agreement.

KAP 1180 4/73

Fig. 7.2 New car order form: terms and conditions

The address for these guides is Glass's Guide Service Ltd., Elgin House, St. George's Ave., Weybridge, Surrey, KT13 0BX. Guides are only sold to motor traders.

(d)   Sales promotions. As with other sections the AIDA principle is required, likewise assessment of promotions when they are concluded. How promotions are arranged, i.e. at the correct time, etc. can have a large bearing upon their success. A salesman needs to know how these are planned and put into operation. With an objective in view some salemen tend to give inflated trade-in prices. This and other factors have to be guarded against.

(e)   Sales campaigns can last 2 to 8 weeks, depending on manufacturers. Various promotional aids can be given, e.g. raffle of a car, free gifts, etc. but the cost must be more than covered by increased profit.

(f)   Buying motives include (1) investment, (2) prestige value of new car, (3) pride of possession, (4) business transaction. Students will be able to list others. A customer will have one buying motive when he enters the showroom. The salesman needs to listen carefully to a customer to determine what the customer has in mind and encourage this by a careful, polite but firm approach. By assessing a customer's requirements by allowing him to converse freely an efficient salesman can direct the customer to the car most suitable and clinch a sale.

(g)   Product knowledge is vital. Speeds of vehicles, acceleration, seating, miles per gallon (km/litre), etc. of cars and commercials he is selling should be at the tips of a salesman's fingers. On the job training and manufacturers' courses all help towards this end. Availability of material in products sold is part of a salesman's general training. A sale is easily lost if a salesman is unable to give comprehensive coverage of the products he is selling. This applies to all aspects of selling such as parts merchandising.

(h)   Prospecting and follow-up schemes. General circulars can be used for car sales. Visits to large fleet operators can be made. Enquiries from all sources can be followed up by letter or telephone. A personal visit can be very useful. Sales records, service records, are all useful lists of prospective customers. Daily prospect calls/letters, new business, demonstration of vehicles, all form part of the daily routine of a car salesman.

(i)   *Sequence of a sale. This is completed as follows*:
   (1) Customer requests demonstration of car performance.
   (2) Approval of car—'Trade in' to be arranged or cash.
   (3) If 'trade-in' then salesman takes the car for a test run along with the customer and determines what needs to be done to put the car in good condition. An 'appraisal form' includes bodywork, paintwork, underbody, boot interior, chrome, interior trim, carpets. Mechanical appraisal includes engine, clutch, transmission, brakes, steering,

suspension, exhaust, oil leaks. Also checked will be battery, starter, wipers and lights as well as all tyres so that cost of all repairs can be achieved. See Fig. 7.3

(4) Trade in allowance approved or cash sale, invoice is made out and hire purchase agreement (if required).

PART EXCHANGE VEHICLE APPRAISAL FORM

CUSTOMER'S NAME	ADDRESS	Tel.No Home Business
MAKE MODEL 2 dr. 4 dr. E/Car Conv. Sports Std./D.L./Super Auto / Manual/ O'D	Reg.No. 1 st Reg Tax Expires D.O.E. Expires	No. of Owners Colours Speedo Chassis No. Engine No.
Accessories fitted		

	ITEM	Good	Fair	Poor	REMARKS	£	p	HIRE PURCHASE
BODY	BODY REPAIR PAINTWORK UNDERBODY BOOT INTERIOR CHROME INTERIOR TRIM CARPETS							Is vehicle subject of H.P. Agreement or other encumbrance ? YES/NO If so with whom ?
MECHANICAL	ENGINE CLUTCH TRANSMISSION BRAKES STEERING SUSPENSION EXHAUST COOLING OIL LEAKS							FOR OFFICE USE Date in stock W/D Value W/S Est. Condition cost
ELECTRICAL	BATTERY STARTER WIPERS LIGHTS							Retail - Trade Actual condition cost Intended retail price
	TYRES	O.S.F.	O.S.R.	SPARE	N.S.R.	N.S.F.		Date sold
	SALESMANS ASSESED COST							
	NET PART EXCHANGE ALLOWANCE							

OTHER NOTES

Fig. 7.3 Part exchange vehicle appraisal form. Variations to this form can be made to suit commercial vehicle trade-in appraisal.

Stock Register - VAT Used Car Scheme

Purchases

1 Stock Number	2 Date of Purchase	3 Purchase Invoice Number	4 Suppliers Name & Address & VAT Number (if any)	5 Vehicle Registration Number	6 Vehicle Make, Model & Type	7 Chassis Number	8 Engine Number	9 Month/Year 1st Reg'd in U.K.	10 Name & Address of last Registered owner in Log Book - if different from 4	11 Last Licensing Authority	12 Date of Sale	13 Sales Invoice Number
												1
												2
												3
												4
												5
												6
												7
												8

Columns 12 and 13 fall under the **Sales** heading.

Fig. 7.4 Stock register: purchases.

Sales		Accounts						Period Ending		Period Ending		Period Ending		Period Ending				
14	15	16	17	18	19	20	21	20	21	20	21	20	21	22	23	24		
Name & Address of Purchaser	Details of any change to 7 & 8	Purchase Price After deducting Refund on Licence	Selling Price or method of disposal	Taxable Margin on Sale	Tax Rate at date of sale	VAT	VALUE Selling Price less VAT (17-20)	VAT	VALUE Selling Price less VAT (17-20)	VAT	VALUE Selling Price less VAT (17-20)	VAT	VALUE Selling Price less VAT (17-20)					
Brought Forward																		
1																		
2																		
3																		
4																		
5																		
6																		
7																		
8																		
Carried Forward																		

Fig. 7.5 Stock register: sales.

VEHICLE SALES INVOICE

Invoice to

Deliver to

Make	Model	Body Colour	Reg. No.	Invoice Date (Tax Point)
Chassis No.	Engine No.	Date of Reg.	Key No.	Stock No.

VEHICLE, SPECIAL BODYWORK & FITTED ACCESSORIES	Amount

	Rate	VAT	
Car Tax			
Total Vehicle & Accessories			
Delivery Charges			
Insurance - Through			
Road Fund Licence for Months			
Petrol			
Total Value Added Tax			
Total Sale Price			
Deduct: Trade-In Allowance Price			
Sub Total			
Add: Outstanding Hire Purchase to			
Total Payment due			
Made up of: Amount due from H.P. Company			
Your previous Deposit			
Leaving a net Balance due from you of			

Details of Vehicle traded in

Make	Model	Body Colour	Reg. No.	Stock No.	
Chassis No.	Engine No.	Date of Reg.	Mileage	Key No.	

SALE

Fig. 7.6 Vehicle sales invoice

(1) CERTIFICATES TO BE COMPLETED UPON THE TRADE-IN OF A USED MOTOR CAR

(A)   TO BE SIGNED BY THE VENDOR OF A TRADE-IN MOTOR CAR

I Certify that the information given overleaf relating to motor car
Registration Number   is to the best of my knowledge and belief correct and I
am the seller of the vehicle at the price stated.

Signature _____   Date_____

Address
        _____

        _____

(B)   TO BE SIGNED BY THE DEALER PURCHASING A TRADE-IN MOTOR CAR

I Certify that I am the Purchaser of motor car Registration Number
detailed overleaf at the price stated.

Signature _____   Date_____

(2) CERTIFICATES TO BE COMPLETED UPON THE SALE OF A USED MOTOR CAR

(C)   TO BE SIGNED BY THE CUSTOMER PURCHASING A USED MOTOR CAR

I Certify that I am the Purchaser of motor car Registration Number
detailed overleaf at the price stated.

Signature _____   Date_____

Address
        _____

        _____

        _____

(D)   TO BE SIGNED BY THE DEALER SELLING A USED MOTOR CAR

I Certify that I am the vendor of motor car Registration Number
detailed overleaf and that input tax deduction has not been and will not be
claimed by me in respect of the car sold on this invoice.

Signature _____   Date_____

Fig. 7.7 Vehicle sales invoice

(5) Paperwork, i.e. excise licence, insurance, test certificates, warranty, etc. are obtained.

(6) When finance is cleared, vehicle is delivered to customer and customer signs for the vehicle.
Note: Courtesy items such as mats, car key rings are usually given to the customer. Before leaving, a customer should be introduced to the Service Receptionist and Service Manager to encourage service work at the station and for correction of any faults should these arise.

A stock register for Used Car Sales is illustrated in Figs 7.4 and 7.5 and a Vehicle Sales Invoice in Figs 7.6 and 7.7.

The basic considerations of salesmanship

To sell is the most important personal requirement of a salesman. To sell his product he must, however, have confidence in the product and know he is offering for sale a useful item. Each member of the public buys a new car at very infrequent intervals. Whilst the salesman sells 2—3 cars a week he can easily become blasé about the job and forget that each and every customer needs to feel he is important. Thus, a customer entering the salesroom should be allowed to browse amongst the cars with the salesman close by as soon as the customer needs him.

A salesman needs to have a number of very important personal characteristics and these are given on the following page. Using these characteristics to his advantage he can.achieve better sales, which is what his job is all about. A salesman must first sell himself to the customer if he is to be successful.

Personal qualities of the salesman

1. Good basic education—'O' levels in English, Mathematics, Geography and similar subjects or C.S.E equivalents.
2. Good response to training and new ideas.
3. Pleasing personality.
4. Smart appearance.
5. Ability to sell.
6. Punctual (for all appointments).
7. Confident and cheerful.
8. Well spoken.
9. Have persuasive nature.

With the above, a good training programme will produce a first class salesman and more profits. By following R.T.I.T.B. recommended training and completing a suitable course on Vehicle Salesmanship, a car salesman will be fully prepared for his job. See page 93 regarding Car Sales Managers which also applies to Commercial Vehicle Sales Managers.

Overheads, operating costs, and profitability

As with other departments, overheads comprise salaries, wages, lighting, advertising, paperwork, rectification of faults on P.D.I., correction of used cars (guarantee 3 months) prior to sale, maintenance of building including cleaning, rent, rates, training—personnel, vehicle running costs for each salesman, stock maintenance, storage and collection expenses. A Budget Control sheet should be complied in a similar way to Fig. 2.7, but detailing sales targets or 'forecasted' costs relevant to the Car Sales Department. As with other departments budgeting commences with a forecast of sales and then forecasting costs. Long Term Planning is usually over 2 years or more. Short Term Planning is usually on a 3, 6, or 12 month basis and this is broken down into monthly control periods and a budget control sheet (see Fig. 2.7) formulated. The advantages of budget control for all departments are: 1) recognition of targets which each department hopes to achieve, 2) policy, plans, and action taken are reflected in the budgetary control system, 3) all personnel are made aware of what is expected from them thus achieving a sound management principle, 4) deviations from the plans are quickly recognized and corrective action can be taken, 5) delegation of responsibilities is given positive recognition by preparation of departmental budgets i.e. service, car sales, parts, forecourt etc; 6) coordination is achieved by the interlocking of all the budgets by having a master budget compiled by a budget controller, e.g. company accountant, managing director etc.

With realistic forecasts and not pious hopes a reasonable estimate of profits from each department can be obtained. The Society of Motor Manufacturers and Traders and manufacturers prepare car and Commercial Vehicle Sales forecasts. With these figures and past experience a forecast of sales can be made. Daily costs can be calculated.

Typical questions used to help formulate a sales target or forecast are:
1) What have I got in stock?
2) What have I sold in x months?
3) What am I likely to sell in the immediate future?
4) What seasonal fluctuations are going to affect sales?
5) What new lines shoud I be stocking?
6) What old lines should I stop stocking?
7) What do the trade organizations and manufacturers recommend in their last forecasts?

Buying for the future targets can be influenced by past performances but it must not dictate the future because of the changing nature of all motor vehicles, parts, and accessories. Obviously all goods must be available for selling at the right time. Salesmanship has been defined as the art of presenting merchandise in an effective manner. Product knowledge, common courtesy, enthusiasm and a cheerful disposition account of half a successful salesman whilst the remainder is having the ability to see a customers' viewpoint along with satisfaction in obtaining an order. Thus service receptionists, partsmen, and vehicle salesmen need these requirements if they are to be successful in their jobs and create profits from sales.

Profits accrue from car sales, the margin on new cars being determined by the manufacturer, usually about 10% of actual purchase price. Around 20% on the sale of used cars should be the aimed profit margin, although 10% is average obtained. Glass's guide is useful for retail price when all repairs have been made. The appraisal form referred to previously would include cost of all repairs, profit required, and actual vehicle price. It will be obvious that 'trade in' vehicles sold directly to the trade will only realise a very small profit—up to 3%.

Layout and equipment of display area

As with all service station operations, a tastefully set out showroom can do much to impress a customer. Literature on new cars should be clearly visible, a centre attraction, e.g. new model, should be well positioned to highlight all its advantages, simple decoration, e.g. small sprays of flowers along with just audible background music all help to make a customer feel he is important and his car sale is important. Cleanliness of the showroom is vital and cleaners should be encouraged at all times to achieve the best possible appearances of cars. Within a car salesroom area an accounts office will be sited, car accessory display, toilet facilities, access to stores and service repair area.

Vehicle hire (See also Appendix IV)

The bulk of the new car market in the United Kingdom is dominated by the company car. In recent years fleet users and small companies have come to rely more and more on the use of cars owned not by themselves but by other people, such as main dealers. Success in vehicle rental depends upon certain key factors, e.g.

(1) The ability to buy and sell the hire cars at the most advantageous prices. Here a motor dealer has a clear advantage over the purely specialist rental operator.

(2) Having access to the right funding sources since the money to run the operation comes out of the profits.

(3) Achieving adequate utilization of the vehicles in the hire fleet. The target ought to be not less than 75 per cent. This means that an adequate marketing programme must be carried out. Overstocking should be avoided as there is no virtue in keeping vehicles in reserve waiting for the odd last-minute customer.

(4) Constructing the right tariff rate. There is no need to undercut major rental companies. A motor trader ought to be able to offer better cars than the major rental companies, and ones with higher standards of presentation in terms of fittings (radios and other accessories) and general upkeep. There are two ways in which costs can be recovered (a) on a mileage basis, and (b) on a time basis. It is customary to charge customers at a certain rate per mile or per hour, whichever is the greatest, with a minimum charge agreed. Daily and weekly rates can be established with longer periods also having fixed charge-out rates.

As with other departments all costs must be recouped. Depreciation, repairs, maintenance, and overheads must be calculated before a profit margin is added. Petrol and insurance charges also require consideration. Established local charge-out rates must be assessed before a price can be fixed for any vehicle. Chauffeur driven hires will require recouping of the driver's expenses, i.e. wages, insurance, and other items.

Car rental is an alternative to selling a car in the traditional manner. It ought to attract the dealer because it offers so much additional profit. Instead of the small percentage gained by selling the vehicle and handling the trade-in, he gathers the ongoing profits of petrol sales, of servicing, of renting out the vehicle, and of gaining a regular supply of good used cars—not to mention increasing his contact with potential car buyers.

Potential customers are available in most towns and cities and these can be summarized as follows:

(1) Companies which are tending to reduce the size of their fleet. Many have scrapped pool cars and reserve cars and prefer to hire when an overload situation occurs. More and more are switching to hire or lease as a standard procedure.
(2) Private motorists, who are relying more than ever on older used cars as their means of transport. So for special occasions (holidays, weddings, etc.) they need to be able to hire smart, reliable, new, showroom-condition cars.

A manager should list all the local companies who are likely to need to hire vehicles. A cold canvass can be made, which is easy for many dealers because there will already be contacts between salesmen and these companies. The objective is to keep the companies informed and reminded that, simply by picking up a telephone, they can have cars available for their use. They should be given copies of the tariff and regular follow-ups should be made.

Getting the message to private motorists requires no more than the techniques used to sell a car. In other words, regular advertising in the local press, circulars, and the operating of an adequate customer follow-up system.

Each vehicle in the hire fleet should be regarded as a demonstration car that is paid for by the customer instead of the trader having to provide it free. A good stock of both young and middle-aged good used cars similar to those operated in a hire fleet should be built up.

Each customer returning after his hire period should be given a thorough audit as to any prospects of his or her company buying a car, new or used. It should be mandatory that no returning hirer ever leaves the premises without being gently 'chatted up' by a salesman.

One advantage of the rental business is that it brings one closer to an appreciation of what matters in acquiring and running a vehicle: that it is not the amount of the original capital investment that determines the issue but the week by week running costs. Rental and leasing are attractive methods of keeping vehicles flowing through the franchise. They can cushion the sales resistance created by the price rises that have been forced upon the manufacturing industry. And in running the vehicles there is an extra profit to be added to the normal sales margin of a vehicle sales department.

As with other aspects of dealership operation, a salesman must know his vehicles and be able to advise all customers of their capabilities.

In the United Kingdom there is general agreement within the motor vehicle rental industry that a rental contract which includes services such as maintenance, relief vehicles, and road fund tax is called 'contract hire', whereas a rental contract which carries no services at all, apart from the basic finance of a vehicle, is called a 'lease'.

This is not really an adequate definition because there are also other considerations. Leasing can be defined more exactly, e.g.

1. A lease is usually for a much longer period than contract hire.
2. A lease usually depreciates the chattel down to nothing and then offers a secondary period of hire at a nominal rent.
3. A lease tends to cover large and varied equipment, with the responsibility for maintenance usually resting with the lessee.
4. In a lease there are usually clauses which enable the lessee to determine the lease at various stages.

So we are left with an accurate definition of medium- and long-term rental, in the motor vehicle industry, 'contract hire'. 'Contract hire' is a perfectly good description of rental business.

The British Vehicle Rental and Leasing Association was formed in 1967 to assist in the development of the vehicle rental leasing, chauffeur drive, and private hire industry. Currently (1983) it has over 600 members, ranging from the very small localized company operating a handful of vehicles to the large international companies operating four-figure fleets. B.V.R.L.A. members themselves operate a total fleet in the region of 150 000 vehicles, and approximately half of these are self-drive rental vehicles, the other half being employed on contract hire work. Some 75 per cent of the contract hire vehicles are cars, 15 per cent light vans and conversions, while the remainder fall into the heavy commercial vehicle, tractor, and trailer categories.

One of the main objectives of the B.V.R.L.A. is to assist its members by making representaitons to Government about legislation and controls which have an adverse effect, or are likely to have such an effect, on the business activities of the members.

Most dealerships providing car contract hire facilities are well aware that the business has to be conducted in accordance with the terms laid down in Statutory Instrument 1973 No 2130 entitled 'Hire Purchase, the Control of Hiring Order'. The fundamental provisions, as far as car contract hire is concerned, are first, that the lessor must take 42 weeks deposit in advance—and not just invoice the lesee and post the amount to a debit account, but be paid the deposit before releasing the vehicle—and, second, that the car may not at the termination of the contract be consigned to the lesee for a previously-arranged sum. A deposit is no longer required for cars acquired for business.

One of the major problems to be overcome by those companies in the vehicle contract hire industry is funding the business. The amount of capital required now to operate the same size fleet each year increases substantially, and there is no doubt that severe inflation affects most vehicle lessors. Large increases in vehicle service and overhead costs, coupled with the fact that used vehicles prices have not kept in step with new vehicle prices, tend to create additional difficulties.

It is vitally important that vehicle contract hire operators adopt a very professional approach to the business—the final profit (or loss) cannot be determined until the end of the contract when the vehicle is returned and disposed of. This is generally a two-year cycle, sometimes three-year. Real experience and the ability to calculate, with reasonable accuracy, vehicle depreciation, maintenance costs, and all the associated overhead costs, are essential. To assist with this professionalism the B.V.R.L.A. organizes seminars for the discussion of these problems and issues a magazine and bulletins for the benefit of its members.

The horse-and-cart days are certainly far behind us; but nevertheless the vehicle contract hire industry is still in its infancy, and both lessors and lessees are likely to experience many changes in the coming years, as the full advantages of contract hire become more widely known and accepted.

Driving instruction

Many dealerships now have their own driving schools. Qualified instructors must be employed to give a first-class service to customers. Current legislation governing driving schools must be known. Vehicles must conform to the Construction and Use Regulations (1978). Driving instructors must be registered with the Department of Transport.

A well planned driving instruction programme should be devised to ensure customer progress and satisfaction. The R.T.I.T.B. should be consulted for course details for staff who may be trained for such work. A pass in the Institute of Advanced Motorists examination is a good basis for driving instructors. Following success with the I.A.M., a driver should receive not less than 120 hours tuition in instructing. It is almost certain that this will become a legal requirement, i.e. instructors must have passed the Department of Transport Instructors Course before payment from learner drivers can be taken. Many school associations exist such as the Motor Schools Association and it can be useful for a dealership to be a member of one of them.

Customers coached to pass their tests are likely to become permanent customers. They can of course be coached to appreciate the value and economy of proper and regular servicing and repair work by recognized dealerships.

Heavy goods vehicle drivers should be encouraged to take the Young H.G.V. Drivers Further Education Certification examinations which the Royal Society of Arts now operate.

Questions

1. (a) State three important qualifications for a salesman (vehicles or parts).
   Which one do you consider to be the most important qualification and
   why?

   (b) State the headings only under which a publicity budget might be apportioned and explain one of these headings (C.G.L.I.).

2. List 4 buying motives and explain how a good salesman can promote
   custom using these motives. (IMI)

3. Name 3 methods of obtaining a 'prospect list' and explain how each of
   these is operated. (IMI)

4. Explain how to recruit and train a car salesman. (IMI)

5. (a) Name 6 essential documents used on car sales.

   (b) Why is Glass's guide a 'guide' only?—give some details.

   (c) Why is 'product knowledge' essential? (IMI)

6. Explain, with the aid of a line diagram, the sequence of a car sale. (IMI)

7. As used vehicle manager in a major distributorship holding a single franchise
   what steps would you take to secure a fast-moving and well-balanced stock
   of used vehicles on show, ready for sale? (I.M.I.)

8. (a) Who in your Dealership should determine next year's Service Department
   Budget?

   (b) What are the advantages of budgeting?

   (c) What are 'daily operating controls' and what information should they
   contain? With what criteria should this information be compared on a
   daily basis? (I.M.I.)

9. Outline the problems of organizing *one* of the following and state the
   advantages and disadvantages which you would expect from the point of
   view of the garage and its staff: Used Vehicle Autumn and Winter Sales,
   with special prizes; Spring Slogan Competitions, with Holiday Vouchers
   as prizes; Free Fault Assessment Weeks; Service Weeks; Summer
   Accessories Sales. (I.M.I.)

10. (a) In connection with vehicle hire, what are the key factors for success?

    (b) Explain how car hire rates can be established.

    (I.M.I.)

11. (a) What provisions for car contract hire are there in Statutory Instru-
    ment 1973 No. 2130 Hire Purchase, the Control of Hiring Order?

    (b) Explain the function of the British Vehicle Rental and Leasing
    Association (B.V.R.L.A.).

12. A managing director decides to investigate car/truck hire from his dealer-
    ship. Explain how this research could be conducted.

CHAPTER 8

PRINCIPLES OF MARKETING AND FORECASTING SALES

MARKETING WORKSHOP SERVICES

Selling workshop services has the same basic principles that apply to all selling, namely; co-ordination of the right goods, in the right place, at the right time, at the right price, for the right people. The Motor Agents Association have issued a voluntary Code of Practice for the motor industry which was drawn up in consultation with the Director General of Fair Trading. Students should obtain a copy of this code from the M.A.A. The Code lists eight areas where recommendations are applied: (1) new car sales, (2) car manufacturers' warranties, (3) used car sales, (4) replacement parts, accessories, and petrol, (5) repairs and servicing, (6) advertising, (7) handling complaints, and (8) monitoring of the Code. The Code of Practice was introduced in 1976 and will, no doubt, be amended as time goes on. It could become the basis for a legal document if traders do not conform voluntarily. In many countries it is illegal for mechanics and other personnel to complete certain work unless they are registered on a government panel. To be registered, evidence of training and education is required. Many traders in the United Kingdom would prefer this method of which would ensure that unscrupulous operators were phased out of business. However, any dealer who operates strictly to the existing code will have no difficulty selling his goods. Customers know where quality control is really applied and are willing to pay for good work. This is an essential part of marketing and is a promotion of a dealership in its own right. Customers will sell a dealership by telling friends and acquaintances when they get what they pay for in the way of service, repairs, new or used vehicles, and so on. Reference should be made to the customer satisfaction check list in Chapter 3.

However, it is necessary to look at marketing in some depth, and see how this can be applied so as to retain existing custom and obtain more.

Marketing

This can be described as the process of discovering a customer's needs up to the point when an actual sale can be made. It is also concerned with retaining the goodwill of existing customers to ensure repeat sales.

Marketing seeks to increase profits by identifying the needs of the customer and exploiting all available opportunities with the available resources of the company.

Marketing involves a number of factors. It is:

(a) a management function—all Departmental Managers are concerned with it in some way;

(b) the co-ordination of the activities of a dealership operation, i.e. selling, delivery, pricing, presentation, and so on;

(c) the assessment of sales potential and customer need;

(d) motivating customers so that they want to purchase the dealership's services and goods;

(e) ensuring the customers can obtain goods and services in the way that suits them best;

(f) the setting and achievement of specified targets such as x number of services, x sets of parts and vehicles, and x profits in a given period of time;

(g) really a definition of attitude within a business which demands total orientation towards the customer.

Market research

The basis of the marketing approach—orientated to the customer—requires a constant analysis and feedback of information from the market place. The Managing Director or Services Director must also monitor trends in the market, and be particularly aware of action taken by competitors. Such market research will assist the Manager in deciding how best to use the resources of his department, and it means that his decisions will be more accurate and scientific.

Research method

In order to increase knowledge of the national and local market, a Manager may build up the answers to a series of questions. Initially, he should look at two basic areas: competitors, and present and potential customers.

Competitors

Who is selling service work, supplying parts, etc., in his area?

Who is supplying service work, etc., and at what prices?

Who are the other main competitors?

What kind of service do they provide?

Have they got a more effective representative system?

Are they operating hours better suited to customer needs?

How are they advertising and promoting their operation?

Customers

Typical analytical questions might be:

Does he know who all his customers are—both cash and credit?
Who are the most valuable ones?
What is the turnover potential of all his customers?
How would they be likely to react to certain promotions?
Who are the main customers?
Do they operate in a particular area?

Techniques of research

Observation

Merely by looking at his competitors' facilities and premises objectively, and browsing through their catalogues, brochures, promotional literature, and discount tables (if available), a Manager will be able to make a fairly accurate assessment of their strengths and weaknesses, and compare them with his own.

Analysis

Use of customer sales records developed under a scientific system will ensure that all the necessary information is available for monitoring sales progress and trends. A store of information can be built up on the service engineering market, and this can become an invaluable basis for future plans, e.g. popular/unpopular services, services that certain customers tend to demand, representative calls per day, vehicle services sold per year, lost-sales records, and so on.

The total current level of trading with customers can be translated into a figure for potential trading by taking into account the following:

The manager's own knowledge of each customer's total business.

Vehicle mileage figures supplied by his Vehicle Sales/Marketing Manager for each customer and accounts over the years.

The ratio of competitive to captive service sales. Analysis of a sample of sales invoices—provided records are sophisticated enough—will provide a potential figure for each of your customers.

Canvassing

When representatives canvass traders, he should get them to find out from whom they are currently buying service work, etc., and establish reasons for this. The answers to these questions will be of great value when he is developing a market platform.

Questioning

If traders and customers are asked for their views, they will generally all be willing to provide suggestions and criticisms if they understand that this will eventually lead to their receiving even better service. They may even be prepared to tell the manager about the service and discounts provided by competitors. Representatives and salesmen of the dealership should not be neglected, and will probably have views on the opinions and needs of present and future customers.

If a survey of customers in a locality is considered, the Market Research Department of the Motor Agents Association, Road Haulage Association, and Freight Transport Association, will be very willing to provide advice and assistance on sample size, questionnaire design, and the use of outside research agencies.

Sales analysis

Sales analysis is important because, on the basis of features and trends obtained from such studies, performance can be examined critically and forecasts made which will guide future action towards success.

Calculating potential and penetration

One use of sales analysis is in the examination of the service/parts/vehicle selling potential, and in the identification of the penetration of the local market.

Many areas form themselves into 'natural catchment areas'. These are normally towns and the surrounding rural areas for which they act as shopping or business centres.

In complex urban areas, a useful starting point is the area into which a significant amount of wholesaling and retailing is done. Local knowledge should be used to conclude whether the area is a reasonable one in which to assess performance, by estimating the strength of competitors in that area and the degree to which they encroach on the activities of a dealership.

The customer sales analysis

The primary benefit from the customer sales analysis is that sales performance and penetration can be monitored and up-dated on a monthly basis. Deteriorating service/sales performance can be identified, and the effects of campaign activity readily assessed. It also enables a comparison of a target achievement with the average achievement of an area and the U.K. as a whole.

Consequently the customers sales analysis can be used:
(1) to highlight services which are below sales target, by comparison between actual and target sales;
(2) to monitor progress towards higher sales and profitability as monthly purchases are adjusted;
(3) to illustrate the profitability of the current operating pattern.

The need for sales forecasting

Service/sales forecasting is important for planning the specific and general direction of a department's operation. It is a vital link between previous and current trends and the creation of the marketing plans and approach.

Some of the many factors which affect service/sales marketing, and which should be quantified where possible are:

(1)   a change in vehicle operations, e.g. inflation i.e. increased petrol costs, lesser mileage;

(2)   trends in competition—wholesale and retail;

(3)   the growth of Operators Licensing and the growth of specialist vehicle loads, e.g. refrigerated containers and their servicing requirements;

(4)   the increase in customer's operating power, e.g. implementation of T.I.R., i.e. international transport operations and services requirements.

From such analysis, decisions on facilities (location, size, etc.) and on marketing tactics (pricing, etc.) can be made. Forecasting will also help management to make decisions on subjects like stock-holding commitments, purchasing, work-load problems, and product sales campaigns. Good sales forecasting is a prerequisite of good budget preparation.

Techniques available

A useful aid in forecasting sales, especially when seasonal variations occur, is the analysis and presentation of 'time series'. This involves plotting or analysing sales revenues or costs, etc., against time (usually weeks or months). Trends and cyclical variations, such as preparation for winter, will be apparent and, if these can be actually quantified along with 'non-recurring' influences like special promotions, Christmas breaks, etc., then a valuable forecast can be made.

Not all variations can be accounted for by known factors, and therefore there is bound to be some inaccuracy in the forecasts. The forecasts can be improved if some form of averaging is used to even out fluctuations. In some cases a three-month moving total or average can be used to show up trends that would otherwise be hidden by random variations. A three-month saving total is one where the figures for the 'oldest' month are replaced by the figures for the 'new' month when they become available. The moving average is simply the moving total divided by the number of months included.

In order to iron out seasonal variations, a moving annual total or average can be calculated. Here the values, totalled and averaged, cover a complete year, so that normal seasonal effects cannot distort the trend. It must always be remembered that a moving average, no matter for what period, will always give a forecast that is behind the market. If the market is falling, the moving average will give a ofrecast that will be above the actual achievement and vice-versa.

Correcting to a constant price

Analysis of historical data can be misleading unless values are compared at constant prices and take into account such things as inflation.

To obtain the annual average price change, year over year, use can be made of the weekly or monthly service department cost sheet.

The importance of market planning

A business is a dynamic thing and conditions both inside and outside the business are constantly changing. It is in this light that a company must plan its future, not just in the short term but also in the long term. No company, if it is to develop, can afford not to produce a market plan, because it is essential to long-term survival that a company knows where it is going and, just as important, how and when it is going to arrive there.

The benefits of market planning

(1)   it encourages systematic forward thinking by management.
(2)   It leads to a better co-ordination of the company's total efforts and makes executives aware of how their responsibilities interact.
(3)   All departmental objectives are clearly defined and performance can be measured objectively against these predetermined controls.
(4)   Adverse trends are quickly revealed and remedial action can be taken.
(5)   It prepares a company better for sudden developments in the market.
(6)   It causes the company to sharpen its guiding objectives and policies.
       When producing a market plan, it is essential that:
(1)   All the persons involved in the implementation of the plan are involved in its formation;
(2)   the objectives set are factual, attainable, and realistic;
(3)   the plan is reappraised regularly and changed if necessary;
(4)   meaningful comparisons are made between objectives and performance by establishing reasons for shortfalls in performance.

The market plan

In order to build up the objectives and tactics for the service or other departments, it is important to take a good look at the opportunities in the market. This will include a careful analysis of the business, social, and government environments, which will involve knowledge of the following areas:
(1)   trade attitude and methods;
(2)   customer attitude and habits, which vary greatly with the company operations;
(3)   the nature of the competition;
(4)   government (national and local) regulations.

As every service market is constantly changing, with new products and competitors emerging, changes taking place in customer needs, and in environmental control (government and legal restrictions), it is vital to keep the methods of each department in tune with the needs of the market and make sure that it reacts to any changes.

The market plan should be the result of decisions made about how the resources of each department are going to be used. The basic direction of these planning activities will be provided by a statement of the department's goals.

These may include:

(1)   achieving certain rates of profit;
(2)   achieving certain sales targets;
(3)   achieving a certain share of the market;
(4)   maximizing sales opportunities.

The actual process of formulating these targets will involve consideration of all aspects affecting a department's competitive situation, namely:

(1)   the potential which exists in the immediate area;
(2)   the potential gain through selling to people who are not customers at present;
(3)   an increase or decrease in local competition.

Also included in the market plan will be details of the facilities which will. be necessary to bring about the sales gain: the size of the sales gain: the size of the advertising budget, the frequency of advertising and promotion, provisions for attendance at local public functions, etc., changes to essential services, telephone facilities, administrative procedures and delivery service, etc. The planned sales and the overhead estimates can then be balanced with one another to produce an over-all profit plan for the whole year.

It is important that these plans and intentions are known to all key personnel so that a combined effort to follow the market plan can be made within a department. The plan should be as specific as possible, particularly on the timing of the proposed actions and the budget to be spent.

Throughout the year the actual achievement should be measured against the budget. The reasons for any differences should be established, and corrections, if necessary, should be immediately put into operation.

The marketing mix

Bearing in mind the previous points, marketing policy can be more clearly worked out within a department. It is against this background of marketing responsibility that the detailed elements or the 'mix' of the marketing plan can be drawn up. Each element should be given a degree of importance in contributing to policy—in order to give the department maximum efficiency and profitability. It is like doing a jigsaw; the relevant pieces are drawn together and put in the right place in relation to each other. The elements to be included in the marketing 'mix' should cover the following areas.

Product planning

This involves discovering what customers' wants are and how these wants can be profitably met. It means deciding what quantities of repair and service work can be sold—to whom, when, where and how—decisions that will have important strategic consequences.

Pricing

Decisions on pricing and the level of discounts to be offered to the users usually fall within the responsibility of a service department. Current charge-out rates are usually adhered to wherever possible.

It is important, however, to recognize that competition varies from place to place. Managers must examine local market conditions before determining re-selling terms.

Advertising

Advertising has the ability to attract new customers and remind the existing customers of the merits of buying service and repair work from an operation, and so boosts sales. When developing the market plan, a decision must be made on how much should be spent on advertising, how this expenditure should be phased over time, what media should be used, what message should be put over, and how the results can be measured. The guide in minimum standards is 1 per cent of service/repair sales revenue for advertising and sales promotion.

Merchandizing

Merchandizing is concerned with 'creating' sales at the actual point of sale. It covers a wide spectrum of promotional activity—particularly applicable to retail selling. Representatives selling service/repair of vehicles need to be educated and trained in the art. R.T.I.T.B. 'training' programmes meet this need and C.G.L.I., I.M.I., and other courses provide the educational aspect of merchandizing. The Institute of Marketing, Moor Hall, Cookham, Berks. can supply a number of explanatory booklets on training and education.

Promotion

Promotions and special offers have the ability to give sales of particular service, work, parts, etc., an added impetus, as well as attracting new customers to the business. The length, style, and direction of such promotions should be worked out as methodically as possible beforehand, and built into the market plan. Reference to Chapter 2 should be made in connection with promotions and their assessment.

Packagaing

In marketing policy, packaging is heavily associated with branding. Although policies on packaging are generally developed by manufacturers, it is important that any packaging used in any business is an effective market weapon with respect to image, design, presentation, impulse purchasing, convenience, and that it clearly represents a company.

Availability

Research has shown the importance of service/repair availability in allowing a department to build up a good reputation in the trade and with customers. Thorough reviews should be undertaken of the range of business, and the effectiveness of control techniques. As mentioned earlier, quality control of all work is an excellent selling commodity.

Delivery

A good delivery service must be sufficiently quick and reliable to satisfy customers, and be capable of attracting new ones. It involves getting goods to the right places, at the right time, and in the right quantities. Service/repair work should be well planned. Efforts should constantly be made to match the speed of service offered by others, and consideration should be given to such ideas as offering high-speed emergency services with lower discounts or with a delivery charge. Workshop loading charts are a means to ensure that vehicles can be delivered on time.

Special delivery services are an expensive luxury, unless extra business is being brought in purely because that delivery service exists.

Service

The standard of service received is obviously vital in its effect on building up customer loyalty and support. An efficient and interested attitude will be rewarded with future sales. Included in this are:

1) politeness on the customers' premises, or over the telephone;
2) offering as far as possible to obtain vehicles that are not actually available;
3) willingness to give customers information and advice.

Telephoning is one of the major activities of the service operation. Apart from being the quickest method by which the trader can inform suppliers of his requirements, it is a sales tool and, as such, should reflect all the aspects of efficiency and image already outlined.

Waiting in a well-designed reception area with courteous and capable staff can be pleasant; a similar wait on the telephone can be irritating. It should be ensured that the right staff and the right number of telephone lines are available, not just for incoming calls but also for canvassing. For example, before a parts vehicle begins its daily journey, telephone calls to customers could produce more sales. If at all possible, sole telephone contacts should be arranged for customers and a personalized service developed.

Sales force

This aspect of the plan involves a decision on the size of the sales force and how it is to be used. It will involve the setting of targets for all sales representatives.

The over-all sales target that will already have been set forms the basis of

the individual sales targets. Given the split in sales between the various customers during the previous sales year, the sales forecast total can very quickly be
allocated to each Manager as an individual target. Ideally, it is better to consult
a Manager about targets rather than attempt to impose the targets. Managers
have to be persuaded that the targets are realistic and achievable. There should
be an incentive of some kind to ensure their enthusiastic and committed sales
support to achieve targets; this support will be more easily gained if the
Manager has been involved in the target-setting process.

Representatives' targets will include making sure that Managers for which
each is responsible achieve their sales turnover targets. The use of league
tables, competitions, and incentives for the sales force are suggested as an
important means of motivating and encouraging their efforts.

Reference should be made to Chapter 6 and sales targets and forecasts.

Monthly and annual sales analysis

Managers responsible for producing targets for the sale of work or products will have clerical assistants to record monthly and annual figures. Each
customer will have a record card. The monthly analysis could have a card
designed to include all relevant details such as name and address, services
sold, repair work sold, and so on.

Annual earnings from main fleet customers which would depend upon
mileage/tonnage their vehicles convey can be scrutinized using a standard
form. The form could have various vertical columns which would be used to
include:
(1) Names of principal customers;
(2) Date when service/repair commenced for each customer;
(3) Type of work completed;
(4) Type of area vehicles serve (e.g. hilly, flat, etc.)
(5) Gross earnings for first year (and second year) from work completed in
     cash terms;
(6) Work completed for first year (and second year) in cash terms;
(7) Remarks.

At the foot of the card total gross earnings and work completed in cash
terms would be recorded. Any hired vehicles could be included in the total
figures on the same card. By analysing fleet operators' requirements it is
possible to give the service needed and boost sales.

All this data is useful when drawing up future forecasts.

Consumer Credit Act 1974 (See also Appendix IV)

When considering marketing, this act must be mentioned. It is not intended to give the full details of the act, since this is outside the scope of this
book. When canvassing for business there are certain rules which must be
followed and full details are given in the Office of Fair Trading booklet

Do you need a Licence? When dealers and their employees canvass off trade premises they would be well advised, when applying for their licence, to apply for a licence which allows them to canvass debtor–creditor–supplier agreements or regulated hire agreements off trade premises. Such licences will not allow the canvassing off trade premises of debtor–creditor agreements or the canvassing of the services of anyone carrying on the business of a credit–broker, debt adjuster, or debt counsellor. Canvassing these agreements off trade premises is a criminal offence.

Booklets about the Consumer Credit Act can be obtained from the Office of Fair Trading, Chancery House, Chancery Lane, London WC2A 1SP, or local Trading Standards Offices and Citizens Advice Bureaus. The act modernizes and rationalizes the law governing the provision of credit and hire to individuals. The term 'individuals' includes both ordinary customers and trade consumers, such as people in business on their own and in partnerships, but it does not cover limited companies who obtain credit or hire facilities.

Individuals will be given wide protection whether they are buying goods on hire purchase or on any other form of credit, seeking loans from banks or finance houses, hiring goods, using credit cards or trading checks, or obtaining credit in other ways.

Virtually all businesses concerned with credit and hire will need a licence from the Director General of Fair Trading in order to continue; the first applications for licences commenced in late 1975.

Section 154 of the act provides that credit brokers, debt adjusters, and debt counsellors cannot canvass their services off trade premises. Thus, it is an offence to set up a meeting with a prospective customer, or to call on him without a prior invitation, and talk to him or anyone else who might be present in order to sell services. But such a conversation is not covered by this Section if it takes place on the business premises of the customer or the canvasser.

Types of business affected by this Section are:
Credit brokers: any person or organization introducing people to sources of mortgage loans to help them buy a home for themselves or relatives.
Debt adjusters: people who negotiate with creditors on behalf of debtors about the discharge of a debt, or take over a debtor's obligations for a fee.
Debt counsellors: people who advise debtors on how to handle debts.

Canvassing by debt adjusters and counsellors is covered by this Section if it relates to the handling of debts arising from consumer credit or hire agreements. A consumer credit agreement is any agreement for credit up to £5000 whether or not it is secured by a mortgage. A consumer hire agreement is defined in a similar way.

Sale of Goods (Implied Terms) Act 1973 (See also Appendix IV)

It is not possible to mention any aspect of selling without reference to this act. *Caveat emptor* (buyer beware) still applies to private sales. If a private motorist sells his car it is the buyer who must guard against any faults in the vehicle.

In a business, however, a customer has many rights against a dealer. These may be summarized:

(1)   the seller must have a proper title to the goods, i.e. he must have the right to sell them;

(2)   goods supplied must correspond exactly to the description;

(3)   all parts, vehicles, and so on must be of merchantable quality, i.e. must be fit for the purpose for which they were purchased. Obviously there is a difference between a new car and one that is five years old but a customer is entitled to a service from the older car which can normally be expected from a car of that age and the mileage it has performed.

A customer, however, has three limitations in connection with the act:

(1)   no refund of money or other redress can be made with regard to the merchantable quality of the goods in respect of defects specifically brought to notice before the sale is made;

(2)   if an examination of the goods was made before buying, and the customer accepts them, he cannot claim for defects which he ought to have seen during the examination.

(3)   No right of redress exists as regards 'fitness of purpose' if the circumstances of the sale show that a customer did not rely on the seller's skill or judgement, or that it was unreasonable for him to do so. This might be the case if a dealer clearly indicated that he had no idea if a car was suitable for certain 'off highway' work.

A dealer should remember that customers' rights cannot be taken away by introducing exclusion clauses, because the law says that in consumer sales such clauses are invalid. A consumer sale is defined in the act as a sale of goods (other than auction or tender) by a seller in the course of business where the goods are:

(a) of a type ordinarily bought for private use or consumption,

(b) sold to a person who does not buy or put himself forward as buying them in the course of his business.

There is always an element of risk at auctions and if someone attempts to get a trade discount by indicating that he is buying the goods for his business, then the buyer's rights may be excluded (except to title). A seller must put faulty goods right if they prove to be faulty, whether bought for cash or on credit.

A retailer needs to bear rights of customers in mind at all times. Customers should certainly not have to fight for something to which they are entitled.

The honest trader has no new commitments under the Sale of Goods Act 1973 as he will continue to provide redress whenever goods sold prove to be defective.

When a customer claims goods are defective the law recognizes a buyer's implied right as being either of 'condition' or of 'warranty'. The law provides that where there has been a breach of condition the buyer is entitled to repudiate the contract and reject the goods. In practical terms the buyer will then be able to recover the price he paid. All the implied terms described here—compliance with description, fitness for purpose, and merchantable quality—are conditions, not warranties. However, if goods are accepted by the buyer and are later found to be defective, any breach of an implied condition will be treated as being a breach of warranty. The buyer 'accepts' the goods when he tells the seller that he has accepted them, or when he keeps them for more than a reasonable time without telling the seller he has rejected them, or (subject to his having had a reasonable opportunity of examining them to ascertain whether they conform to the contract) when he treats the goods in some way that shows he no longer regards the seller as being the owner. But even when the buyer has lost his right to reject the goods he is still entitled to compensation.

Individual claims can be settled by giving a refund of the price paid, which will frequently restore the *status quo* in the case of a breach of condition and may represent the measure of damages recoverable for a breach of warranty. Alternatively, as the cost of repair may often be the measure of damages recoverable for breach of warranty, it is possible in such cases to offer to repair the goods free of charge. But the buyer may be entitled to claim, among other things, for loss of use, or for the cost of hiring a replacement, or for any other loss which he may have suffered because of the breach.

It is impossible to lay down hard-and-fast rules as to how long goods can be expected to give good service. Clearly the period during which an article ought to remain in good condition or give trouble-free service must vary. Goods which function adequately when sold may, in fact, not be of merchantable quality (one does not expect a consumer durable to be fitted with a part which has an unreasonably short life). And it may not, of course, become apparent for some time that the goods sold were not fit for a particular purpose for which the seller knew they were being bought at the time of the sale.

In the case of a breach of condition the buyer is not obliged to return defective goods, unless he has previously agreed with the seller to do so. He is only obliged to tell the seller that he refuses to accept the goods. In the case of a breach of warranty it will depend on what is reasonable in the circumstances of the particular case, but any direct and predictable expense can be claimed by the buyer, and this could include the cost of transport. In some instances the buyer may well get the defects remedied by someone else and claim the cost from the seller as damages for breach of warranty.

Responsibility for defective goods can be passed on to the supplier, as long as a dealer has not agreed to give them up. The dealer can claim the same rights from a supplier as the customer can claim from a dealer. If a contract with a supplier (e.g. conditions of sale) does not contain a clause excluding your rights, you can look to him for redress for defective goods which have been the subject of complaint by customers. Exclusion clauses in (or on the back of) order forms, invoices, statements, catalogues, and other trade literature should be very closely examined. Even where a dealer has agreed to give up rights, the law now provides an important new safeguard. Take the case, for example, where it is believed that a dealer has been supplied with defective goods and his supplier relies on an exclusion clause in order to deny him redress. The dealer can now sue him for breach of contract and contend in court that it would not be fair or reasonable for his supplier to be allowed to rely on the exclusion clause. In applying the 'test of reasonableness' the court is required by the 1973 Act to take into account all the circumstances of the case, and to pay particular attention to such matters as the relative bargaining strengths of the buyer and seller, whether the buyer received any special inducement to accept the exclusion clause (e.g. a special discount), whether the goods or suitable alternatives could be obtained from another source without an exclusion clause, and whether the goods were made to the buyer's specification. This new right is particularly valuable to small retailers who have often found it difficult to obtain goods from powerful suppliers, except on the latter's terms.

Questions

1. (a) What areas does the M.A.A. Code of Practice cover?
   (b) Why must this code be observed?
   (c) How would you ensure customer satisfaction? (I.M.I.)
2. (a) Explain the basic rights of customers in connection with the Sale of Goods Act (Implied Terms) 1973.
   (b) Define consumer sale.
   (c) Give three limitations to customers' rights. (I.M.I.)
3. Briefly explain the purpose of the Consumer Credit Act 1974 and state which of the sales staff should be aware of its implications. (I.M.I.)
4. (a) What factors are involved with marketing?
   (b) List some of the factors which could affect service/sales forecasting.
   (I.M.I.)
5. Explain the benefits of market planning and detail the points which need to be observed in a market plan. (I.M.I.)
6. 'Customers will sell dealership services.'
   (a) What is meant by this statement?
   (b) How would you ensure customers were retained? (I.M.I.)
7. A manager, director, and service manager decide to implement monthly and annual sales analysis of fleet operators who have work completed at their dealership. Explain in detail how you would complete such work and the purpose of it. (I.M.I.)

CHAPTER 9

VEHICLE TESTING

Department of Transport tests

For the newcomer to this field of work a brief clarification of the official tests is needed. Originally the Ministry of Transport (M.O.T.) were responsible for vehicle testing. The department's name was changed when it became part of the Department of the Environment (D.O.E.) It was changed again in 1976 when it became the Department of Transport (D.Tp.). Hence the various names used to describe the tests. M.O.T. is predominant but D.Tp. is likely to become more well known in the future, unless of course, by one more step, D.Tp. reverts back to M.O.T.!

The object of all vehicle testing, whether it is a public service vehicle, commercial vehicle, or a car, is to find out whether the vehicle is as mechanically sound as the law requires. Some years ago a 1937 saloon car was struck by a slow moving van at a junction of busy cross-roads. The van remained virtually undamaged but the car almost totally disintegrated. The old body, rusted and suffering from metal fatigue, could not stand the impact. It burst open, scattering bits and pieces all round, and left the driver sitting in a seat with not one of the doors or wheels still in place. Modern cars are generally designed with a body life of seven years but experienced mechanics and testers know full well that, for instance, salt on our roads in winter can seriously corrode important safety items on vehicles and reduce body life considerably. Some mono-construction cars have body sills and other units which act as load-carrying members, and corrosion of these units seriously weakens the strength of the car.

In 1977 the Ford Motor Co. estimated from a research programme that at least 2 500 000 vehicles were too unsafe to be allowed out on the roads in the United Kingdom., and the 1976 regulations will almost certainly ensure safer vehicles on our roads.

Public Service Vehicles (P.S.V.) have had stringent examinations since 1930, and a Condition of Fitness Certificate for every P.S.V. has been a legal requirement since that time. Tests for cars should have been introduced by the end of 1960 but were postponed until 1961. These tests were introduced under the Motor Vehicles (Tests) Regulations 1960, Section I of the Road

Traffic Act 1956. There have been numerous changes over the years, e.g. the 1968 regulations were amended seven times and a new set of regulations came into force on January 1st 1977 (price 60p.). These regulations were made under powers conferred to the Secretary of State under Sections 43 and 44 of the 1972 Road Traffic Act. The new regulations are entitled 'The Motor Vehicles (Tests) Regulations 1976, (No. 1977)'. Students should always refer to current documents on this subject, which are available from H.M.S.O. In the coming years vehicle tests are almost certain to become more stringent and include many items which do not form part of current tests. Commercial vehicle tests will be dealt with later in this chapter. Let us now look at the 1976 regulations.

The vehicles covered as as follows:

Class 1: light motor bicycles (cylinder capacity up to 200 cc.)

Class 2: motor bicycles (two wheels, with or without sidecars).

Class 3: light motor vehicles (motor car, unladen weight up to 408 kg, or motor cycle which is not a motor bicycle).

Class 4: motor cars and heavy motor cars (not being Class 3 or 5).

Class 5: large passenger-carrying vehicles (more than 13 seats, not being public service vehicles (R4)).

Motor caravans are included in the regulations and will be eligible for test on the 1st January 1978 and thereafter.

Applications and authorizations

Businesses having the required equipment may apply, on specified forms, for authorization to test the relevant vehicles (R5) to the Area Traffic Office in the area of which the business is situated (R7). After any necessary inspection of the facilities the Secretary of State (the Department of Transport) may authorize the applicant to carry out the tests on any or all of the classes, which are specified in an authorization (R8). Stringent conditions (R9) are laid down. These may be summarized as follows:

1. The examiner must carry out the regulation tests on specified vehicles, either personally or by personal supervision, in accordance with the conditions, and sign test certificates, or delegate the signing to competent staff, who must be authorized.

2. The examiner must notify the Department of Transport, via the Area Traffic Office, of all the alterations to his list of authorized testers or to the constitution of his firm or company within seven days of the change.

3. The examiner must show the official sign (Schedule 1) conspicuously outside the premises (flat against a wall and not more than 4·57 metres (15 feet) above the ground—maximum of one sign per road frontage).

4. The examiner must show conspicuously inside the premises a list of testers authorized to conduct the tests and sign certificates.

5. He must be prepared, on three days' notice, to allow official inspectors to examine his vehicle-testing station, equipment, books, (etc.) on an appeal against a refusal of a test certificate.
6. Authorized testers must first pass a test of competence approved by the Department of Transport (R9) to conduct tests and sign certificates: authorizations are in writing.

Prescribed statutory requirements

This is the jargon for the tests which must be carried out on specified vehicles (R10); these are listed in Schedule 2 and (very briefly) cover: brakes, steering gear; lights and tyres (condition and maintenance); seat belts and anchorages; windscreen wipers and washers (now obligatory on virtually every vehicle used on the roads); exhaust systems; horns (or other warning instruments); and the general condition of bodywork and suspension. The manner of carrying out the tests is laid down in R13 and Schedule 3. Every specified part must be examined, but there must be no dismantling of any part by means of tools, and the examination must be undertaken in an area with sufficient lighting and over a pit or on a ramp or hoist. Further and more extensive details are set out in Parts II to XII of the Schedule 3, and the objectives are to see that all parts are sound, in good condition, and that they work effectively (R13).

The examiner's equipment must be effectively maintained and where measurements are involved must work 'accurately within reasonable limits of tolerance' (R24). The Schedules are closely linked to the Construction and Use Regulations, and there are many exceptions to the detailed requirements. It is desirable to have equipment arranged so that a flow of vehicles from stage to stage can be made.

Appointments for examinations

These may be made in any normal way, by telephone, letter or personal visit. Once an appointment has been made the test must be carried out, unless there are circumstances 'beyond the control of the examiner'. With an unannounced call the examiner has the right to do the job there and then, i.e. during the business's normal working hours, or to agree a future time (R11).

Appointment details must be written down and should include date, time, and the name of the person making the appointment (R11). Local authorities may be authorized examiners (R11), in which case they are known as 'designated councils'.

Applicants' duties

At an appointment the applicant must produce, if required by the examiner, the 'registration document' or any other evidence of the date of first manufacture of the vehicle. The vehicle must also be reasonably clean, and it must be supplied with enough fuel and oil for any road test. Any cargo must be removed on the examiner's request so that the vehicle may be properly tested (R12), and if any of these conditions is not complied with the examiner is not obliged to carry out the test.

Examiners' responsibilities (insurance)

The position with regard to responsibility for damage and third party liability is exactly the same as for any other garage service, with the additional proviso that the applicant, the customer, must not be asked to indemnify the examiner, or accept any responsibility for loss, damage, or injury caused by the examiner (R14), except once the test has been completed and the applicant has been told to remove the vehicle, or in respect of suggested or requested repairs or maintenance. An examiner's insurance policy should contain specific cover for the tests covered by these regulations, and an examiner should also be on his guard against such dangerous parts as an exhaust system which is on the point of crumbling to dust.

Examination results

Test results must be documented on the same day as the work has been carried out, i.e. a 'test certificate' or a 'notification of the refusal of a test certificate' (R15). The standard format of a test certificate is reporduced in Scheudle 4, the refusal form (VT21) is not: form VT21 must be used. Test certificates blanks may be obtained from the Department of Transport, which may make a charge of £14 for 100 forms. The refusal form must show the vehicle-testing station number, the amount of the fee, the vehicle registration number (or a chassis number), and the date of the refusal and the reasons for it (R15). Certificates must be signed by the authorized tester (R15), and duplicates may be issued when the original has been lost or defaced (R23). The applicant must apply to the relevant Area Traffic Office, with the statutory fee of 50p, and if the Area Traffic Office is satisfied that the loss or defacement is genuine then it will issue a duplicate, but it will not do so in respect of certificates more than eighteen months old.

A certificate may also be refused if a tester, having inspected a vehicle, is of the opinion that it is so defective in construction, condition, equipment, or accessories that it would be dangerous to carry out a braking test (R15), and this reason must be stated—this time on official form VT22. The rest of the test must, however, be completed.

Fees for tests

These are now very much simpler than they were in the past, (R17) Schedule 5, and from 1 December 1978 were as follows:

Motor bicycle, without sidecar   £2.70
Any other vehicle covered by the regulations   £4.50
Students should obtain current charges for such vehicles.

A vehicle, having failed the test, may be left at the vehicle-testing station for the necessary repairs to be carried out, and in that case there is no further fee to be paid when the remedial work has been done (Schedule 5). When a vehicle is removed from a vehicle-testing station after a failure, but brought back to the original test station within fourteen days, then the fee payable is halved, providing an authorized test station carried out the repairs. Re-tests after 14 days from original test, and, if repair work is not completed by an authorised test station, require a full fee. Nothing is laid down in the regulations as to when or how the statutory fee is to be paid and there is no right of lien on a test examination. Examiners should insist on the payments being made before a test and include this condition in their terms of business.

Vehicles must be removed from the testing station by the end of the second day after an examination, or within two days of the applicant having been notified, in writing or orally, that an examination has been carried out (R20). It should be noted, however, that an examiner must make his own arrangements to get a vehicle moved when the customer makes no attempt to move it himself, since there is no penalty for non-removal.

Appeals against refusals

Any person who feels aggrieved at a test refusal may appeal to the relevant Area Traffic Office within fourteen days of the notification, or after a longer period at the discretion of the Department of Transport; there is a special appeal form for the purpose. On receiving the appeal, the Area Traffic Office notifies the appellant of the time and place (which may be a vehicle-testing station or any other premises), where he must present the vehicle for the appeal examination. He must also give the examination officer whatever information may be required for the purpose of the re-examination, including production of the refusal notification.

The examination officer then re-tests the vehicle, and either issues a test certificate or a refusal R18. There is no further appeal after a second refusal. The same fee as for an original test must be paid and sent with the appeal form, and without the fee the re-test is simply not carried out. The Secretary of State has, however, the power to refund the appeal fee, or part of it, if he considers that the applicant had grounds for complaint.

If the appellant changes his mind and gives the Area Traffic Office two clear days' notice of his decision not to submit the vehicle for an appeal test he is entitled to the return of the appeal fee (R19).

When the Area Traffic Office sees fit to use a vehicle-testing station other than the original, in an appeal case, that station operator is entitled to a fee of one half of the normal for the use of his services and facilities, but even this fee is not payable if the examination appointment is cancelled with one clear day's notice, either verbally or in writing (R21).

Records, documentation

All examiners must install and maintain a duplicate record of all examinations at the vehicle-testing station (official form VT12). Each entry must be made not later than seven days after the test (R22), and one copy of the record must be sent to the Area Traffic Office preferably on the first working day of each month, but at least not later than the fifteenth day. Nil returns are required. The copies must be retained for possible inspection for at least eighteen months.

Inspections

A vehicle-testing station may be inspected at any time without warning by an authorized officer of the Department of Transport; the officer may demand production of documents; examine equipment; watch any test, including a road test; and question the staff (R24). If he is dissatisfied with any aspect of the vehicle-testing station the Secretary of State may withdraw the authorization (R26) on at least 28 days' notice. The 28 days' notice may be dispensed with in serious cases, e.g. of proven fraud. The examiner has a right to 'make representations' to the Secretary of State within 14 days of the notice, a procedure which stops somewhat short of usual appeal procedures, although the Secretary of State is bound to take those representations into consideration. Authorizations must also be withdrawn in the case of bankruptcy or the liquidation of a company and, of course, on the death of the examiner. The authorized examiner may also terminate his appointment himself.

Forms

Only official forms may be used (R25) and all must be returned to the Area Traffic Office on the termination of an authorization. The Department of Transport must refund the cost of any unused test certificates (R27).

VEHICLES

Not covered by the regulations

There are a number of classes of vehicle not covered. These are tractors and locomotives; heavy goods vehicles over 1525 kg unladen weight, and works trucks; articulated vehicles; pedestrian-controlled vehicles; invalid carriages, whether built for the purpose or adapted, up to 306 kg unladen weight; invalid carriages between 306 kg and 510 kg supplied by the Department of Health and Social Security; hackney carriages. Also excluded are vehicles on their way to a port for export, foreign armed-forces vehicles, vehicles exempted from duty under S7(1) of the Vehicles (Excise) Act, 1971 (R30). Police vehicles maintained in approved police workshops and electric vehicles under 1515 kg unladen weight are also excluded.

No licence required

While a vehicle is on its way to or from a statutory test which has been booked by appointment or while it is at a test it needs no excise licence, but it must be insured. Similarly, it needs no licence while it is being delivered to or from a repair garage by appointment for the purpose of putting right those items which earned it a notice of failure. A repairer carrying out a post-repair test may use trade plates for the purpose.

Test Manuals

H.M.S.O. issue two manuals which form part of all vehicle-testing operations. One is entitled *Vehicle Testing–The M.O.T. Tester's Manual* and includes 'Explanatory Notes on the Statutory Provisions and Regulations for Testing of Motor Vehicles (except Motor Cycles) and Light Goods Vehicles under Section 43 of the Road Traffic Act 1972', (price £3.50, 1983). The second document is entitled *Vehicle Testing–A guide to the operation of the M.O.T. test.* (price 85p, 1983). All the forms used are well illustrated, and both documents should be obtained for detailed study. Full details of exactly what is required of all testable items are given. A typical example is a vehicle with four wheels–the footbrake must be at least 50% efficient and the hand-brake 25%. With few exceptions only roller brake testers will be used in the future to measure braking efficiency. Another example is seat belts. The method of inspection consists of a visual check to see that belts are provided for the appropriate seats, and also each belt is tested by pulling it manually to ensure that anchorages are sound and properly attached to the structure of the vehicle. Seat belts must not be cut, or have seriously deteriorated webbing, or fractured or worn fittings. Locking mechanisms must function correctly.

When 'refusal' certificates are issued some dealerships insist that a second examiner should confirm the first examiner's report. This helps to avoid disputes with customers, and is also a safeguard should the customer appeal–as he has every right to do. Needless to say, it also makes sure that the first examiner was correct in his examination.

As a project a student or manager could obtain the tester's manual From it he could plan the layout of essential equipment, e.g. roller brake tester, headlamp alignment equipment, lift or pit, inspection lamps, etc. The total area required for vehicles waiting for test, completing the test, and parking could be calculated. Such layouts must take into account the work study methods mentioned in this book which enable staff to work as efficiently as possible so that the tests do give a profit to the dealership. Part of the project could include the design of a check list to cover every item in the test. Broadly speaking the test covers steering, tyres, lighting, and brakes, but the tester's manual and amendments must be obtained to ensure that all units coming within the test are inspected. The check list would be drafted according to the system adopted. For example, in Stage I if steering gear was to be examined then all parts should be listed, such as track rods, steering arm, drag links, and so on. Adjacent to these could be two columns headed 'pass' and 'fail'. These would be ticked by the examiner according to the condition of the unit. A remarks column could be useful for indicating to the customer that attention to such things as brake-pads was likely to be required in the following two or three months. This would help to create good customer relations as the customers would then feel the dealership 'cared' about them. It would also, of course, help to bring more work into the dealership.

The D.Tp. official check list must be used to hand to the customer and copy retained to reference.

A summary of the project would be (a) calculate area; (b) obtain area required for equipment/tools and place them in the most efficient position; (c) decide how many examiners are going to man the area and where they will be stationed; (d) make out a detailed check list which will match the area for specific test items.

HEAVY GOODS VEHICLE TESTS

Vehicles subject to plating and testing are, with certain exceptions:
- (a) tractive units of articulated goods vehicles,
- (b) rigid goods vehicles over 1525 kg (30 cwts) unladen weight,
- (c) goods-carrying semi-trailers,
- (d) goods carrying drawbar trailers over 1020 kg (1 ton) unladen weight.

Since these tests were introduced in 1967, many amendments have been made. The Road Traffic Act 1972 Part II Section 45 deals with testing procedures. Applications for initial tests must be made to the Goods Vehicle Centre, 91/92 The Strand, Swansea SA1 2DH. The form used is V.T.G.1.L. (motor vehicles) or V.T.G.2.L (trailers) and the current test fee must be enclosed. Local testing stations will notify applicants of the time and date when the test will take place. Students are advised to obtain current application forms from a general post office or the test station, and study the details.

Applications should always be made at least one month before the vehicle is due for annual test. Application forms (V.T.G/40L) are necessary for re-tests. Alterations to vehicles affecting plating requires form V.T.G.10 to enable a new plate to be affixed when approved by D.Tp. examiners.

The items which are tested are described in the *Goods Vehicle Tester's Manual*, price £3.00, (1983) which is available from H.M.S.O. At the test station the items are examined as illustrated in Fig. 9.1. At the back of this form is a refusal certificate which is filled in if any item is not up to D.Tp. standards.

Some dealerships offer a Pre D.Tp. Guardian Test Service. All items covered in the test are examined, and worn parts are replaced. Before the day of the actual test the condition of the vehicle should be checked to ensure it is roadworthy. It should be cleaned underneath and on top, and the

INSPECTION CARD FOR MOTOR VEHICLES – FIRST AND ANNUAL TESTS
Department of Transport Road Traffic Act 1972 Section 45 Examination of Goods Vehicles

FORM VTG 4A

Day Month Year
19

Registration number of vehicle

Station fees
Schedule number

Line

Station
ref. number

Notification of
refusal issued

Test certificate
issued

OL number

GVw

Station Number	Week Number	DTp Number	DTp STATS	TEST TYPE	S.C.		
0 0	0 0	0 0 0 0	DGV Tanker	1st	1	4	
1 1	1 1	1 1 1 1	DGV Other	Ann.	2	5	
2 2	2 2	2 2 2 2	VTG 12		3		
3 3	3 3	3 3 3 3	Dept fail		+	−	
4 4	4 4	4 4 4 4	FTA	VTG 10	1	1	
5 5	5 5	5 5 5 5	Plate issued	Clear GV 9	2	2	
6 6	6	6 6 6 6	GV 9 issued	Other	3	3	
7 7	7	7 7 7 7	GV 10 issued		IP	DP	
8 8	8	8 8 8 8	Test day changed	2 Axles	1	1	
9 9	9	9 9 9 9		3 4 5	2	2	

1 2 3 4 5 6 7 Fee received
1 2 3 4 5 6 Spl returns
3 | 3

AGE Pre-65 C D E F G H J K L M N P R S T V W X Y

BODY TYPE: Tract / Flat / Box / Refuse / Tip / Skel / Petrol/Oil Tank / Other Tank / Other

DTp number

For official use

6	7	8	9	10
11	14	15	19	36
37	48	49	50	

Brake type DD T

A
1 Legal plate position
2 Legal plate details
3
4
5 Smoke emission
6 Road wheels and hubs
7 Tyres (size and type)
8 Tyres (condition)
9 Bumper bars
10 Spare wheel carrier
11 Trailer coupling

14 Wings (condition)
15 Cab mountings
16 Cab doors
17 Cab floor and steps
18 Driving seat
19 Body (security)
20 Body (condition)
21
22 Mirrors
23 View to front
24 Glass (condition)

25 Windscreen wipers and washers
26 Speedometer
27 Audible warning
28 Driving controls
29 Tachograph
30 Play at steering wheel
31 Steering wheel
32 Steering column
33
34 Air/vacuum warning
35 Air/vacuum build up
36 Mech brake hand levers
37 Service brake pedal
38 Service brake operation
39 Hand op brk control valves
40

B
41 Chassis (condition)
42 Elec wiring and equipment
43 Engine mounting
44 Oil leaks
45 Fuel tank and system
46 Exhaust system
47
48 Spring pins and bushes
49 Susp'n units (condition)
50 Susp'n units (attachment)
51 Shock absorbers

52
53 Stubs/Wheel bearings
54 Steering linkage
55 Steering box
56 Power steering
57 Transmission
58
59 Mech brake components
60 Brake wheel units
61 Brake pipes, res, etc

C
62 Rear markings
63 Oblig side lamps
64 Oblig rear lamps
65 Oblig reflectors
66 Direction indicators
67 Headlamp vert aim
68 Oblig headlamps
69 Oblig stop lamps

D
71 Serv brake performance
72 Sec brake performance
73 Prk brake performance
74
75
76
77

Notes relating to defect markings

Serial number
1411662

TEST RESULT: Pass / Pass–After rectification at Station / Fail

Lane 1 2 3 4 5

K+J

Fig. 9.1 This is the D.Tp. inspection card which is 'clipped' as inspection proceeds. The card is in triplicate – one copy for D.Tp. head office, one for the owner of the vehicle and one for the H.G.V. Test Station. The back of the card is used for refusal of a certificate if necessary. On the card certain items have a line against them. These are free re-test items which must be done on the same day or next working day. Pass or fail is marked on the test sheet. Numbers without 'items' on the sheet will be used for additional test items in the future. No. 3 item for example i.e. seat-belts, was added in 1983.

chassis or serial number shown in the registration book must be clearly shown on the chassis or structure.

On the day of the test:

(1) Sufficient fuel and oil should be available to ensure the vehicle can get through the test;

(2) Ensure that the driver leaves in good time—a late arrival could mean a new application;

(3) Instruct the driver to follow the instructions of the station staff;

(4) Ensure a trailer is taken, if required;

(5) Ensure the vehicle carries any stipulated load;

(6) If required, complete and send form V.T.G.15 which deals with conveyance of dangerous goods;

(7) Remember a vehicle left at a D.Tp. station after hours is left at the owner's risk.

At the test station details of the vehicle will be checked. Regulation 146 of the Motor Vehicles (Construction and Use) Regulations 1978 states that each axle of a goods vehicle must have the correct size and type of tyre for the plated load. Needless to say, any incorrect tyres fitted should be picked up during normal inspections at dealerships or road hauliers or during pre-D.Tp. tests.

A test centre will refuse to accept a vehicle for test for any of the following reasons:

(1) The vehicle was not submitted for examination within thirty minutes after the appointed time for the examination.

(2) The applicant did not produce, after having been requested to do so:
 (i) the examination appointment card for the vehicle;
 (ii) the registration book or other evidence as to the date of first registration of the vehicle (motor vehicles only);
 (iii) evidence as to the date of manufacture of the vehicle (Motor vehicles not registered before the 1st January 1969 and trailers only);

(3) The particulars relating to the vehicle as shown on the application form were found to be substantially incorrect.

(4) The vehicle was not accompanied by a trailer as requested in the examination appointment card or, where the vehicle for examination is a trailer, it was not accompanied by a motor vehicle suitable in its construction and equipment for drawing that trailer.

(5) The vehicle was not marked with the chassis or serial number shown in the registration book or the Department identification mark allotted to the vehicle, or that number or mark was not permanently affixed to the chassis or main structure of the vehicle in a conspicuous and easily accessible position so as to be readily legible.

(6) The vehicle or a part of the vehicle or its equipment, or, where the vehicle is a motor vehicle accompanied by a trailer, the trailer or a

part of the trailer or its equipment, was in such a dirty or dangerous condition as to make it unreasonable for the examination to be carried out.

(7)   The applicant did not produce a certificate, as required by the last examination appointment card, that the vehicle, being a vehicle used for carrying toxic, corrosive, or flammable loads, had been properly cleaned or otherwise rendered safe.

(8)   The vehicle or, where the vehicle for examination is a trailer, the motor vehicle accompanying the trailer was not provided with sufficient fuel and oil to enable it to be driven to the extent necessary for the purposes of carrying out the examination.

(9)   In the case of a motor vehicle dur for examination, that vehicle or any trailer which accompanied it, or, in the case of a trailer due for examination, that trailer did not comply with the conditions specified in the last examination appointment card or otherwise requested, as to submission without a load or with such load as was specified.

(10) The vehicle for examination being a trailer, it was not possible to complete the examination of the vehicle without the accompanying motor vehicle being driven on a public road and no licence under the Vehicles (Excise) Act 1962 was in force for the motor vehicle.

(11) It was not possible to complete the examination due to a failure of a part of the vehicle or a part of any motor vehicle or trailer accompanying the vehicle which rendered the vehicle incapable of being moved in safety under its own power or, where the vehicle is a trailer, under the power of the accompanying motor vehicle.

(12) In the case of a vehicle being submitted for a periodical test or a retest following such a test, the driver of the vehicle, or where the vehicle is a trailer, the driver of the motor vehicle accompanying the trailer, did not produce the last plating certificate (or a photo-copy) and the last test certificate (or a photo-copy) issued in respect of the vehicle.

It will be seen from Fig. 9.1. and Fig. 9.2 that a check list forms part of the inspection. Such check lists should be used for all tests and inspections. This helps to ensure that nothing is overlooked.

If the vehicle on the test fails any of the listed items a failure certificate will be issued. Appeals against such failures can be made and form V.T.17 is used.

A manufacturer's plate means a plate which must be fitted to all post-1967 vehicles showing the weights at which the manufacturer of the vehicle considers the vehicle may be safely operated and includes the manufacturer's name, vehicle type, engine type, chassis or serial number and the number of axles. A useful explanatory booklet is available from the D.Tp. entitled *Plating and Testing of Goods Vehicles—Guide for Vehicle Operators.* This

D. Tp. COMMERCIAL VEHICLE TEST

ITEMS TO BE INSPECTED	STAGE	STAFF	EQUIPMENT
COLUMN 2 (left) C 1 LEGAL PLATE POSITION 1; C 2 LEGAL PLATE DETAILS 2; 3 SEAT BELTS 3; 4 ... 4; C 5 SMOKE EMISSION 5; R 6 ROAD WHEELS & HUBS 6; R 7 TYRES (SIZE & TYPE) 7; R 8 TYRES (CONDITION) 8; K 9 BUMPER BARS 9; C 10 SPARE WHEEL CARRIER 10; C 11 TRAILER COUPLING 11; 12 ... 12; 13 ... 13; K 14 WINGS 14; K 15 CAB MOUNTINGS 15; K 16 CAB DOORS 16; K 17 CAB FLOOR & STEPS 17; K 18 DRIVING SEAT 18; K 19 BODY (SECURITY) 19; K 20 BODY (CONDITION) 20 **(right)** 21 ... 21; K 22 MIRRORS 22; K 23 VIEW TO FRONT 23; K 24 GLASS/WINDOWS 24; K 25 WINDSCREEN WIPERS & WASHERS 25; K 26 SPEEDOMETER 26; K 27 AUDIBLE WARNING 27; K 28 DRIVING CONTROLS 28; 29 ... 29; R 30 PLAY AT STEERING WHEEL 30; R 31 STEERING WHEEL 31; R 32 STEERING COLUMN 32; 33 ... 33; B 34 AIR/VACUUM WARNING 34; B 35 AIR/VACUUM BUILD UP 35; B 36 MECHANICAL BRAKE HAND LEVERS 36; B 37 SERVICE BRAKE PEDAL 37; B 38 SERVICE BRAKE OPERATION 38; B 39 AIR/VAC HAND CONTROLS 39; 40 ... 40	A	1 H.G.V. tester	Various hand tools
COLUMN 2 (left) C 41 CHASSIS FRAME 41; C 42 ELEC WIRING & EQUIP. 42; C 43 ENGINE MOUNTINGS 43; C 44 OIL LEAKS 44; C 45 FUEL TANKS, PIPES & SYSTEM 45; C 46 EXHAUST SYSTEM 46; 47 ... 47; R 48 SPRING PINS & BUSHES 48; R 49 SUSPENSION (CONDITION) 49; R 50 SUSPENSION (ATTACHMENT) 50; R 51 SHOCK ABSORBERS 51 **(right)** 52 ... 52; R 53 STUBS 'WHEEL BEARINGS 53; R 54 STEERING LINKAGE 54; R 55 STEERING BOX 55; R 56 POWER STEERING 56; C 57 TRANSMISSION 57; 58 ... 58; B 59 MECH BRK COMPONENTS 59; B 60 BRK. WHEEL UNITS 60; B 61 BRAKE PIPES, RES., ETC. 61	B	1 H.G.V. tester assisted by Stage C tester	Various hand tools, rail mounted pit jack, inspection lamp, wheel shakers, micro—phone and speaker
COLUMN 2 L 62 REAR MARKINGS 62; L 63 OBLIG. SIDE LAMPS 63; L 64 OBLIG. REAR LAMPS 64; L 65 REFLECTORS 65; L 66 DIRECTION INDICATORS 66; L 67 HEADLAMP VERT AIM 67; L 68 OBLIG. HEADLAMPS 68; L 69 OBLIG. STOPLAMPS 69; 70 ... 70	C	1 H.G.V. tester	Headlamp alignment equipment
B 71 SERVICE BRK. PERFORMANCE 71; B 72 SEC BRK PERFORMANCE 72; B 73 PARK BRK PERFORMANCE 73; 74 ... 74; 75 ... 75	D	1 H.G.V. tester	Roller brake tester load simulator

Fig. 9.2 D.Tp. Commercial Vehicle Test. Each stage can take up to 10 minutes but at stage B 5 minutes per axle is allowed for underneath inspection thus increasing time allowed for multi axle vehicles. Approximately 15 metres × 4 metres is allowed for each stage. A large waiting area is provided. Staff can be rotated from stage to stage every two weeks.

explains in detail what is meant by plating, e.g. maximum gross weights, axle weights, and in certain cases 'train' weights. The Plating Certificate is form V.T.G.7. The booklet also gives details of such things as block bookings. Unlike cars, commercial vehicles are subject to test after their first anniversary and thereafter on an annual basis. Cars have to be three years old before they are tested, but this is almost certainly to be reduced in the future.

Some haulage operators have very strict inspection schedules, e.g. once a week on each vehicle. Whilst the inspection may only take 20 minutes, the items examined are crucial for high-mileage vehicles. Road haulage operators depend upon well maintained vehicles for their livelihood. All vehicles with serious faults picked up on the road or elsewhere may be served with prohibition notices, such as form G.V.9, in various forms, e.g. immediate, delayed, etc. Copies of these are sent to the local traffic commissions and an operator could have some or all of his vehicles taken off the road. Vehicle safety has reached a new era and operators or dealers concerned with heavy goods vehicles must ensure their staff are highly trained and re-trained as required. It is the only way to remain in business.

Educational and training establishments can usually arrange visits to D.Tp. Vehicle Test Centres by contacting the manager of the station. This can be extremely valuable to all personnel concerned with such work. To enable the visit to be objective, students should compile a check list of questions prior to the visit which might include such things as:

1. Make an outline sketch of the station and explain why this arrangement was chosen.
2. How long does a normal test take, what items are inspected and where are these items inspected, i.e. location of inspection on the line?
3. Explain in detail the plating procedure at this station.
4. What is the minimum braking efficiency for the handbrake and pedal braking systems? Explain how this is checked.
5. Explain how smoke emission and tyre checks are made to ensure they comply with the regulations.
6. State the permissible noise level for a plated goods vehicle exceeding 3½ tons gvw and explain how this is tested.
7. Detail the main items which result in a certificate's being refused.
8. Name all the forms involved with goods vehicle testing, from application forms to issue of a final certificate. What are current test fees?
9. What is a GV9, who issues this and for what reasons?
10. How are engineering tolerances applied to vehicle inspection and what permissible wear is allowed for king pins and bushes?
11. What details are required on a current plating certificate?
12. How many items are currently examined on a heavy goods vehicle?

Department of Transport

We live in a very developing and rapidly changing society. Consequently testing of vehicles is changing and new legislation brought onto the statute book. An example of this is the Motor Vehicle Test Extension Order which became law on January 1st. 1983. This order makes light vehicles with 8 or more passenger seats eligible for an annual test from first registration.

All personnel involved with all forms of legal testing of vehicles should contact the Department of Transport, Bristol for current requirements. It is proposed that from 1st. July, 1983, the H.G.V. and P.S.V. tests will be completed by Lloyds Register Vehicle Testing Authority. A P.S.V. Inspection Manual (price £5.70, 1983) is available from H.M.S.O.

Questions

1. A D.Tp. 'Notification of Refusal' has been issued to a customer.
   (a) What complications can the examiner expect?
   (b) Suggest a remedy to safeguard the interests of the dealership.
   (c) What is involved with 're-tests'? (I.M.I.)
2. Detail all items which could lead to a D.Tp. Heavy Goods Vehicle Test Station refusing to complete a test.
3. (a) What is meant by Operators' Licensing?
   (b) How can a licence be revoked?
   (c) What can be done to ensure a license is made safe? (I.R.T.E.)
4. A commercial vehicle is due for test.
   (a) Explain what you would do the day before.
   (b) How does the D.Tp. carry out such tests? (I.R.T.E.)
5. List at least six requirements in connection with applications and authorizations for light vehicles test stations (I.M.I.)
6. The management of a large garage is contemplating investing £20,000 in order to improve the efficiency and consisting of light vehicle testing and of expanding M.O.T. testing facilities at the workshop from June 1979.
   (a) State six changes in the Ministry's testing regulations which will become effective from that date.
   (b) Explain how the money should best be spent on new equipment, etc., in order to meet the D.Tp. requirements and also develop a greater demand for the service. State the approximate cost of any major items of equipment recommended.
   (c) What associated benefits should serve as a direct result of this investment.

APPENDIX I

Invoices

The Value Added Tax (General) Regulations 1972 require that, as from 1st April 1973, a trader registered for V.A.T. who makes a taxable supply to another taxable person must provide him with a tax invoice. The issue of a tax invoice in respect of a zero-rated supply is optional.

Except as indicated below, a tax invoice must contain the following particulars:
1) Identify number and date of issue.
2) Tax point (date of supply).
3) Name, address and V.A.T. registration number of the supplier.
4) Name and address of the person to whom the goods or services are supplied.
5) Type of supply i.e., sale, hire purchase, credit sale, conditional sale or similar transaction, loan, exchange, hire, lease or rental process (i.e. goods made from customer's materials), sale on commission, or supply on sale or return or similar terms.
6) Description sufficient to identify the goods or services supplied.
7) Quantity of goods or extent if services and amount, excluding tax, payable for each description.
8) Gross total amount payable excluding tax.
9) Rate of any cash discount offered.
10) Rate of tax in force at time of supply.

Now for amounts not exceeding £10 (including tax), retailers and other taxable persons supplying goods and services direct to both the general public and other taxable persons may issue tax invoices showing the following particulars only:
1) Name, address and registration number of the supplier.
2) Tax point (date of supply).
3) Description sufficient to identify the goods or services supplied.
4) Total amount payable including tax.
5) Rate of tax in force at time of supply.

CREDIT NOTES AND V.A.T. A supplier who gives a customer a credit relating to taxable supplies for which a tax invoice was issued, must issue a credit note showing the following particulars:
1) Identifying number and date of issue.
2) Supplier's name, address and V.A.T. registration number.
3) Customer's name and address.
4) Reason for the credit (e.g. returned goods).
5) Description sufficient to identify the goods or services for which credit is being allowed.
6) Quantity and amount credited for each description.
7) Total amount credited excluding V.A.T.
8) Rate and amount of V.A.T. credited.

The number and date of the original tax invoice must also be shown on the credit note but if this is not possible the supplier must be able to satisfy Customs and Excise in some other way that he accounted for tax on the original supply.

Local Customs and Excise offices can supply a full range of explanatory booklets concerning all aspects of V.A.T. Suppliers of printed invoices will always send specimen invoices for all aspects of service station operation. The Motor Agents Association has a complete range of forms for all aspects of service station work.

N.E.D.O. have produced an excellent book entitled *Financial management for the smaller garage,* price 95p, available from H.M.S.O. This booklet is an invaluable aid to all concerned with accounts in dealerships.

APPENDIX II

List of Institutes and Associations

Institute of the Motor Industry (Inc.),
'Fanshaws',
Brickeden, HERTS.

A professional institute with various grades of membership which are usually obtained by examination and other requirements. The aim of the institute is to raise and maintain the status of the motor industry as a whole.

Institute of Road Transport Engineers,
1 Cromwell Place,
London, S.W.7.

A professional institute with various grades of membership depending on examination success and job responsibility. The aim of the institute is to improve all aspects of vehicle operations within the transport industry.

Road Transport Industry Training Board,
Capitol House,
Empire Way,
Wembley, MIDDLESEX HA9 0NG.

A government body which imposes a levy on all transport and garage organizations. The size of the levy depends upon the number of employees. Grants are payable to firms who operate satisfactory training programmes. On request, the R.T.I.T.B. will supply data concerning all aspects of training.

City and Guilds of London Institute,
76 Portland Place,
London, W1N 4AA.

An independent institute which offers certificates which can be obtained by examination passes. The C.G.L.I. is recognized throughout the world.

National Economic Development Office,
Millbank Tower,
21–41 Millbank,
London, SW1P 4QU.

A government office which can supply on request, many valuable booklets dealing with motor vehicle distribution and repair.

Motor Agents Association,
201 Great Portland Street,
London, W1N 6AB.

This is an association of garage employers and represents them on various committees such as wage negotiation. Employers can use the M.A.A. for legal and other advice.

Garage Equipment Association,
Forbes House,
Halkin Street,
London, SW1X 7DS.

This is a body which represents manufacturers, distributors and other people concerned with garage equipment. Advice on equipment and garage layout is given to members.

Society of Motor Manufacturers and Traders,
Forbes House,
Halkin Street,
London, SW1X 7DS.

A society which has members drawn from manufacturers of vehicles, components, accessories and allied trades. The society represents the interests of its members by formulating economic and other policies associated with the motor industry. The N.E.C. Motor Show is organized by this body.

Vehicle Builders and Repairers Association,
Belmont House,
102, Finkle Lane,
Morley,
Leeds, LS27 7TW.

Membership of this association is open to all vehicle body builders and repairers whose premises and standards comply with those laid down by the Association.

Motor Industry Research Association,
Watling Street,
Nuneaton,
Warwickshire, CV10 OTO.

All manufacturers of vehicles can obtain membership and obtain advice in connection with vehicle performance. Research into all problems connected with transport are conducted at the proving ground.

Her Majestys Stationery Office,
Atlantic House,
Holborn Viaduct,
London, EC1P 1BN.

All legal publications and other government journals are obtainable through this office or through a local stationery office which can be found in big cities. The Factories Act and similar controlling documents can be obtained from H.M.S.O. Prices of such documents are available upon request.

British Standards Institution,
2 Park Street,
London, W1A 2BS.

Manufacturers and other interested parties form committees to set standards for all kinds of work. Copies of such standards can be obtained from the institution. A price list is available upon request.

Institute of Mechanical Engineers,
1 Birdcage Walk,
London, SW1 9JJ.

A professional institute which has an Automobile Division. Membership is available upon passing appropriate sections of the Institute's examinations along with other requirements.

197

Road Haulage Association,
22 Upper Woburn Place,
London, WC1H 0ES.

An employers' association which has information to deal with all problems affecting road transport organizations.

Engineers' Registration Board,
2 Little Smith Street,
London, SW1P 3DL.

A national body organized by the C.E.I. (Council of Engineering Institutions). Designatory letters C.Eng., T.Eng., and Tech. can be used by registrants. Details obtainable from the E.R.B. or its member bodies, such as the Institute of Motor Industry or the Institute of Road Transport Engineers.

Council for Vehicle Service and Repair,
94 Park Lane,
London, W1Y 3TR.

Formed in 1974, the government-sponsored council aims to achieve and maintain high standards of quality in the servicing and repair of motor vehicles and to safeguard the interests of customers of vehicle servicing and repair workshops. Full details can be obtained from the council, which consists of representatives of the A.A., R.A.C., British Insurance Associations, Institute of Trading Standards. Administration, Lloyd's Motor Underwriters' Association, M.A.A., S.M.T.A., S.M.M.T., V.B.R.A., some oil companies and assessors from departments of prices and consumer protection, industry, and the environment. N.E.D.O. is the controlling authority.

Department of Transport,
St. Christopher House,
Southwark Street,
London SE1 0TE.

Various divisions exist within this department to deal with D.Tp. tests, vehicle engineering construction, and so on. Enquiries can be made direct to the department. Various publications are issued and are obtainable from H.M.S.O. All enquiries regarding H.G.V., P.S.V., Light Vehicle, Motor Cycle Tests should be directed to D.Tp. Vehicle Inspection Division, Tollgate House, Houlton St., Bristol BS2 9DJ.

Ronald Sewell and Associates Ltd.,
1 Queen Square,
Bath, BA1 2HE.

This is a management consultancy agency that runs short courses and has many books for sale relating to the motor industry. Dealerships can register with the organisation for a fee and obtain current literature and information.

Association of Vehicle Recovery Operators Ltd.,
1 Stockbury House,
Church Street, Stannington, Pulborough,
West Sussex, RH20 4LD

AVRO was formed on November 3rd 1977. It has a large number of Operator Members. A journal is issued bi-monthly. A membership grade is issued according to recovery equipment available. Top grade requires a vehicle with 55 tons GTW, lifting 8.5 tons minimum over rear axle along with other equipment. AVRO can supply details of training courses and qualifications relevant to this form of work.

There are many other associations which represent the public and motor industry as a whole. Some of these are Automobile Association, Royal Automobile Club, Institute of Advanced Motorists, Motor Schools Association, British Trade Association, Tyre Manufacturers' Conference Limited, National Tyre Distributors' Association, Retread Manufacturers Association, The Motor and Cycle Trades Benevolent Fund.

Trade journals

Keeping up to date with equipment and techniques is possible by studying trade journals. There are a large number but the most popular are the *Motor Trader*, *The Service Station*, *The Garage and Motor Agent*, *Motor Transport*, *Garage and Transport Equipment* and *The Motor Industry*. Journals are issued by the various associations listed and two well known weekly magazines are *The Motor* and *The Autocar*. *Engineering, Materials and Design* is a monthly magazine.

A student would do well to peruse all the journals listed and decide which journal is essential for him. To keep abreast of new techniques in management and administration a particular journal can be selected which is relevant to the work he is doing.

199

APPENDIX III
C.G.L.I. Courses

Many changes have occured in course numbers in recent years. To avoid confusion, 1983 course numbers are given in the text. To enable readers to compare the old courses the old numbers with current courses and 1983 numbers the following list has been compiled.

Course	Pre 1970 Number	1970's Number	1983 Number
Construction Plant Mechanic	418	620	620
Motor Vehicle Technician	170	390	390
Motor Vehicle Mechanic	168	375	–
Motor Vehicle Electrician	169	375	–
Vehicle Parts Personnel	384	386	384
Motor Vehicle Craft Studies Part I	550	380	381
Light and Heavy Vehicle Mechanic Craft Studies Parts II and III	551,559	381	381
Motor Vehicle Electricians Craft Studies Part II	552	381	381
Vehicle Partsmen's Craft Studies Part II	554	381	–
Vehicle Salesmanship	555	382	– –
Vehicle Body Ctaft Studies Parts I, II and III	554,549	385	385
Vehicle Body Engineering Technician	318	395	–
Compression Ignition Engine Mechanic	447	379	–
Panel Beating	295	377	All part
Vehicle Body Building	294	378	of V. Body
Vehicle Painting & Industrial Finishing	296	378	Craft
Vehicle Body Trimming	297	378	Studies No. 385
Vehicle Body Work	298	378	above
Motor Vehicle Service Reception	559	383	381–629
Motor Cycle Mechanic	–	389	389

Note: The old course numbers are now a historical fact but are useful for managers, personnel staff and others for reference purposes. Further changes are inevitable. For example, the 390 Motor Vehicle Technician Course has been scheduled to run until 1986 and may continue beyond this date. However, the new Technician Diploma and Certificate in Vehicle Engineering and Higher Diploma and Technician Certificate in Vehicle Engineering Management are now well established and will eventually replace the 390 course.

The Licentiateship of the C.G.L.I. (L.C.G.) is also a very important qualification indicating a well trained and educated person (see pages 111-2). A trained and tested craft person can obtain C.G.L.I. Parts I, II and III of his specialism, then, along with a career extension course such as 390 Part III or 771 Organisational Studies, can apply for his L.C.G. direct to C.G.L.I. who will send an application form and current requirements.

National Craft Certificates are offered by the National Joint Council for the Motor Vehicle Retail and Repair Industry for the occupations of Light Vehicle Mechanic, Heavy Vehicle Mechanic, Auto-Electrician and Light Vehicle Body Repairer. Other trades will become eligible in due course. Qualifying conditions usually include: (a) An approved apprenriceship or accepted equivalent for at least 3 years. (b) Success in Stage III practical skills test with RTITB. (c) C.G.L.I. success in appropriate part II examination.

A certificate holder may apply for election as a graduate member of the Institute of the Motor Industry (G.I.M.I.). The craft certificate is also evidence of practical skills for the L.C.G. of the C.G.L.I.

APPENDIX IV

Recent Legislation

The Petrol Prices (Display) Order 1977 came into force on 12 August 1977 and compels retailers clearly to indicate the actual price of 2-, 3-, and 4-star petrol. The order does not apply to the sale of diesel engine road vehicle (DERV) fuel oil. Paraffin is also exempt. The price of paraffin was controlled by legislation until July 11th 1979, when The Paraffin (Maximum Retail Prices) was revoked. Prices are now controlled by Market forces.

The Petrol Prices (Display) Order 1977 refers to premises where petrol is 'exposed for sale' and this means virtually any petrol forecourt where petrol is sold. Some forecourts offer sub-grades of petrol, i.e. octane ratings which can be slightly above those of 90, 94, or 97, e.g. 90·5, 94·5, or 97·5, and a higher price is charged per gallon. Where 2-, 3-, or 4-star petrol with sub-grades is sold, the highest price must be displayed for customers entering a point of sale. Some dealers also used to offer a discount on every full gallon and make customers pay the full price for every part of a gallon. An amendment to the existing order came into being in December 1978 to make this practice illegal, so that discounts must now be on the total amount of petrol sold or a clear notice shown to indicate the higher price for part of a gallon.

Penalties for contravening these regulations can result in fines up to £400 and students and managers are urged to contact the local weights and measures office to obtain current information. In these days of dynamic change managers must keep themselves up to date if they are to survive.

The Motor Fuel (Lead Content of Petrol) Regulations 1976. This states the maximum amount of permitted lead per litre of petrol. From 1 January 1978 the regulations were amended and the current amount of lead permitted is 0·45 grams per litre of petrol. Whilst dealers will not normally be concerned with increasing lead content and thereby improving octane rating, some may be tempted to sell tetra-ethyl-lead for older engines to run on the out-of-date 5-star (99+ octane) petrol. Persons found with excess lead content in the petrol could be convicted of an offence under the above regulations.

The Trading Stamps Act 1964. This has had no amendments since its inception, but has brought about minor amendments to the Sale of Goods Act, i.e. sale of stamps. Two requirements are that the value of the stamp must be shown on the face of the stamp, e.g. 0·5p, and for traders, a need to display a notice to give details of value of the stamp. Where a catalogue is issued a current edition must be available.

The Theft Act 1978. This is an act which enables the police to prosecute a person who steals from a dealer, e.g. a person filling up with petrol and driving off without paying. Prior to this act it was always difficult to proceed with a civil action, but this new act allows a criminal prosecution to take place when the evidence is there to support it.

The Unfair Contract Terms Act 1977 received Royal Assent in October 1977 and came into force on 1 February 1978. It controls the avoidance of liability by means of contract terms and notices. Amongst other things it regulates the use, as between businessmen, of exemption clauses which are part of the written standard terms of business, and of terms or notices which exclude or restrict liability for negligence and breach of contract. We could say that small print could mean big trouble for traders! The act bites in connection with liability for negligence, as it is now illegal to exclude liability for death or personal injury in any contract or notice, e.g. 'the Company is not liable for loss of life or injury whether caused by negligence or otherwise'. This type of clause is now void. Similarly loss or damage caused by negligence cannot be avoided in guarantees given with consumer goods, except where a shop rather than a maker gives its own guarantee. Likewise those clauses, in contracts for the supply of goods for hire and contracts for work and materials, which restrict liability for quality, fitness for purpose, or correspondence with description or sample, are void if they attempt to exclude responsibility.

An example of a void clause for car hire is as follows: 'The garage excludes all conditions and warranties relating to the fitness for use or road-worthiness of the car and the consequences of any breakdown or repair must be borne by the hirer'. An example of a void clause for work and materials would be one similar to: 'The company does not make any payment if any parts supplied are defective whatever the reason'. Obviously all managers concerned with parts, materials, and work must be made aware of the importance of such clauses.

Within the act are clauses subject to a 'reasonableness' test and these could be listed:

(1) One of these is the clause which restricts a trader's liability for breach of contract, e.g. a term in a trader's contract limiting liability for failure to complete on time to a stated sum of money.

(2) Clauses which claim to entitle the trader to render a contractual performance substantially different from that which was reasonably expected of him, e.g. the right is reserved to offer an alternative vehicle if this becomes necessary.

(3) Clauses which require the consumer to indemnify the trader or another person in respect of their liability for negligence or breach of contract, e.g. a trader who requires the consumer to indemnify him against a claim from a third party if a worker, in negligently handling a consumer's car, causes damage to a third party's car.

Bold and uncompromising statements by a trader, e.g. 'not responsible for loss or damage due to negligence' are just as misleading as using void terms, as the consumer will know that such statements are subject to a reasonableness test. It could well be that void terms will become illegal in the future, therefore dealers should ensure they are not contravening the 1978 Act in any way.

All business dealings which use standard forms of contract, e.g. printed conditions and all trade contracts with consumers, must meet the test of 'reasonableness' if the contract attempts to avoid responsibility for breaking the contract or for providing something substantially different from what was promised.

Exceptions include insurance and some international contracts, but, because the act defines negligence as any lack of care or skill, the Act in effect encompasses a wide range of activities. Thus, managers of workshops and other departments would do well to ensure their contracts for service or repair work do not have any unfair disclaimers, as they will be open to prosecution. Likewise they will ensure all work done is completed to a high standard. Effective quality control and this new Act will ensure that the honest dealer will survive.

The Consumer Transactions (Restrictions on Statements) (Amendment) Order 1978. This order, which forms part of consumer protection legislation, prevents the display of any notice which attempts to remove a person's rights under the Sale of Goods Act. If a notice, for example, in a service or parts department, states that money will not be refunded and only a credit note issued, this would now be illegal if the goods being returned were not of merchantable quality. Therefore notices displayed must not under any circumstances take or attempt to take away the rights of a person in connection with the Sale of Goods Act.

Control of Hiring Order (1977). This order came into effect on 1 June 1977. Cars acquired for business use no longer require deposits on hire purchase agreements or 42 weeks advance payment on leasing arrangements.

Open-ended leasing can also form the basis of a legal contract. The effect of this is that although the customer cannot gain legal ownership of the vehicle at the end of the agreement he can contract an entitlement to share in the benefits of selling the vehicle if it can fetch a higher sum than the residual value written into the agreement. The result of all this is to make leasing by far the cheapest method of acquiring business vehicles. It means that Hire Purchase will be of little interest except to private motorists.

Monthly instalments on leasing are about half that of Hire Purchase because

(1) tax shelter funds can be used in leasing;

(2) whilst hire purchase requires a customer to pay the full cost of a vehicle over 2 years, etc., a leasing agreement is based on the difference between the cost of the vehicle new and what it is likely to be worth at the end of the agreement, i.e. leasing is based on depreciation which is about half the cost new.

If the residual price improves the customer again benefits. Fleet users will be particularly interested in this development and Car Sales Managers must be able to develop leasing of their vehicles to potential customers by having the ability to explain the value of leasing agreements.

Health and Safety at Work Act 1974

From 2 October 1978 new legal powers came into force to strengthen the 1974 Act. Over 150,000 trade union appointed representatives now help to monitor safety at work. Shop-floor safety committees are now appointed and they can have time off work on full pay to carry out their work and undergo training.

About 700 people die at work each year and 300,000 have serious accidents annually, which costs the community an estimated £2,000 million pounds. As there are only 1,000 Factory Inspectors to cover over 300,000 workplaces many work areas are not inspected as regularly as they should be.

As indicated elsewhere in the book (p. 70) management has special responsibilities when safety at work is being considered. Management cannot allow any unsafe practices to take place. The Abrasive Wheel Regulations (1970) make it an offence for any unqualified person to fit, dress, or otherwise deal with grindstones on fixed or portable hand machines. To enable an employee to replace or dress any grindstone wheel they must attend a recognised course at a college or manufacturer. The certificate obtained must be filed in the appropriate section of the factory act register. Failure to do so will mean heavy fines.

Fire is also a special risk in dealerships and the section of the book dealing with this should be carefully studied.

Shop stewards and safety committees should be familiar with all the provisions of the 1974 Act. In the Code of Practice approved on 12 September 1978 the following statements make it quite clear what is expected of safety representatives.

1. The function of safety representatives appointed by recognised trade unions as set out in Section 2(4) of the Health and Safety at Work Act 1974, to represent employees in consultations with employers about health and safety matters. Regulation 4(1) of the Safety Representatives and Safety Committees Regulations (SI 1977 No. 500) prescribes other functions of safety representatives appointed under those Regulations.

2. Under Regulation 4(2)(b) of those Regulations the employer has a duty to permit those safety representatives such time off with pay during the employee's working hours as shall be necessary for the purpose of 'undergoing such training in aspects of those functions as may be reasonable in all the circumstances'.

3. As soon as possible after their appointment safety representatives should be permitted time off with pay to attend basic training facilities approved by the TUC or by the independent union or unions which appointed the safety representatives. Further training, similarly approved, should be undertaken where the safety representative has special responsibilities or where such training is necessary to meet changes in circumstances or relevant legislation.

4. With regard to the length of training required, this cannot be rigidly prescribed, but basic training should take into account the functions of safety representatives placed on them by the Regulations. In particular, basic training should provide an understanding of the role of safety representatives, of safety committees, and of trade union policies and practices in relation to:
(a) the legal requirements relating to the health and safety of persons at work, particularly the group or class of persons they directly represent;
(b) the nature and extent of workplace hazards, and the measures necessary to eliminate or minimise them;
(c) the health and safety policy of employers, and organisation and arrangements for fulfilling those policies.
Additionally, safety representatives will need to acquire new skills in order to carry out their functions, including safety inspections, and in using basic sources of legal and official information and information provided by or through the employer on health and safety matters.

5. Trade unions are responsible for appointing safety representatives and when the trade union wishes a safety representative to receive training relevant to his function it should inform management of the course it has approved and supply a copy of the syllabus, indicating its contents, if the employer asks for it. It should normally give at least a few weeks' notice of the safety representatives it has nominated for attendance. The number of safety representatives attending training courses at any one time should be that which is reasonable in the circumstances, bearing in mind such factors as the availability of relevant courses and the operational requirements of the employer. Unions and management

should endeavour to reach agreement on the appropriate numbers and arrangements and refer any problems which may arise to the relevant agreed procedures.

The recommended report forms in the Code of Practice are illustrated at the end of this Appendix.

It is as well now to summarize the main objectives of the Health and Safety at Work Act. Firstly, a company safety policy should be established and a safety committee formed. The committee should consist of members with a specialised knowledge of a particular area with particular risks, e.g. service manager, parts manager, bodyshop manager, and so on. The committee will also have trade union representatives and the chairman of the safety committee should be a senior member of the company. With large companies, it may be necessary to create sub-committees to enable them to function well. A record of minutes should be kept by a secretary. The main objectives of the committee will be as follows:

1. It will need to ensure that the company's premises, operations, and working environment are safe and healthy. When we say operations, we include operations outside the premises as well as inside.
2. It will need to set up an administrative system to maintain the company's premises, operations, and working environment in this safe and healthy condition.
3. It will need to set up some kind of information system—internal and, where necessary, external—on all matters relating to health and safety.
4. It will need to ensure that employees receive adequate training in health and safety matters.

These four objectives should appear on the agenda of the first safety committee meeting and be constantly repeated to ensure apathy does not creep in.

A Code of Practice for the company should be established which should have committee approval, and all personnel should receive a copy. The R.T.I.T.B. recommend a format of the three R's and an example given in one of their booklets is as follows:

Code of Practice for Service/Repair Workshop

Item: Vehicle Jacks and Stands

Requirement:
    (a) No work will be carried out under a jacked-up vehicle until it has been secured on axle stands (or blocks or frames).
    (b) All axle stands should show their load capacity and should have the correct type of pin attached by chain.
    (c) An adequate supply of axle stands will be provided.

Record:
    (a) Training record.
    (b) Maintenance record.
    (c) Equipment inventory.

Responsibility:
    (a) All workshop personnel.
    (b) Workshop maintenance staff.
    (c) Workshop manager.

Other items of equipment should be appraised in a similar way. It is not unusual to have a Code of Practice for premises and another for personnel.

Regular inspections of all equipment as outlined in the Safety Practices Check Form on page 34 has always been essential but is now a legal requirement. Failure to meet the requirement of the Act can result in imprisonment for up to 2 years or an unlimited fine or both of these punishments!

To summarize an employer's duties, these could be briefly listed by stating he must provide and maintain
    (1) safe equipment,
    (2) a safe place of work with safe access and egress,
    (3) safe systems of working,
    (4) a healthy working environment,
    (5) welfare arrangements, e.g. washing facilities, rest rooms, and so on,
    (6) adequate training, with time off for this activity as required.

An employee's duties could be summarized as
    (1) to take reasonable care for his own safety and the safety of others who may be affected by his acts or omissions,

(2) to co-operate with his employer or any other person on whom a statutory duty or requirement is imposed to enable that duty or requirement to be complied with.

These requirements mean that the objectives of the act can be met. The objectives are

(1) to repeal, replace, or modify existing regulations,
(2) to maintain or improve standards of health, safety, and welfare of people at work,
(3) to protect people, other than workers, against any risks to their health or safety arising out of the activities of people at work,
(4) to control the keeping and use of dangerous substances including explosives and highly flammable material,
(5) to control the emission of noxious substances into the atmosphere.

The Fire Precautions Act 1971. This act is not part of the Health and Safety Act. The act is self-contained and is concerned with means of escape in case of fire, fire-fighting arrangements, and fire warning arrangements. A fire certificate is required if 20 or more people are employed at ground level, or 10 or more people above the ground level, or highly flammable materials are used or stored. Obviously this includes all dealerships and the local fire officer should be consulted on all matters relating to this consolidated act.

Supply of Goods and Services Act 1982

Part I. This gives members of the public who hire items, buy them in part exchange or have them supplied together with a service (such as spare parts) the same protection that other shoppers now have. Forms of redress are now available if the goods supplied are, in fact, faulty.

Part II. This spells out the basic rights of consumers under common law when they obtain a service (such as having their car repaired). The Act emphasises that the work must be done with reasonable care and skill unless otherwise agreed, within a reasonable time scale and at a reasonable cost.

Number

Safety representative: report form

Notification to the employer (or his representative) of conditions and working practices considered to be unsafe or unhealthy and of arrangements for welfare at work considered to be unsatisfactory.

Date and time of inspection or matter observed	Particulars of matter(s) notified to employer or his representative (include location where appropriate)	Name(s) of safety representative(s) notifying matter(s) to employer (or his representative)	Remedial action taken (with date) or explanation if not taken. This information to be relayed to the safety representative(s) This column to be completed by the employer

Signature of employer (or his representative)

(This report does not imply that the conditions are safe and healthy or that the arrangements for welfare at work are satisfactory in all other respects)

Signature(s) of safety representative(s)   Date

Record of receipt of form by the employer (or his representative).

Signature: Date:

Number

Safety representative: Inspection form

Record that an inspection by a safety representative or representatives has taken place

Date and time of inspection
Area or workplace inspected

Name(s) and signature(s) of safety representative taking part in the inspection

Name(s) and signature(s) of employer (or his representative) taking part in the inspection (if appropriate)

(This record does not imply that the conditions are safe and healthy or that the arrangements for welfare at work are satisfactory)

Record of receipt inspection form by the employer (or his representative)

Signature: Date:

INDEX